Terrorism: A Challenge
to the State

Terrorism: A Challenge to the State

edited by

JULIET LODGE

St. Martin's Press • New York

© Chaps. 1, 7 & 9 Juliet Lodge; Chap. 2 Geoffrey Pridham; Chap. 3 Paul Furlong; Chap. 4 Philip G. Cerny; Chap. 5 Valentine Herman and Rob van der Laan Bouma; Chap. 6 E. Moxon-Browne; Chap. 8 David Freestone; all 1981.

St. Martin's Press, Inc., 175 Fifth Avenue, New York, NY 10010
Printed in Great Britain
First published in the United States of America in 1981

ISBN 0-312-79230-1

Library of Congress Cataloging in Publication Data

Main entry under title:

Terrorism: a challenge to the state.

    1.   Terrorism — Addresses, essays, lectures.
    I.   Lodge, Juliet.
    HV6431.T459   1981   303.6'2   80-24237
    ISBN 0-312-79230-1

Contents

Abbreviations

APO	Ausserparlamentarische Opposition
ARB	Armée Révolutionaire Bretonne
BGS	Bundesgrenzschutz
BKA	Bundeskriminalamt
BR	Brigate Rosse
CDU	Christlich Demokratische Union
CFDT	Confédération Française Démocratique du Travail
CFT	Confédération Française du Travail
CRS	Compagnie Républicaine de Sécurité
CSU	Christlich-Soziale Union
DC	Democrazia cristiana
DDR	Deutsche Demokratische Republik
DKP	Deutsche Kommunistische Partei
DST	Direction de la Surveillance du Territoire
EDF	Electricité de France
EEC	European Economic Community
ETA	Euzkadi Ta Askatasuna
FDP	Freie Demokratische Partei Deutschlands
FLB	Front de Libération de la Bretagne
FLN	Front de Libération Nationale
FLNA	Front de Libération Nationale d'Algérie
FRG	Federal Republic of Germany
GAP	Gruppe di azione partigiana
GARI	Groupement d'action revolutionaire international
GINI	Groupe d'intervention des narcisses interurbains
GSG	Grenzschutzgruppe
INLA	Irish National Liberation Army
IRA	Irish Republican Army
KNIL	Koninklijk Nederlandsch Indische Leger
KPD	Kommunistische Partei Deutschlands
MEP	Member of the European Parliament
MRPO	Movimento di Resistenza Proletario Offensivo
MSI	Movimento Sociale Italiano

NAP	Nuclei Armati Proletari
NAPAP	Noyaux armés pour l'autonomie prolétarienne
NATO	North Atlantic Treaty Organization
OAS	Organisation de l'Armée Secrète
OIRA	Official Irish Republican Army
OPEC	Organization of Petroleum Exporting Countries
ORTF	Office de Radiodiffusion-Télévision Française
PCI	Partito Communista Italiano
PFLP	Popular Front for the Liberation of Palestine
PIRA	Provisional Irish Republican Army
PL	Prima Linea
PLI	Partito Liberale Italiano
PLO	Palestinian Liberation Organisation
PRI	Partito Republicano Italiano
PSDI	Partito Socialista Democratico Italiano
PSF	Provisional Sinn Fein
PSI	Partito Socialista Italiano
RAF	Red Army Faction
RIC	Royal Irish Constabulary
RMS	Republic Maluku Selatan
RPF	Rassemblement du Peuple française
RUC	Royal Ulster Constabulary
SDS	Sozialistischen Deutschen Studentenbund
SdS	Servizio di Sicurezza
SID	Servizio Intelligenza di Difesa
SISDE	Servizio Informazione Sicurezza Democratica
SISMI	Servizio Informazione Sicurezza Militare
SPD	Sozialdemokratische Partei Deutschlands
SRP	Sozialistische Reichspartei
TD	Teachta Dala
UN	United Nations
UNR	Union pour la Nouvelle République

Notes on the Contributors

PHILIP G. CERNY has been a Lecturer in Politics in the University of York, England, since 1970. Born in New York, he graduated from Kenyon College (Ohio) and also attended the Institut d'Etudes Politiques in Paris; he took his doctorate at the University of Manchester, where he was a teaching assistant. His interests include the comparative politics of democratic capitalist societies (Western Europe and the United States), French politics since 1940 and foreign policy studies. He is the author of *The Politics of Grandeur: Ideological Aspects of de Gaulle's Foreign Policy* (1979), and co-editor (with Martin A. Schain) of *French Politics and Public Policy* (1980). He has published articles in a number of journals, including *Government and Opposition, The Review of Politics,* the *British Journal of International Studies,* the *British Journal of Political Science, Il Pensiero Politico* and the *Scottish Journal of Sociology,* as well as in *The Guardian* newspaper. He is currently working on a comparative study of the influence of institutional and systemic constraints upon the competition and coalition behaviour of political parties in party systems.

DAVID FREESTONE read law at the Universities of Hull and London. He now teaches international law and European Community law at the University of Hull.

PAUL FURLONG studied at the Gregorian University, Rome, at Lincoln College, Oxford and at the University of Reading, England, before taking up his present post as Lecturer in the Department of Politics at the University of Hull, where he lectures in Italian and West European Politics. He has published work on electoral behaviour in Italy and has a particular interest in the politics of the Catholic Church in Italy. He is at present working on a study of state intervention in the Italian economy.

VALENTINE HERMAN is a Senior Lecturer in Political Science in the Faculty of Social Sciences, Erasmus University, Rotterdam, the Netherlands. Previously he taught at the universities of Essex, England, and Aarhus, Denmark. He is author of *Parliaments of the World: a Reference Compendium* (1976); co-author of *The European Parliament and the European Community* (1978), *Direct Elections to the European Parliament: A Community Perspective* (1980), and *Workbook for Comparative*

Government (1972); and co-editor of *The Backbencher and Parliament* (1972), *Cabinet Studies* (1975), *The European Parliament and National Parliaments* (1979), and *The Legislation of Direct Elections to the European Parliament* (1980).

ROB VAN DER LAAN BOUMA is a teacher of economics. Previously he was a researcher at Erasmus University, Rotterdam, the Netherlands. He has written a number of articles on terrorism in the Netherlands, and is currently working on a study of the relationship between terrorism and public opinion in Western democracies.

JULIET LODGE is a Lecturer in Politics at the University of Hull. She was formerly a Lecturer in West European Politics at the University of Auckland, New Zealand, and a Visiting Fellow at The London School of Economics and Political Science. She is the author of *The European Policy of the SPD* (1976); co-author of *The New Zealand General Election of 1975* (1976), *The European Parliament and the European Community* (1978) and *Direct Elections to the European Parliament: A Community Perspective* (1980). She has contributed chapters to several books, and her articles have been published in the following journals of political science and international affairs: *Orbis, International Organization, Canadian Journal of Political Science, Revue d'Intégration Européenne, British Journal of International Studies, Political Studies, Parliamentary Affairs, The Parliamentarian, Journal of Common Market Studies, European Journal of Political Research, West European Politics, Res Publica, Australian Outlook, Politics, Political Science, World Review, The World Today, Beleid & Maatschappij, Common Market Law Review, Cooperation and Conflict, Futures, Jerusalem Journal of International Relations, New Zealand International Review, Contemporary Review, Commonwealth, The Round Table* and *European Community*.

EDWARD MOXON-BROWNE is a Lecturer in Political Science at Queen's University, Belfast, Northern Ireland. He read history at the University of St Andrews, Scotland, and then did graduate work in international relations at the University of Pennsylvania where he was a Thouron Scholar (1967—70). His research interests include the European Parliament, Ireland and the EEC, and Northern Ireland politics, and he has published several articles on these topics. He reviews books for *International Affairs,* and broadcasts regularly on BBC local radio.

GEOFFREY PRIDHAM has been a Lecturer in European Politics at Bristol University, England, since 1969. His special interests are political parties and party development in the three areas of West Germany, Italy and the European Community. Apart from publishing articles in a number of journals, he has published the following books: *Hitler's Rise to Power: the*

Nazi movement in Bavaria, 1923—33 (1973); Documents on *Nazism, 1919—45*, with Jeremy Noakes (1974); *Christian Democracy in Western Germany* (1977); *Change and Continuity in the Italian Party System: the Case of Tuscany in the 1970s* (1980); and *Transnational Party Cooperation and Direct Elections to the European Parliament*, with Pippa Pridham (1980).

CHAPTER 1

Introduction

Juliet Lodge

Numerous attempts have been made to define terrorism[1] and to distinguish it from forms of political violence associated with the conduct of a legitimate campaign against a repressive regime — usually of a despotic, military or fascist type — or from revolutionary violence, which also has been seen to be, in some way, legitimate. However, recent attempts to construct typologies of terrorism tend either to categorise terrorism as a sub-specie of revolutionary violence (and terrorists themselves may argue that they are revolutionaries seeking the overthrow of a corrupt government) or to define it as a distinct and possibly new phenomenon, owing nothing to historical antecedents of violence by non-governmental people in pursuit of political ends of the revolutionary or anarchist mould. While it is outside the scope of this book to detail the various typologies of terrorism, it will be useful to outline briefly some definitions of terrorism. As will become apparent, a consensus seems to be emerging that the resort to violence by non-elected groups for achieving political ends in liberal democracies is an illegitimate and unjustifiable use of force; that the means do not justify the ends; and that terrorist acts in such societies constitute criminal rather than political offences, and should be prosecuted as such.[2] Repudiating the notion of 'state violence' as illegitimate, Conor Cruise O'Brien argues that 'the *force* used by a democratic state against the terrorist is legitimate, while the *violence* of the terrorist is not legitimate';[3] and that terrorist groups' claims to be liberation movements or groups engaged in 'guerrilla' warfare are attempts to inject terrorist groups with the legitimacy that most contemporary terrorist movements lack.[4]

Laqueur argues that the difficulty with defining terrorism lies in the fact that its character has greatly changed over the last century. For him,

> terrorism is not an ideology but an insurrectional strategy that can be used by people of very different political convictions . . . [It] is not merely a technique . . . its philosophy transcend(s) the traditional dividing lines between political doctrine. It is truly all-purpose and value-free.[5]

1

However, terrorism in Western Europe, as elsewhere, is not value-free. Like Servier,[6] Laqueur sees terrorism, historically, as but one of several different political strategies. Concentrating on the main stages in the development of terrorism and terrorist doctrine (which he sees as *post hoc* rationalisation of the resort to terrorism[7]), as well as on its central features, he traces the evolution of systematic terrorism (rather than terrorism as a legitimate means of resisting despotism dating back to antiquity[8]) to the second half of the nineteenth century. He argues that terrorists of the 'left' or 'right' now assume the deed to be more important than words; believe any change to be for the better; are contemptuous of liberalism and 'bourgeois' democracy; and have a sense of historical mission for the chosen few.[9]

Others have isolated additional characteristic attributes of terrorism. Jenkins argues that terrorism is

> the threat of violence, individual acts of violence, or a campaign of violence designed primarily to instil fear — to terrorize . . . Terrorism is violence for effect; not only, and sometimes not at all, for the effect on the actual victims of the terrorists. In fact, the victim may be totally unrelated to the terrorists' cause. Terrorism is violence aimed at people watching. Fear is the intended effect, not the by-product of terrorism.[10]

However, even if this notion of terrorism for effect, terrorism as theatre or public spectacle is accepted, it must be remembered that this is not its *sole* objective. Terrorists do have goals over and above attracting media coverage for their activities and instilling fear among the public. Indeed, the latter, as shown by Pridham in Chapter 2 of this book, can be related to terrorists achieving their goals. This is especially so if terrorist action elicits a government response involving the introduction of security measures impinging upon generally accepted civil liberties that may then be interpreted, rightly or wrongly, by terrorists as an illegitimate abuse of authority by the government.

In a similar vein, Wolf argues that

> [the terrorist's] strategic intent is to destroy the confidence a particular minority has in its government by causing [it] to act outside the law . . . to bring about the moral alienation of the masses from the government until its isolation has become total and irreversible . . . to make life unbearable for a democratic government as long as [terrorist] demands remain unsatisfied.[11]

This may overstate the case, and Wolf's definition relates primarily to the use of coercive powers by a government against a particular section of society with which terrorists may try to identify[12] or to incite to disobedience or rebellion (especially against measures introduced in response to terrorism), which may then be extolled as legitimate resistance. In such instances, the terrorist goal — 'to register a calculated impact on a target population and on other groups for the purpose of altering the political balance in favour of the terrorists'[13] and discrediting the authorities — is realised.

However, discrediting and questioning the right of the legitimately elected authorities to act against terrorism can be, and in the West German case has been, linked with rhetoric aimed at convincing the masses that the state embodies violence, and acts illegitimately; that violence can only be counteracted by violence; that 'the people's' violence is justified and proper;[14] and that the 'oppressive authorities' must be overthrown. At the very least, internal terrorism cannot but be regarded by the legitimate governmental authorities as challenging and undermining their authority and legitimacy. Moreover, this impression may spill over to the public if the government proves unable to prevent or limit such terrorism.[15]

It is true that many terrorist acts may be aimed at the redress of specific grievances,[16] the release of jailed terrorist colleagues, the acquisition of funds, the taking of hostages,[17] and so forth. However, where terrorist demands are couched in broader terms and linked with ideas of revolution, the question of whether terrorism is guerrilla warfare[18] or takes a 'revolutionary'[19] or 'sub-revolutionary' form has been raised. Wilkinson, for example, distinguishes between three broad types of terrorism: 'revolutionary' terrorism, aimed at political revolution; 'sub-revolutionary' terrorism, having political motives other than revolution; and 'repressive' terrorism, aimed at restraining certain groups, individuals or forms of behaviour deemed to be undesirable.[20]

Adapting this, Sloan suggests that 'revolutionary' terrorism aims at effecting a complete revolutionary change within the political system, and that 'sub-revolutionary' terrorism aims at effecting various changes in the structural—functional aspects of the particular political system, in the body politic. Instead of 'repressive' terrorism, he refers to 'establishment terrorism'; this he argues may be applied externally by the government against other nation states and internally 'to repress various forms of domestic opposition/unrest and/or move the populace to comply with [the] programmes/goals of the state'.[21] Although Sloan couples all his definitions with reference to the threat and/or resort to 'extranormal forms of political violence',[22] his three types of terrorism do not advance our understanding of the various forms terrorism takes, and the third type seems to embrace international aggression and measures to suppress internal dissent. In the first instance, 'extranormal forms of political violence' may not seem extraordinary, especially if employed by states not respecting conventions regarding human rights; whereas in the second instance, the use of extranormal forms of political violence would appear inconsistent with the values espoused by governments, and particularly those of liberal democratic persuasion.

A further attempt to classify terrorism and to differentiate its various forms from each other by alluding to the various goals towards which each is oriented is made by Bowyer Bell. He isolates several aspects, which he concedes overlap, of 'revolutionary' terror. These concern the internal and external dimensions of 'revolutionary' terror, and range from matters regarding the initiation of group members and the maintenance of group loyalty, to the instillation of fear (and with it compliance) among either the population at large or specific sectors of it and action in pursuit of terrorist goals. (To some extent, these concerns affect not simply terrorist bodies but other movements that resort to violence or to tactics that reject moral constraints and norms valued or upheld by a given society. While the concerns may be particularly significant to terrorist groups, they are not exclusive to them and are not, therefore, straightforward criteria enabling one to classify a group as terrorist.) Bowyer Bell refers to the first aspect of 'revolutionary' terror as 'organizational terror'. This he regards as the matter 'revolutionary' organizations face in maintaining internal discipline, inhibiting penetration and punishing errant members.[23] The second aspect, 'allegiance terror', he argues is 'a less restrained variant of organizational terror' involving the use of violence to create mass 'support' in the form of funds obtained through extortion or 'support' in the form of actions like strikes, boycotts and civil disobedience obtained by threats of vengeance.[24] The third aspect he describes as 'functional terror', involving actions to gain strategic advantages or the isolation of a category of victims by virtue of their function as targets for assassination (he refers to the undercover agents murdered on Bloody Sunday in Northern Ireland).[25] A fourth aspect is defined as 'provocative terror' (identified also by Laqueur as a strategy rather than form of terrorism[26]) concentrating on 'exploiting the deed and escalating its impact';[27] while a fifth variant — 'manipulative terror' — is characterised as 'the creation of a bargaining situation' in which threats are made to destroy assets or kill hostages unless certain demands are granted. 'Manipulative terror rests on the dread, if not the certainty, that such threats are real.'[28] Finally, Bowyer Bell describes what he terms 'symbolic terror', where the victim is selected because (s)he 'represents the epitome of the enemy'[29] — however the latter is interpreted.

For Bowyer Bell terrorism can take forms other than that depicted as 'revolutionary' terrorism. He refers to 'psychotic' terrorism involving bizarre, 'ostensibly political actions with uncertain or irrational outward motivations' committed for personal, internal reasons.[30] He then categorises certain tactics — such as hijacking and kidnapping — as 'criminal terror'.[31] Certainly, such acts are regarded internationally as criminal offences (See Chapters 7 and 8 for details). Apart from identifying the different forms that terrorism may take when practised by non-governmental authorities, Bowyer Bell isolates three other types of terrorism that he associates with governmental authorities (or with those purportedly acting on their behalf) — and so with the notion of state terror and state violence. These forms of terror, he suggests, are 'endemic terror' — the collapse of a state into barbarism; 'authorized terror' — 'the set of conventions concerning the use of state power for coercive purposes'; and 'vigilante terrorism' — arising where volunteers, instead of the regime that is under threat from within, act to curb or eliminate dissent.[32] All appear to be linked with forms of internal repression and violence, and all lack a clear international dimension. The problem with some of these characterisations is that they appear almost indistinguishable — except in respect of their duration and intensity — from the general terms like 'civil strife'[33] and 'political violence' when they are associated with notions of deviance or illegitimacy, including — according to Gurr — revolution, guerrilla wars, coups d'état, rebellions and riots.[34]

I have referred to but a few contemporary attempts to define terrorism. Some illuminate aspects of terrorism, mostly with reference to goals whose realisation those practising terrorism purport to seek. For our purposes, terrorism is seen as the resort to violence for political ends by unauthorised, non-governmental actors in breach of accepted codes of behaviour regarding the expression of dissatisfaction with, dissent from or opposition to the pursuit of political goals by the legitimate government authorities of the state whom they regard as unresponsive to the needs of certain groups of people. Moreover, terrorism — even indigenous terrorism — transcends national boundaries in its exercise, effects, ramifications and prosecution. As will become apparent from the following chapters, many terrorist groups have international links, and the problem of combating terrorism occupies international rather than just national organisations.[35] International terrorism can be defined as

> the threat or use of violence for political purposes when (1) such action is intended to influence the attitude and behaviour of a target group wider than its immediate victims, and (2) its ramifications transcend national boundaries (as the result, for example, of the nationality or foreign ties of its perpetrators, its locale, the identity of its institutional or human victims, its declared objectives, or the mechanics of its resolution).[36]

Each of the case studies presented in this book highlights the international dimension to terrorism in Western Europe by dint of the locale, the aims of terrorist acts and the terrorists' nationality, source of arms and links with other terrorists outside a given country. Mainly concerned with the rationale and reasons advanced by terrorists for their actions, their goals, the nature of terrorist attacks and government responses to terrorism, the case studies do not delve in detail into the socio-psychological aspects or possible 'causes' of terrorism. Attempts have been made elsewhere to probe these matters, and suggestions made that the causes of various forms of terrorism lie with one or more psychological, economic, political or social factors.[37] Such factors may provide plausible explanations for and/or rationalisations of terrorist activity but they have so far been of little predictive value in indicating when the next likely terrorist attack will occur and what its goal or purpose and institutional or human target(s) will be in a given state, and so in assisting efforts to combat terrorism.

Instead, the attempts to combat terrorism have involved the recourse to improved security measures;[38] the establishment of mechanisms for controlling governmental resources with a view to ensuring efficient and rapid responses by the authorities to terrorist incidents; and the refining of data collecting and retrieval systems to assist in identifying terrorist suspects and to help expedite decision-making by making relevant information quickly available to any governmental crisis teams and authorities established to deal with terrorist incidents. These may be supplemented by emergency measures 'taken to delimit the terrorist act in a physical sense and to decouple it in a psychological sense from the intended political conse-quences', or to redress the situation by ending the incident.[39] The emphasis on security measures rather than on alleviating socio-economic problems (where relevant) is partly due to the expectation that they can be relatively expeditiously enforced, at least at the national level. Moreover, the recourse to security measures may help to reassure the public that the legitimate authorities are 'in command' of the situation. Even in places like Northern Ireland, where some attempts have been made to reduce socio-economic deprivation in areas of high unemployment deemed likely to support terrorism, little headway seems to have been made.[40]

Although socio-economic factors — including poverty, unemployment and low education — may help to explain aspects of support for terrorism in Northern Ireland and the Netherlands, they do not help in respect of terrorism in West Germany where terrorists are believed to conform to the 'typical sociological profile'[41] of terrorists and terrorist groups.[42] Russel and Miller found the typical terrorist to be single, male, aged 22—24, having at least a partial university education, often in the humanities, with an affluent middle- or upper-class family background, and deriving much of his impetus from frustration mixed with anarchist or nihilist notions.[43] This is true also of prominent female terrorists who are especially active in West Germany.[44] According to Clutterbuck, the exception to this profile of a terrorist is to be found among the ranks of the Provisional IRA (PIRA) and extremist Protestant groups, which he claims 'are the only terrorist organizations in the world which even in their leadership have practically no intellectuals.'[45] Macfarlane and Russel and Miller find this consonant with the fact that, because of the socio-economic position of Catholics in Northern Ireland, 'many cadre members and the leadership within the [PIRA] are not drawn from the middle- and upper-classes'.[46]

The fact that terrorism seems entrenched in divided nations (Germany and Ireland) where the legitimacy of the government authorities can be queried with reference to the division does not appreciably help to account for either its form or frequency. Space limitations preclude a detailed analysis of the possible psycho-socio-economic causes of terrorism in the states under scrutiny, so we have chosen in our concluding chapters first to investigate how at a regional level within the European Community the governments have attempted to find a collective response to international terrorism (see Chapter 7), and second to consider the legal niceties that make the conclusion of seemingly rational and superficially easy and limited international agreements — even among EEC member states — highly problematic (see Chapter 8). We are concerned not with how or why governments chose to meet terrorist violence with force,[47] but rather with efforts at improving procedures to ensure the prosecution of terrorist suspects. It becomes apparent that legitimate government authorities in Western Europe have chosen for the most part, with the arguable exception of Ireland, to view terrorism as a criminal rather than political offence. Each of the case studies examines the nature of and government response to terrorism in EEC member states. The cases have been chosen because they illustrate how different Western European liberal democracies have coped with various levels of terrorist activity. Sometimes this activity is designed to challenge and undermine the claim to legitimacy of the elected government, as in West Germany, or of the authorities in office, as in Northern Ireland. In the Netherlands, terrorist activity by the South Moluccans is clearly goal-centred and aimed at redressing a long-standing political grievance. In Italy, the goals are more diffuse and the practitioners drawn from both ends of the political spectrum, whereas in West Germany terrorism has arguably had a greater 'ideological/philosophical' content amd has been oriented towards discrediting the government, persuading the public that those in authority have no right to govern and, latterly, to goals associated with securing the release of captive terrorists.

By contrast, in France there has been a lower level of political violence, with terrorists having a wide variety of goals and disparate ideological roots. Unlike in either West Germany or Italy, or more recently in Northern Ireland, there has been but a small number of groups with the ambition to emulate the Red Army Factions, and even then they have lacked the requisite material and organisational resources. Instead of a clear-cut terrorist movement emerging, different foreign terrorist groups have operated in France, regional groups have engaged in symbolic bombing campaigns against symbols of state domination and various levels of political violence have been employed by rival political groups. The forms terrorism has taken differ from country to country although some common underlying notions emerge.

However, the aim of this book is not to provide some comparative 'theory' of terrorism. Instead, we have chosen the case study approach in order to permit an analysis of terrorism in specific national contexts and to allow for a more detailed assessment of terrorism in individual Western European liberal democracies. Since all the states under scrutiny have increased efforts to combat terrorism since the 1960s, since all are members of the

European Community, and since the international character of contemporary terrorism has led to pressure for an international response, we have also chosen to examine the European Community's efforts to combat terrorism.

In adopting the case study approach, the contributors have endeavoured to cover a number of common areas — including the origins, organisation, 'philosophy', rationale, motives and goals of the various terrorist groups, their international links, state responses to terrorism, attempts to legislate against terrorism and public reaction towards terrorism and towards anti-terrorist measures — insofar as each is relevant to the particular country under investigation. The penultimate chapter is devoted to analysing legal responses to terrorism and illustrates the close dependence of the legal order on the political order at the national, supranational and international levels.

Notes and References

1. For an outline of some of them, see S. Sloan, Conceptualizing political terror: a typology. *Journal of International Affairs, 32* (1978) p. 7.
2. See C. C. O'Brien, *Herod: Reflections on Political Violence* (London: Hutchinson, 1978) pp. 24—39.
3. *Ibid.,* p. 33.
4. *Ibid.,* p. 72.
5. W. Laqueur *Terrorism* (London: Weidenfeld and Nicolson, 1977), pp. 4—5.
6. J. Servier, *Le Terrorisme* (Paris: Presses Universitaires de France, 1979).
7. Laqueur, *op. cit.,* p. 77.
8. *Ibid.,* p. 21.
9. *Ibid.,* p. 75.
10. B. Jenkins, *International Terrorism: A New Mode of Conflict* (Los Angeles: Crescent, 1975), p. 1.
11. J. B. Wolf, Controlling political terrorism in a free society. *Orbis, 19* (1975/76), p. 1290.
12. *Ibid.,* pp. 1289—90.
13. *Ibid.,* p. 1289.
14. See M. Funke (ed.), *Terrorismus* (Düsseldorf: Athenaüm, 1977), pp. 9—36 and R. Zundel, Gerechtigkeit als Aggression. *Liberal, 10* (1974) pp. 726ff. For a discussion of the state as violence and violence against the state, see L. J. Macfarlane, *Violence and the State* (London: Nelson, 1974), pp. 55—129.
15. On Ulster, see Macfarlane, *op. cit.,* p. 114.
16. Laqueur, *op. cit.,* p. 79. Also see D. Fromkin, 'Die Strategie der Terrorismus', in Funke (ed.), *op. cit.,* pp. 83—99.
17. U. Pesch, 'Diplomaten-Entführungen als terroristisches Kampfmittel', in Funke (ed.), *op. cit.,* pp. 100—17; D. C. Rapoport, *Assassination and Terrorism* (Toronto: Canadian Broadcasting Corporation, 1971); M. Havens *et al. The*

Politics of Assassination (Englewood Cliffs, NJ: Prentice Hall, 1970); C. Edler Baumann, *The Diplomatic Kidnappings: A Revolutionary Tactic of Urban Terrorism* (The Hague: Nijhoff, 1973); J. A. Arey, *The Sky Pirates* (New York: Scribners, 1972); and P. Clyde, *An Anatomy of Skyjacking* (London: Abelard Schuman, 1973).

18. See W. Hahlweg, 'Moderner Guerillakrieg und Terrorismus: Probleme und Aspekte ihrer theoretischen Grundlagen als Widerspiegelung der Praxis', in Funke (ed.), *op. cit.*, pp. 118—39.

19. M. C. Hutchinson, The concept of revolutionary terrorism. *Journal of Conflict Resolution, 16* (1972) pp. 383ff.

20. P. Wilkinson, *Political Terrorism* (London: Macmillan, 1974), pp. 36—40.

21. Sloan, *op. cit.*, pp. 9—10.

22. In turn defined as 'very extreme and brutal tactics that would be considered even beyond the conventions of war if they were used in a declared war between two nations. Examples would include blowing-up a school with children present, torture of political prisoners, kidnapping, execution, etc. . .'

23. J. Bowyer Bell, *Transnational Terror* (Stanford: AEI—Hoover Institute, 1978), pp. 15—16.

24. *Ibid.*

25. *Ibid.*

26. Laqueur, *op. cit.*, p. 81.

27. Bowyer Bell, *op. cit.*, p. 17.

28. *Ibid.*, p. 18.

29. *Ibid.*

30. *Ibid.*, pp. 10—12.

31. *Ibid.*, p. 12.

32. *Ibid.*, pp. 13—14.

33. See T. Gurr, *Why Men Rebel* (Princeton, NJ: Princeton University Press, 1970), pp. 573—4.

34. *Ibid.*, pp. 3—4. See also T. Gurr and M. McClelland, *Political Performance: A Twelve Nation Study* (Beverly Hills and London: Sage, 1971), pp. 17—47; H. Eckstein, *The Evaluation of Political Performance: Problems and Dimensions* (Beverly Hills and London: Sage, 1971), pp. 32—64; and T. Nardin, *Violence and the State: A Critique of Empirical Political Theory* (Beverly Hills and London: Sage, 1971).

35. See Y. Alexander (ed.), *Terrorism: National, Regional and Global Perspectives* (New York: Praeger, 1976); and D. Carlton and C. Schaerf (eds), *International Terrorism and World Security* (London: Croom Helm, 1975).

36. *International Terrorism in 1977: A Research Paper* (National Foreign Assessment Center, CIA, RP 78—102554, August 1978) p. 1, footnote 1.

37. See, for example, Sloan, *op. cit.*, p. 11. Also see J. Becker, *Hitler's Children* (London: Michael Joseph, 1977).

38. For an interpretation of United Kingdom measures, see C. Scorer, *The Prevention of Terrorism Acts 1974 and 1976* (London: NCCL, 1976).

39. R. H. Kupperman, Treating the symptoms of terrorism: some principles of good hygiene, *Terrorism, 1* (1977) pp. 46—7.

40. See, for example, E. Hyams, *Terrorists and Terrorism* (London: Dent, 1975).

41. See S. Sloan and R. Kearney, Non-territorial terrorism: an empirical approach to policy formation. *Conflict 1* (1978) pp. 134—5.

42. See C. Dobson and R. Payne, *The Weapons of Terror: International Terrorism at Work* (London: Macmillan, 1979), pp. 1—16 and pp. 40—60 on typical 'ideal' type groups from an organisational point of view and on the motivation for terrorist action by different groups.

43. C. A. Russel and B. H. Miller, Profile of a terrorist. *Terrorism, 1* (1977) pp. 17—34; and C. V. Hassel, Terror: the crime of the privileged — an examination and prognosis. *Terrorism, 1* (1977) pp. 1—16.
44. See Becker, *op. cit.*; H-J. Horchem, West Germany's Red Army anarchists. *Conflict Studies* (June 1974); and Dobson and Payne, *op. cit.*, pp. 46—9. They note that the nature of female terrorism has been interpreted as an extension of sexual liberation.
45. R. Clutterbuck, *Terrorism ohne Chance* (Stuttgart: Seewald, 1975), p. 174. Cited by Russel and Miller, *op. cit.*, p. 28.
46. Macfarlane, *op. cit.*, p. 95; and Russel and Miller, *op. cit.*, p. 27. Also see B. Crozier, *Ulster: Politics and Terrorism* (London: Institute for the Study of Conflict, 1973).
47. C. Cruise O'Brien discusses these concepts in his *Herod: Reflections on Political Violence* (London: Hutchinson, 1978).

CHAPTER 2

Terrorism and the State in West Germany During the 1970s: A Threat to Stability or a Case of Political Over-reaction?

Geoffrey Pridham

COMPARATIVE AND HISTORICAL PERSPECTIVES OF WEST GERMAN TERRORISM

Two introductory points may be made immediately in presenting a case study of terrorism in the Federal Republic of Germany: the Baader—Meinhof Group or Red Army Faction (RAF), the 2nd June Movement, the Revolutionary Cells and other such groups can be categorised straight-forwardly as a branch of terrorism in general; and it provides a valuable example of the political dimensions of terrorism studies for a number of historical, political—cultural and ideological reasons. However, on closer examination many of the methodological problems in assessing terrorism as a phenomenon nevertheless apply. Whilst they must be confronted, these analytical problems are somewhat contained in looking at the specifics of a particular instance of terrorism, thus confirming the usefulness in this field of the case study approach.

West German terrorism conforms broadly to various classifications of terrorist activity. Qualitatively, Lösche identifies five categories in a study of international terrorism: national or anti-colonialist liberation movements; regional or separatist movements; social-revolutionary movements in industrialised societies; defensive associations to protect group privileges; and opposition movements in dictatorial systems.[1] Although German terrorists have themselves made a case for being anti-dictatorial — in their arguments about 'structural violence' in the Federal Republic and their professed aim to expose the 'constitutional mask' of the political authorities, — and have also derived some strength, moral and material, from their self-acclaimed association with Third World liberation movements, the third category of social-revolutionary as an analytical line of pursuit is obviously the one applicable to the German example of terrorism. Quantitatively, a basic doubt must be cast on the possibility that German terrorism has possessed any features of a movement. If one distinguishes here between the progressively diminishing forms of a movement, an active expression of sub-cultural protest or fringe-group activity, one must opt for the last case, even though German terrorism of the 1970s historically had a derivative albeit tortuous relationship with the extra-parliamentary protest movement of the late 1960s. Finally, to use Laqueur's distinctions of modern terrorism, the German example relates geographically speaking to patterns of terrorism in Western Europe, North America and Japan, which grew out of the failure of the 'New Left', as distinct from Latin American rural guerrilla activity inspired by the indigenous conditions of that continent or from the vibrant nationalist terrorism located in the Middle East.[2] In short, lacking any ethnic, religious or viable social basis, German terrorism is first and foremost a *political* (in the view of some observers a psycho-political) phenomenon rather than a socio-political one (compared with terrorism in Italy, which has attracted a certain sub-cultural consent and has been distinctly less isolated from society as a whole). It nevertheless remains to be seen how far terrorism in the Federal Republic has been really revolutionary.

Following this classification, the basic approach to German terrorism must be on the political level of analysis with reference where necessary to relevant sociological and psychological factors. This assumption is confirmed by the way in which terrorism developed as a problem or issue during the course of the 1970s. Above all, the public and especially party political discussion of terrorism that ensued hardly ever omitted some reference to the question of the *Rechtsstaat* or the challenge to West Germany's constitutional order. A whole host of fundamental questions were automatically introduced into the debate, such as the quality of political tolerance (e.g. the controversy over 'sympathisers') and the broad matter of the individual rights of citizens in relation to the increasing requirement for internal security measures (did these involve a move towards the negation of the *Rechtsstaat*?). Terrorism undoubtedly came to be perceived as a 'crisis' in the Federal Republic as the abundant references to 'Weimar conditions' indicated.

But did terrorism really involve a serious threat to political stability, and if so how and why? For the purposes of this chapter, I draw a distinction between the 'objective' performance record of the postwar system in West Germany and the 'subjective' impact of historically conditioned political attitudes and complexes. Such a distinction may of course be applied to other parliamentary states, but the unique feature of the German case is the marked discrepancy between these two dimensions in looking at the progress of the Federal Republic. 'Model Germany' has been accompanied by its irrational leitmotivs, and these were uncomfortably brought to the surface by the terrorist issue.

The starting-point for appreciating this problem is obviously historical. The historical connection either provides traditions, patterns or precedents for a particular form of political behaviour, or it conditions its presentation or responses to it. Thus, on the first count one can identify a Marxist tradition in modern German history, though one highly complicated by the successive experiences of Weimar (birthmarked by the shadow of the Russian Revolution), the Third Reich and the establishment of the East German state, the DDR. Of anarchism, the other ideological stream associated with terrorism of the 1970s, there is a less evident tradition compared say with Spain. Perhaps it is more relevant as an historical theme to refer to elements of German romanticism, notably a utopian search for absolute values, to which youth movements have been especially prone. However, the salient background feature is the role of political violence (to use this loose term for the moment) in modern German history. This was undoubtedly apparent during the Weimar Republic — as a form of political intimidation, in the shape of political assassination, as an expression of underlying and later explicit political instability and of course as a method employed 'informally' by the Nazis in conjunction with their strategy of 'legality' (a combination that was to haunt the fathers of the West German *Rechtsstaat*). Furthermore, the role of political violence/terror is one of the constant themes in explaining the operation of the Third Reich, confirming only too well the terrorists' thesis of 'structural violence' that they applied provocatively to the Federal Republic. It goes without saying that these two 'emotive' periods in German history, which preceded the creation of the West German state, were bound to condition postwar political attitudes.

In looking directly at the Federal Republic this is clear when one remembers that, unlike postwar Italy, West Germany's adoption of parliamentary democracy was not prefaced by any intervening experience of a mass resistance movement, which could have acted as a purgative in the way that anti-fascism became the common ideological denominator among the various Italian political forces. Celebrations of the July Plot, while an official occasion, have not been free from ideological reservations, especially in conservative circles, over such questions as treason against the state. In a broader historical context, Germany has never undergone a real revolution — though some stillborn examples like 1918—19 fostering complexities associated with the afore-mentioned 'subjective' dimension — that, absorbed into the national historical bloodstream, might have allowed for a less loaded response to social and political pressures. Therefore with the coming of the Federal Republic there remained a number of unresolved ideological conflicts deriving from historical experience. One might add to this historical perspective several conditions pertaining to the Bonn republic: its provisional status at birth, the Cold War circumstances at the time and the related 'German question' in its postwar version of the 'two German states in one

German nation'.

Hence, the problems of 'overcoming the past' and the peculiar factors relating to the Federal Republic's legitimacy — and therefore the framework surrounding its developing political stability — accounted to a large degree for the discrepancy between the 'objective' and 'subjective' dimensions, despite the Federal Republic's relatively sound parliamentary—democratic record. This problem has notably arisen in the perception of what constitutes a 'crisis'. In a comparative context West Germany has been noticeably exempt from the major political or economic crises of some of her European partners, although events like Erhard's collapse of authority as Chancellor in 1966 and the Brandt government's loss of its majority in 1972 were assumed to be 'critical'. Historical parallels were drawn on the occasion of the *Spiegel* affair of 1962 (a scandal arising from the arbitrary arrest of leading members of the editorial staff of this magazine and resulting in the ministerial resignation of Strauss; it provoked strong public disquiet and was perceived as a challenge to the freedom of the press) and the economic recession of 1966—67. Similarly, the intermittent occurrence of terrorism in West Germany during the 1970s produced comparable responses, with one contemporary observer going so far as to comment during the Lorenz kidnapping in 1975 that it was a question for the West German state of 'not merely representation or self-presentation but of self-assertion, as for the first time since its existence it was challenged in a completely new and existential way to act as a state and show what it is'.[3] Equally, the 'year of terrorism' in 1977 produced a more intensified debate than ever before on the need for democracy to defend itself internally, which occasioned inevitable parallels with Weimar. In view of such problems in interpreting the nature of West German democracy — which became unavoidably linked with the terrorism question — the initial position of this study is to emphasise that there are different national versions of parliamentary democracy in both the political—institutional and political—cultural sense. Such matters will be discussed further below with reference to the political and institutional responses to terrorism.

Finally, mention should be made of various methodological problems in analysing terrorism systematically as they apply to the West German example. These may be divided into the interpretative and those relating to the nature of evidence. In the first case, Laqueur's point that no truly scientific theories about terrorism have emerged[4] is as much applicable to West Germany as to any other case. The absence of adequate comparative tools does inhibit investigation, as the very academic controversy over defining the term 'terrorism' denotes.[5] In the emotive atmosphere occasioned by terrorist events this word has become a polemical football in the Federal Republic, both in public references to the terrorists as well as in inter-party arguments over the causes of this relatively new phenomenon in German politics. One thought process by no means confined to the political right followed the sequence of terrorism = subversion = communism, under-standable in the light of the historical link between the Federal Republic's legitimacy and the problems of inter-German relations but one that all the same obstructed a differentiated assessment of the issue. For the purposes of the German case study, the term 'terrorist' rather than 'guerrilla' is applicable in the sense that the former is very clearly politically motivated with the ultimate goal of revolution employing a variety of methods of which one common feature is the maximisation of fear. The object of attack in this case is the West German state and 'system' and everything it stands for. Although some terrorist activity in the world may pursue guerrilla methods, such as a more discriminating concentration on specific political or military targets, the West German groups do not really fit into this definition.

Probably the most useful standpoint to adopt in trying to place West German terrorism in a comparative setting is simply to start with the obvious hypothesis that its form of politics is 'unconventional'. That is to say, comparative terminology relating to the ideology or socio-political importance of terrorism is not easy to apply, although it is necessary to use it qualifiedly as a basis for systematic discussion. However, concentrating this discussion on a political level does allow at least in the German case for a more compact treatment than would say a purely psychological or cultural—historical approach with their neglect of socio-political factors and a certain partiality for moralistic judgements. The case study method, with all its limitations, does allow for an assessment of the problem in the light of the national circumstances that might or might not have promoted it and that have conditioned its operation. Since much of the general literature on terrorism has in effect been a cursory review of numerous cases of its appearance, there are strong arguments for looking at individual examples more thoroughly.

The other methodological problem in looking at West German terrorism is that although its activities are better documented than many other examples there nevertheless remain various difficulties of evidence. This ranges in general from the microscopically detailed to the tendentious or sensationalist and the impressionistic. One of the reasons is that 'conventional' sources are both partial and partially informative, inevitably affected by the tenor of debate about the terrorism issue in West Germany. But there is still a variety of evidence that altogether makes a reasoned survey possible. First, the very discussion within the Federal Republic of terrorism and its political implications stimulated by the later 1970s a growth of publications from political and academic circles, sometimes as a result of special conferences on the subject, with some of this informed debate featuring in the press (notably the weekly *Die Zeit*). Second, contemporary observers such as the media have throughout the 1970s reported extensively on terrorist activity and strategy — particularly *Der Spiegel* on a fairly regular basis but also the daily press during terrorist events. Third, there is direct evidence from the terrorists themselves. This has been in the form of theoretical works or tracts on urban guerrilla warfare or revolutionary aims, especially by the original RAF leaders, similar evidence offered by terrorists for publication in the press, the confessions of a few 'defectors' who have been willing to talk and the polemical literature of 'New Left' groups sympathetic to the aims of the terrorists. Fourth, official documentation such as the annual reports of the Interior Ministry on internal security and special government reports on terrorist events (such as the *Schleyer-Dokumentation*) contribute to the picture, although naturally selective in information about the details of government consultations during them. One might also add here the official material produced for the purposes of informing the public about different aspects of German terrorism and about the security structure of the state.

THE DEVELOPMENT, IDEOLOGY AND SOCIOLOGY OF TERRORISM IN THE FEDERAL REPUBLIC

Since it is clear that the rise and impact of terrorism cannot be viably treated outside the particular circumstances of the society in which it has chosen to operate, the aim of this section is to examine the course of terrorism as a phenomenon and problem in the context of West German politics from the late 1960s. If by 'conventional' standards terrorism in that country must be regarded as politically marginal — i.e. in terms of its very limited attraction as a form of activity outside the small groups engaged in it — the question still has to be faced as to what has motivated the German terrorists, how they have operated and what exactly is their relationship with society at large. For this it is necessary to establish some reference points for a discussion of terrorist development, which may be done by focussing on the following aspects: the origins and history of terrorism, including its different patterns of activity; the theoretical dimension, such as whether one may speak of an ideological orientation among the German groups and how terrorist doctrines and strategies related to terrorist actions; and the sociological aspect, where the main points of interest are any particular features of those involved in terrorism, whether they may be regarded as representing a form of fringe sub-culture or indeed how much one may make reasonable generalisations about these groups.

The Origins and History of German Terrorism

While it is accepted there is no simple explanation for the appearance of terrorism, a number of different factors relating to its origins can be deciphered. One of these often neglected in the discussion of German terrorism and its causes is the domestic political context in which it arose. This is worth emphasising because, although the Vietnam question undoubtedly became a classic object for youthful indignation,[6] the early terrorists spent more time in polemical attacks on the Federal Republic (albeit sometimes described as a 'colony' of the USA) rather than on 'American imperialism' as such. The desire to create a 'Vietnam feeling' did feature prominently in leaflets distributed by them in connection with the first actions in 1968—69. Some of them were later to claim that the motive for the Frankfurt department store fires of April 1968 had been 'to light a torch for Vietnam', just as Gudrun Ensslin, one of them, asserted: 'We did it out of protest against the indifference towards the war in Vietnam'.[7]

All the same, the chief 'enemy' for the terrorists remained West Germany itself and its postwar system and this continued to be so once their actions became a trend from 1970. Various political developments inside the Federal Republic, as confirmed by some terrorist writings of the time, seemed to help ignite their determination to embark on their course of violent protest — above all, a general disillusionment with the constitutional left, as represented by the Social Democrats (SPD), which could be traced back to the break between the party and the Socialist Student Organisation (SDS) in the early 1960s but which came to a head with the Grand Coalition of the SPD with the Christian Democrats (CDU) and Christian Socialists (CSU) (especially over the issue of the emergency laws) and thereafter was fostered by the general failure of the much promised 'inner reforms' once the SPD became the principal governing party from 1969. Since the SPD's coalition with the CDU/CSU was clearly viewed by the radical student movement as a fundamental challenge, several later terrorist figures then involved in minority activist circles within the SDS (notably Horst Mahler and Ulrika Meinhof) were influenced by this viewpoint. Meinhof was then editor of *Konkret,* a mouthpiece for these circles, in which she accused the SPD of wanting 'to prostitute itself', a step which had 'been prepared systematically since Godesberg'.[8] This feeling soon broadened into an overall rejection of what the party represented:

> all Leftists have run over to the Right to boil the common pot and cook in it, there is nothing but one anger, one hatred, one lament . . . and the exclusion, the hereticising, the bedevilment of what remains has sired a kind of Left. A 'New Left' as it calls itself, so as to doubly signal its appearance.[9]

The importance of the Grand Coalition as some kind of turning-point in the eyes of early terrorists was later repeated in the detailed questionnaire answered by Baader, Meinhof, Ensslin and Raspe for *Der Spiegel* in early 1975, where they selected the emergency laws of 1968 as the start of a 'fascistisation process' in the Federal Republic.[10] Furthermore, the neglect and inoperativeness of most reforms despite the enthusiasm they engendered under the new social—liberal coalition, aside from a few positive examples, appeared to confirm these assumptions about the need for a basic change in the 'social order'. I agree with Lösche's comment that West German terrorism cannot in part be understood without reference to 'the disappointment over the reform policy since the end of the sixties which came to a standstill at the outset'.[11]

The thought arises at this point how much these political events might have been used as an *ex-post facto* justification for later terrorist activities. This leads to the question of their ideological motivation, which will be discussed below, but remaining on the historical level of explanation it is necessary to clarify the relationship between the terrorist groups and the New Left movement of the late 1960s. While evidently this movement belongs to the lineage of the terrorists, the relationship was far from being the uni-causal linear one claimed by conservative opinion during the 1970s. This is because whatever the impact of German terrorists as a whole, especially with reference to their early years of involvement, they did not themselves represent a movement in any conventional sense. The New Left, or the Extra-Parliamentary Opposition (APO) as it was formally known, faded rapidly before the 1969 change of power in Bonn, and its participants went in a variety of directions: a substantial number, so far as they remained in politics, were absorbed into the SPD, a much smaller number into orthodox communism, some became anti-communist publicists and only a miniscule proportion became engaged in any way in terrorist activity. At the same time one should not underrate the symbolism of '1968', for whatever the APO's failure as a movement it was bound to have indirect political consequences of some kind. The student background of many individual terrorists and the involvement of some in the vogue habits of commune-living and the drug scene suggested a link with the mood of radical protest against conformist bourgeois society, but the specific relationship between APO and the later terrorists demands closer examination before any general points can be inferred.

What emerges is that the APO/terrorist relationship was at best a tenuous one. First, the New Left as a movement in West Germany was itself not cohesive. Kurt Shell usefully divides the APO typologically into three tendencies — radical—democratic—liberal, Marxist—revolutionary and anarchist—direct—actionist[12] — which, not being clearly demarcated from each other, indicated the problems it faced in trying to formulate political positions, most relevantly over the employment of illegal methods of protest and generally the role of force in politics. Those who were potentially sympathetic or open to terrorist activity were primarily grouped under the third tendency; but even here they formed a dissenting minority, for as Shell emphasises those uncompromisingly determined to put their feelings into action ran 'contrary to the mainstream' of New Left thinking.[13] His conclusion is apt that the New Left's theoretical leaders 'did for a long time ignore the unintended but implicit consequences of their theories and utterances; and they did neglect to anticipate or clearly counter plausible misinterpretations of their positions'.[14]

Second, it is instructive to record the reactions of certain key terrorist figures to the New Left, as these revealed a less than wholehearted response to the aims and methods of that movement. Jillian Becker's detailed narrative shows that Ulrike Meinhof's evolution from a pacifist position through marriage with an orthodox communist to her gradual acceptance of the use of violence included a stage when she was a publicist expressing scepticism about the indiscriminate or 'noisy' forms of protest of student radicals (she was a good decade older than the average student then) despite some early sympathy for their outlook.[15] More significantly, Horst Mahler's later comment made during his trial in early 1973 on the motives for forming the RAF underlined the terrorists' sense of profound disappointment with the failure of the APO in the face of 'the power barriers of the state institutions':

> It can only be termed deeply frustrating to recognise the necessity of a revolution with growing clarity and yet be unable to know who and where the revolutionary class, in other words the beneficiaries of this upheaval itself, actually are. That is bad, and how easily can such a state of affairs lead to a mood of desperation! From this point, via a completely abstract identification with the liberation struggles in the Third World, the further course led to out-and-out adventurous concepts.[16]

Indeed, the original Baader—Meinhof leaders had also cited as a motive for the Frankfurt fires of 1968 their intention to 'prevent the voice of the Extra-Parliamentary Opposition from not being able to find a hearing'.[17] The absolutist negative sentiment prevalent among the early terrorists did differ somewhat in quality from the serious and intensive theoretical preoccupations of the New Left of 1967—69, whose main contribution to the history of the Federal Republic was to initiate the first open discussion of radical Marxist theory since the War.[18] One could therefore offer at this point a distinction between the extreme tenuousness of the political/sociological link of APO with terrorism (especially over the form of political activity adopted) and a greater continuity with respect to their ideological link.

Third, even this ideological link cannot pass statement without mention of the critical attitude towards terrorism and the general use of violence on the part of some prominent theoreticians of the New Left. The most notable case was Jürgen Habermas of the Frankfurt School of neo-Marxist thinking who in early days crossed dialectical swords with those seeking to derive violent conclusions from his ideas by referring to the dangers of a 'left-wing Fascism':

> Demonstrational force is that with which we force attention to arguments, and so establish conditions for a discussion where it is needed. But if I am to understand provocation in the sense of provoking violence hidden in the

institutions into declared and manifest violence, then systematically undertaken
provocation by students is a game of terror (with Fascist implications).[19]

Similarly, Theodor Adorno as another leading light of the same school
deplored the fact that 'I have presented a theoretical model, but how could I
suspect that people would want to put it into effect with Molotov cocktails'.[20]
Herbert Marcuse, the chief father figure of New Left thinking, went further
than his spiritual colleagues in his radical critique of modern capitalism and
industrial society and his projection about its social forms of 'Fascist
suppression'. However, Marcuse noted in his later years his own reservations
about the New Left experience, particularly its 'unrealistic' features:

> the reluctance to re-examine and to develop Marxian categories, the tendency
> to make a fetish out of Marxist theory, to treat the Marxian concepts as reified,
> objective categories, instead of becoming finally conscious of the fact that
> these are historical and dialectical concepts which cannot simply be repeated,
> which have to be re-examined in accordance with changes in society itself.[21]

His judgement may seem over-tinged with belated regret about the outcome
of the New Left, but this description is certainly applicable at least to the
outlook of the German terrorists to whose own ideas we now turn. One
feature already apparent in the debate over the New Left, and which
surfaces again in the controversy over terrorism in the 1970s, is the mutually
antagonistic use of the term 'fascism' by opposing sides with its unavoidably
emotive connotations in the postwar German context.

The Ideological Dimension

The ideological dimension of West German terrorism, as indeed of terrorism
in general, broaches the kind of interpretative problems mentioned initially,
for it raises the question of the 'unconventional' nature of terrorist politics.
Laqueur's point that 'it is certainly not true that scratching a terrorist will
necessarily reveal an ideologue'[22] is probably correct, but the specific
ideological content or orientation of terrorism, or cases of it, is still open to
discussion. In the German instance ideology is by no means absent from the
scene, and in view of the introductory remarks about ideological perspectives
in modern German history it is an essential aspect of the subject. A first
glance at German terrorism would certainly locate its ideological home on
the left, or as more left than anything else in the sense that its main
ideological targets and phobias were distinctly 'right wing', e.g. Nazism/
fascism, American imperialism and Vietnam, bourgeois opposition to the
'class struggle', capitalist society. The historical link with the New Left, the
political background of individual terrorists and the fact that their circles of
'sympathisers', both active and passive, all came from the political left
suggested the same ideological location. West Germany did not undergo any

phase equivalent to Italy's period of neo-fascist inspired violence in the early 1970s. Violent activities (for 'terrorism' is too strong a word here) deriving from the extreme right have occurred spasmodically in the Federal Republic through the 1970s, with some fluctuation and occasional growth in incidents,[23] but they cannot *in toto* be considered and have not been perceived as presenting the same challenge as 'red' terrorism.

Yet, the problem of identifying specifically the ideological left-wingness of the German terrorists remains and is underlined by their complicated relationship, or really lack of it, with the constitutional left. A good illustration of this problem is Willy Brandt's commentary in his speech to the Bundestag during the debate on terrorist legislation in March 1975:

> It is customary to speak of the terrorists as of the 'left'. This is a use of speech which has been taken over only too thoughtlessly, also by me and therefore I criticise not only others but also myself. There is certainly a reason behind this in some cases — therefore two comments. Firstly, those who decree the terrorists the title of 'left' in the sense of the proper political spectrum of our country — I emphasize, political — are doing them an honour to which they have no right. This includes them in a schema — about which one can of course argue — that is taken from the parliamentary sphere. I say emphatically: the terrorists are everything other than 'left' in the sense of the political and parliamentary spectrum of parties. They have nothing to do with it. They are rather people who play into the hands of reaction. Secondly, those who nevertheless characterize them as 'left' in an ambiguous way are defining consciously or unconsciously the parliamentary left so as to place it, again consciously or unconsciously, close to the terrorists. In the name of the parliamentary left — and this is the role of Social Democracy, also when it is part of the new centre — I reject firmly these views.[24]

This ideological demarcation of the SPD from terrorism, a determined viewpoint fully shared by the Young Socialists in the party,[25] touched on a sore historical nerve because of the SPD's at times complicated relationship with the state through different successive political systems in the twentieth century (the above quotation omits sarcastic and alluding interjections from CDU/CSU members). It is also significant that for a different reason the orthodox Communist Party (DKP) attacked terrorist violence for promoting reaction,[26] for clearly this ran counter to their own methods of infiltration and in their view distracted attention from their different political aims as well as strategy (one of the relative strongholds of the DKP was the universities, also a catchment basin for terrorist sympathisers).

So far as the terrorists themselves were concerned it could be said they represented unorthodox variations based on Marxism. This assertion is only possible because of the political divisions of the Marxist tradition in German history. The terrorists themselves laid claim to 'Marxist' or even 'communist' inspiration, firmly rejecting the 'anarchist' label, in which their ideological loyalty was to Mao-tse-tung or Che Guevara rather than Lenin — as in their criticism of the DKP for being 'embourgeoised' and not wanting to overthrow the state.[27] Insofar as they had any German historical reference points, these were the 'purist' martyrs of Rosa Luxembourg and Karl Liebknecht. Yet it is also possible to add that insofar as they resembled features of German romanticism they were more akin to right-wing politics. All the same, by any usual standards it is still difficult to measure the ideological dimension of German terrorism. Various authorities or observers have commented that for the terrorists ideology has provided a 'camouflage' or that it is eclectic and taken at face value, that at best it is utopian (or 'criminal utopianism') and finally that it is theoretically weak as it offers no clearly defined alternative society, only the belief that the system should be 'different'. There is some element of truth in all these remarks but it still remains to identify more specifically the ideological content and orientation of the German terrorists. While their politics are obviously 'unconventional', familiar analytical yardsticks have to be employed at least as a starting-point for lack of other suitable ones.

The method adopted here is to identify various leitmotivs in terrorist thinking, and then to comment on its general features and importance for the development of terrorist activity. Three overarching leitmotivs may be said to have contained the various key concepts in terrorist thinking on the grounds of their common or regular inclusion in terrorist tracts and underground publications or their apparently central relevance to the terrorists' motivation:

(a) *The concept of the 'armed struggle' and the model of Third World liberation movements.* This probably had the greatest individual influence on terrorist thinking, especially as it gave the groups a sense of international solidarity in the face of their lack of popular following in the Federal Republic. However, this leitmotiv had a definite history of its own deriving from the New Left (e.g. the hero-worshipping of Che Guevara), and it undoubtedly provided the salient 'theoretical' basis for terrorist activity. Numerous terrorist booklets, manuals or statements gave expression to it: 'The concept of the urban guerrilla' (1971, written by Ulrike Meinhof), 'Concerning the armed struggle in Western Europe' (allegedly authored by Horst Mahler), 'Serve the people — Red Army Faction: urban guerrilla and class struggle' (sent to *Der Spiegel* for publication in April 1972) and 'Lead the anti-imperialistic struggle — Create the Red Army — the action of Black September in Munich' (November 1972).[28] It was repeated by other shorter statements from the RAF's two ideological leaders, Horst Mahler and Ulrike Meinhof, on various occasions.[29] Briefly, while identifying with 'oppressed' people in the Third World in opposition to 'US imperialism', the theory involved following Carlos Marighela's application of guerrilla warfare to urban areas and drew succour from the theoretical blessing given by Frantz Fanon to violence as an intrinsic element of revolution. The terrorists' fervent adherence to these concepts had something of a simplistic ring when applied to German conditions, as in 'The concept of the urban guerrilla':

> If it is right that American imperialism is a paper tiger ... and if the thesis of the Chinese Communists is right that the battle is being fought in all corners of the world, so that the forces of imperialism are splintered and have become defeatable ... then there is no reason to exclude any country or region from the anti-imperialist struggle.[30]

This clearly involved a fundamental rejection of legal methods and parliamentarianism, but two further points are worth a mention. The absolutist and cathartic view of violence, in asserting that the destruction of the existing order was an essential precondition for a 'free' society, was nevertheless hedged with conceptual ambiguities in a German context. These derived in part from historical experience, but also semantically from the fact that the term *Gewalt* makes no distinction between 'power' and 'violence', e.g. in a loose sense *'Gewalt'* had become something of a conceptual catchword among New Left circles in the late 1960s. The other point concerned the terrorists' idea of their relationship with the masses. These theories contained an automatic belief that 'armed struggle' would inspire mass support, but here they were criticised from within the 'unconventional left' — Jean-Paul Sartre emphasised their failure to construct a mass basis, and eventually Mahler left the RAF on these grounds. In answer to such criticism they argued that it was not a question of 'supporters' or 'fellow-travellers' but of the 'effects' of their politics in 'changing people's attitude to the state' following the government's anti-terrorist measures.[31]

(b) *The Nazi 'connection' and 'formal democracy' in the Federal Republic.* Although Nazism was defeated militarily in 1945, it was in the view of the terrorists still living 'spiritually' and politically. This basic association of the postwar democracy with the Third Reich — whereby the Federal Republic was only 'formally' a democracy (a term borrowed from the New Left) because it served only the interests of the 'bourgeoisie' — was of course, in the intensity with which it was applied, a special feature of the German version of terrorism for obvious historical reasons. As an emotively charged concept it involved not so much a theory as a theoretical assumption and it covered a variety of other or related attitudes, e.g. problems of generational conflict, postwar Germany's 'neglect' of the 'spiritual' education of the young and above all the thesis of 'structural violence' on the part of the existing system (a concept elaborated theoretically by Galtung at this time) and the need to oppose it with counter-force. This socio-political anti-Nazism, expressed through the frequent use by the terrorists of the term 'resistance' to describe their own activities,[32] was said to be influenced by their personal complexes about the past,[33] but it also clearly drew on the revival of anti-authoritarianism in the late 1960s as a virtually sub-cultural attitude of the younger generation by no means confined to the New Left though vehemently promoted by it. Meinhof's assertion about 'that type of person who wears a uniform' ('der Typ in der Uniform') who as a representative of authority deserved nothing but being shot was a violent interpretation of this viewpoint.[34] On a more directly political level, the terrorists' main claim was that anti-communism from the time of the Cold War had opened the way for 're-fascistisation' in the Federal Republic, especially as Germany had unlike many other European countries experienced no 'mass-scale armed anti-fascist resistance'.[35] This particular thesis of the terrorists predictably aroused more controversy in West Germany than many of their other ideas, with perhaps the most pertinent argument coming from the political historian Bracher that the terrorists were making the mistake of confusing 'totalitarianism' and 'fascism', so that the discussion centred around the confrontation of fascism versus socialism while ignoring the difference between parliamentary and totalitarian rule.[36] It is worth noting that on a psychological plane the views of the terrorists occasioned much debate focussing on the thesis of their being 'Hitler's children'.[37] This thesis worked in two different directions: on the one hand, that they were reacting against the recent past and sought to compensate for it, and on the other that they were sub-consciously identifying with it. The latter interpretation produced the idea that the terrorists were 'left-wing fascists', although as a concluding point it is worth distinguishing in political terms between their ideological anti-Nazism and the fact that their *methods*, violent as they were, resembled those employed by Nazis.

(c) *The rejection of consumer society.* This leitmotiv overlapped somewhat with the preceding two both because of the terrorists' sympathies with the Third World 'proletariat' and because they were influenced by New Left theories about what Habermas called 'a form of modern, noiseless fascism', above all Marcuse's critique of capitalist society as having a 'fascist' potential sociologically speaking in its 'degradation' of humanity. This anti-capitalist leitmotiv again allowed an outlet for generational conflict because of the terrorists' attack on the materialistic preoccupations of the parental generations, and provided a further basis for overthrowing the established system. For this reason they have been called 'refugees from affluence' or 'the spoiled children of the economic miracle' (a reference to the prosperous middle-class background of many of them). Generally speaking, terrorist thinking on this matter hardly offered anything new or original.[38]

In looking now generally at the ideological content of German terrorism, different features are already evident and may be summarised. These ideological leitmotivs and the various concepts they included were largely negative, certainly utopian and very much second-hand. Because of these characteristics doubts have to be cast on how far terrorist thinking involved any integral or systematic assessment of the wrongs and deficiencies of West Germany. One particular problem is that terrorist language, while familiar in its use of jargonistic terminology, has been both confused and confusing as a means of communicating ideas.[39] It did indeed sound highly eclectic, as the following description by an observer of Ulrike Meinhof's evidence at Mahler's trial in late 1972 suggested:

> The 38 year-old former journalist . . . walked in shouting 'Freedom', refused to sit down on the witness bench and stood instead. When being given the usual talk on the duties of a witness she interrupted the presiding judge and called him such names as 'pig' and 'Fascist', refused to answer questions as to her identity, and said that she was an 'anti-Fascist' by profession. Her hearing turned, in fact, into a dialogue between Herr Mahler and Frau Meinhof on the concept and ideology of the 'Red Army Faction', on which the two did not always agree. Observers had a hard time following this baffling dialogue. The names of Marx, of Herr Genscher, the Minister of the Interior, Herr Brandt and President Heinemann cropped up, anti-semitism was broached as well as Fascism, the capitalistic social order and the Government coalition. Eventually, there was a kind of summary by Frau Meinhof of what the goals were: to hit the system in the face; to mobilize the masses; and to maintain international solidarity.[40]

This eclecticism is a pointer to the ideological orientation of the terrorists, for the structural weakness of their theories derived from the fact that their motivation was by no means exclusively ideological. From one point of view they were of course extremely ideological, in the sense of their rigid attempt to apply ideological beliefs in practice,[41] but other features indicated a relativisation of the importance of ideology. It is usually agreed that the two prominent ideologists of German terrorism were Mahler and Meinhof, the first-generation RAF leaders, but that others in the same group (notably Andreas Baader)[42] were more motivated by a cult of violence, with ideology as a subsidiary factor, and that later terrorists were much less interested in theories. It is therefore significant that direct evidence of terrorist thinking, as noted above, is based predominantly on the writings and statements of the early RAF, and that similar material from either the RAF successors or the other groups (save intermittent broadsheets from the Revolutionary Cells) has been scarce. Among the latter there have been signs of a certain scorn for theory and an emphasis on the value of 'propaganda by deed', although it is understood they have adhered to the same revolutionary aims as the early terrorists. However, a full picture of the terrorists' ideological orientation can only be completed by turning to their patterns of activity and some discussion of the sociological aspects of German terrorism.

It is not the intention here to examine in detail the full range of terrorists activities in West Germany,[43] some of which will again be considered in the case studies of government policy during terrorist crises. In view of the political focus of this study, it is however useful at this point to identify some particular features of German terrorist activity before touching on the groups' relationship with society as a whole. These may be treated fairly briefly.

Taken altogether, terrorist actions have not differed significantly in their methods compared with those adopted in most other West European countries: bombings and arson, 'expropriation' (especially bank robberies), the 'liberation' of captured terrorists from imprisonment, kidnappings and the instituting of 'people's prisons' (first tried with Peter Lorenz, early 1975, and of course with Hans Martin Schleyer in the autumn of 1977) and assassination (the Buback and Ponto murders in 1977). From the political angle, a relevant distinction may be made between the total of terrorist actions and those that were dramatic because of their direct political effect. With the former there has been a greater regularity or consistency although the overall totals have fluctuated from year to year, as the official figures in Table 2.1 show. In this connection, a difference emerges between the first

TABLE 2.1 *Terrorist Actions in the Federal Republic, 1973—76*

	1973	1974	1975	1976
Murder attacks	6	5	5	2
Kidnappings/taking of hostages	—	—	2	—
Explosions	19	37	21	12
Cases of arson	42	57	13	13
Robberies	3	5	5	3
	70	104	46	30

Source: Bundesinnenministerium, *Verfassungsschutz 1975* (1976) p. 108; *Verfassungsschutz 1976* (1977) p. 127.

phase of terrorist activity during 1970—72 with the original Baader—Meinhof group (with their concentration on robberies, bombings and fires) and the successor and other groups, who while continuing the same methods also followed the more alarming practice of attacks on prominent public figures (beginning with the murder of Günter von Drenkmann, president of the West Berlin high court, by the 2nd June Movement in November 1974). In the eyes of the terrorists all such criminal acts are regarded as 'political', as part of their overall strategy, but nevertheless actions involving public figures had a more immediate effect, presented a more overt political challenge and required a different form of government response. Another feature of German terrorist activity during the 1970s is that it was marked by long intermissions, assumed to be for the purpose of preparations for a further phase of attacks: during 1972—74 following the arrest of the leaders of the RAF, again in 1975—77 before the 'year of terrorism' (notably the attacks on the Chief Federal Prosecutor Buback, the banker Ponto and the industrialist Schleyer) and in the couple of years following the Schleyer affair. During these pauses less large-scale actions continued, notably bank robberies for financing further activities.

It is no secret, and obvious from the nature of their planned actions, that the terrorists have usually been well organised. Their methods of preparation have been systematic with various common features such as the procurement of arms from abroad or by stealing from military depots, the renting of so-called 'conspirative flats' usually in anonymous blocks, a strong mobility with the use of fast cars and other details like the forging of passports and driving licences. One key factor has of course been finance, a vital precondition of all these expensive modes of operation. Aside from the pattern of bank robberies (which produced DM 5.4 million during 1970—78 with another DM 6.2 million from other forms of robbery[44]) as the main source, financial demands have been made on active sympathisers, there has been some blackmailing of those implicated in small ways with assisting the terrorists who prefer this not to become known and apparently material support from international terrorist contacts, notably the Palestinians. These international links have been an important backdrop to German terrorism for other reasons since various leaders have at times received guerrilla training in the Middle East,[45] some German terrorists have participated in actions abroad (e.g. the attack on the OPEC headquarters in 1975) while, more notably, Palestinian terrorists have sometimes played a central part in German activities (the Munich Olympic massacre in 1972, and the Lufthansa hijacking during the Schleyer affair in 1977).

In the later 1970s this efficiency seemed less evident, for a principal change had by then occurred in the structure of German terrorism. Whereas in the first phase of 1970—72 the terrorist scene had been dominated by the centralised and nationwide RAF, in the latter half of the decade several autonomous groups were operating, although all committed to a form of 'strategic' agreement. The mere dynamism of terrorism itself, together with the fact that the West German security authorities were now 'biting', made it in any case unlikely that its structural nature would remain stable. This more hydra-headed leadership situation made it in turn more difficult for security to be effective in tracking down the terrorists. Already by 1975 a lack of contact and coordination was apparent between the different groups: the so-called 'Central Info-Office' had been disbanded, terrorists were more cautious in avoiding contact with other groups and there developed a preference for a strict division of labour through smaller units, which could easily disperse when necessary.[46] One could add to this a further qualitative difference and speak of a second generation of terrorists, for many of them were distinctly younger than the original Baader—Meinhof group — born in the late 1940s or early 1950s rather than 1930s or early 1940s — and therefore had no direct experience of participation in the student protest movement of the late 1960s. It is possible to suggest that they were differently influenced, if at all, by the ideological assumptions of the New Left. The 'belief system' of the terrorists was seemingly inherited by later groups, but what is clear is that they drew inspiration from the very act of terrorism itself with the Baader—Meinhof acting as trail-blazers.

Generally, there were two main groups with others, including a new RAF, putting in an occasional appearance. The most notorious was the 2nd June Movement, which had been responsible for most terrorist activities in West Berlin since 1970 (except those attributed to the RAF) and became renowned once it kidnapped Peter Lorenz, the Berlin CDU leader, during the state election campaign in 1975. The group was named after the date of the police killing of the Berlin student Benno Ohnesorg during an anti-Shah demonstration in 1967 (one of the trigger events of terrorism). The Movement tended to be far more localised than the original RAF, with its actions focussed on the city of West Berlin. Although it drew some supporters away from the leaderless RAF, it adhered more strictly to anti-authoritarian views, rejecting the authoritarian methods of the RAF in favour of leadership with no 'orders' or 'directives'.[47] It also contained a greater proportion of proletarian members than the very middle-class Baader—Meinhof Group. The other main branch of second generation terrorism was the Revolutionary Cells, active from 1973 but prominent from 1976. As with the 2nd June Movement, they accepted the general ideological tenets of the RAF — the concept of the urban guerrilla featured in their irregular polemical newssheet *Revolutionärer Zorn* — but they differed over tactics, with a more informal or 'spontaneous' organisation and the habit of acting as 'after hours terrorists' (i.e. maintaining a bourgeois existence during the day).[48] With this changed situation in the terrorist world it was not entirely surprising that there should have been some signs of internal criticism between the different groups over the tactical use of violence in relation to ideological aims.[49] The need to give political 'meaning' to actions, a theme frequently aired in *Revolutionärer Zorn,* was a possible breaking-point between some of the terrorists, especially the RAF successors and their sympathisers in the various 'K' groups (extreme left Marxist groups).

The sociological dimension

This problem leads directly to the question of the sociological dimension of German terrorism. Again, it is relevant to clarify some features in order to provide insights into terrorism as a political phenomenon. Several of these have already been alluded to in the preceding discussion but need further elaboration. First, the predominantly bourgeois background of the terrorists[50] and the prominence among them of women[51] accord with patterns in other West European countries. While it is outside the province of this study to comment psychologically, it is worth noting in the German case that the particular complexes of the bourgeoisie over the Nazi experience and the strong patriarchal values in traditional family life had some bearing on these features. The intensely utopian bent of the terrorists' outlook supports the claim that only the leisure class can afford abstract idealism — as in the *Schili* ('Chic Left') connections of many terrorists, and almost caricatured by Baader's taste for expensive cars — and one is reminded of Horst Mahler's assertion that revolutionary theory can only be developed by those who can 'interpret and conceptualise lessons from the past'.[52] Second, the relative political isolation of the terrorists naturally had its social side. As we have seen, it has been necessary to differentiate between the various tendencies in the West German political left — between the constitutional/ anti-constitutional left in general and among the extreme left between orthodox and 'unconventional' communists — because these historical divisions derive from conflicting aims for German society and divergent means of achieving them. The country's long background of fratricidal antagonism between these divisions created added pressures for the deliberate isolation of the radically activist minority within the left. Moreover, the terrorists' reminder of the Nazi past in such brutal terms was hardly comfortable to those outside circles committed unswervingly to their beliefs. Consequently, recruitment into terrorism involved an act of finality that expressed itself in the absolutist demands of the various groups.

One final question in this context is the degree to which the German terrorists as a phenomenon may be said to have social roots, that is with which social groups they have had any relationship and which may provide a potential recruitment basin. This touches on a highly controversial matter in the German public discussion of terrorism, to which I shall return in the next section (see below, pp. 42-4). The most valid point to make at this stage is to distinguish between the 'active' and the 'passive' among the 'sympathisers'. The former would include those involved in some form of practical assistance for the terrorists, notably in providing temporary accommodation; while 'passive sympathisers' comprised the much larger audience receptive of the terrorists' theories (which after all had never been confined to the terrorists) but who had reservations about or disagreed with their violent methods. Even this distinction had its weaknesses as a sociological description, not only because of inevitable overlap but also on account of the variety and complexity of motives that led some people into active support (and maybe even terrorism) and others close to its border but never actually across it.[53] Various official estimates have been given at different times of the numbers of 'sympathisers', sometimes confusingly totalling them all together, with ranges of up to several thousand 'active' supporters around a hard core of some 60—200 terrorists. They have been drawn from the intelligentsia or academic and professional classes (e.g. doctors, lawyers, some priests, but above all students), but clearly they have been a fluctuating and unquantifiable number.

The three dimensions discussed in this section — the historical, ideological and sociological — have all been essential in not only presenting the different characteristics of German terrorism, but also providing a necessary background to the following discussion of the treatment of terrorism as a political problem in the Federal Republic. They facilitate an understanding of the strong public reaction to this problem and of the particular difficulties faced by the government in dealing with it, some indications of which have already been given. For the common factor among these three dimensions is that German terrorism, while being 'objectively' marginal, related very evidently to the 'subjective' aspects of postwar German politics.

THE POLITICAL AND INSTITUTIONAL RESPONSES TO TERRORIST ACTIVITY

One unqualified generalisation from the foregoing discussion is that terrorism became an emotive issue in West Germany in the 1970s for a variety of political reasons deriving predominantly from the modern historical past. The fact that terrorism as an issue was widely perceived in 'subjective' terms by both party elites and the general public underlined this factor. What follows now is an assessment of the Federal Republic's responses to this new issue, the way in which terrorism came to be seen as posing a fundamental challenge to the authority and credibility of the West German state, a closer examination of party-political and public reactions to this problem and finally an analysis of the variety of institutional procedures and responses in the handling of terrorist crises.

The Emergence of Terrorism as a Political Issue

In saying that terrorism was a new issue of the 1970s is to beg a few secondary questions. As a consequence of the political and sociological phenomenon of urban guerrilla and other forms of modern terrorism since the late 1960s, not only in West Germany but also internationally, the issue may be described as a new area of government policy concern in the 1970s. Matters of law and order and especially security had however been regular affairs of state since the founding of the Federal Republic, not without implications for potential political stability. This link with such a fundamental question had hovered in the background, if not always the foreground, of political attention. The CDU/CSU as the main governing party for the first twenty years of the postwar republic had accorded the theme of 'security' the greatest prominence in its electoral appeals apart from its traditional emphasis on the Chancellor.[54] This theme was interpreted in a very broad sense for it applied to the Federal Republic's international position, expressed the party's basic anti-communism and amounted generally to a defence of the *status quo.* Prior to the 1970s the situation was that the political threat to the West German state was seen as coming from both extremes of right and left (i.e. orthodox communism), for terrorist acts of the kind that developed in the third decade of the republic's history were not experienced before then. Terrorism in the 1970s was therefore a new issue because it was regarded not as a sub-division of 'law and order' but as a problem in its own right.

This change of policy perception was reflected in the nature of government security reports during the period under discussion. Since the beginning of the 1960s the Ministry of the Interior had published annual reports on extreme right- and left-wing activities in the Federal Republic. However, from 1968 these became a more comprehensive review of the work of the Office for Protection of the Constitution including the area of political radicalism, following the protest actions of the Extra-Parliamentary Opposition. The review for 1968 argued this was necessary 'in order to be able to judge better the stability of our basic democratic order and the dangers which threaten it'.[55] This report included a separate section on 'other left extreme groups' such as the Socialist Student Organization (SDS) and its protest actions, in addition to that on orthodox communism. In the earlier 1970s, the part of the annual review on extreme Left activities came to include a further section on 'force and terror'. Thus, in the report on 1975, Werner Maihofer, the Interior Minister, remarked in the introduction that 'protection against extremism, but also against terrorism . . . was besides fighting espionage the main preoccupation of constitutional protection'.[56] Already, in his New Year address for 1975 Helmut Schmidt had selected the Baader—Meinhof Group as one of the five most threatening developments of 1974 together with world inflation, the oil crisis, the Guillaume affair and unemployment.

The emergence of terrorism as a major political issue is similarly visible in its growing prominence as an electoral matter. In the 1969 Bundestag election campaign neither of the two main parties had lent it special attention, simply because it did not yet exist. In the CDU programme the question of left- and right-wing radicalism received only a passing mention in the section on fighting crime, which was the last but one of thirty items.[57] The SPD only referred to 'fighting growing criminality' among several questions relating to 'reform of the state order' towards the end of its own programme.[58] By the time of the next Bundestag election in November 1972 the Baader—Meinhof Group had made their dramatic appearance, but even so protection against terror was only the fifth among priority issues for the public during the last month of the campaign. Admittedly the RAF leaders had been captured several months before, but the Munich Olympic massacre did occur in September.[59] By the 1976 election the greater salience of terrorism as an issue was very evident as a new wave of attacks on public figures had developed in the meantime. The SPD programme, for instance, contained a section called 'Preserving and extending the *Rechtsstaat*' with detailed proposals for combating terrorism.[60] In that election the various 'K' groups, as those most associated with terrorist ideas, mustered no more than 0.1 per cent of the popular vote. In other words, the threat from terrorism was seen as coming from strictly outside the normal constitutional framework.

Compared with the threat from traditional political extremism (e.g. the neo-Nazi SRP and Maoist KPD had been banned in 1952 and 1956 respectively as party organisations working within the constitutional system), this difference presented special difficulties for government handling of terrorism as an issue. While during a terrorist crisis all government actions are often closely observed by the public with extensive coverage by the media, it is very difficult to establish workable yardsticks for measuring official performance because the outcome of a particular crisis may be very open to subjective interpretation. Schmidt was insistent during the Stockholm embassy attack that there was 'no patent solution' to the affair; indeed there is an inevitable case-by-case approach in responding to different crises, for the luck factor cannot be totally contained by detailed and systematic planning. However, there has tended to be something of a 'high-noon' style of drama about major terrorist crises where any wrong move may wholly alter the situation, just as a kaleidoscope jolted slightly may produce a quite different picture. At the level of principle, the choice is usually between remaining hard or giving in, but there are many incalculables. For instance, tactics are not easy to marry with strategy because in both respects there are strong risks that the situation will slide (or further slide) out of the government's control. If an overriding priority is given to saving those kidnapped, there is the probability that the terrorists will be encouraged to repeat their action on other occasions, with damaging consequences for the government's authority and the state's credibility. The alternative option also introduces possible escalation, achieving the terrorists' aim of provoking draconian measures by the state and thereby undermining its popularity through accusations of 'police-state methods' (which have a particular poignancy in the German case).

Ultimately, the problem points to the question of political leadership, which cannot be simply defined as exhausting constitutional powers to the full. Matters of timing, perception and political judgement are equally important. All these various aspects of crisis management were illustrated in one way or another by the four terrorist events to which attention is now given: the Munich Olympic massacre of September 1972, the Lorenz kidnapping of February—March 1975, the attack on the West Germany embassy in Stockholm of April 1975 and the Schleyer affair of September—October 1977. These case studies will necessarily have to be brief, concentrating on those aspects that demonstrate the problems of government response.

The Munich massacre, when guerrillas belonging to the Palestinian Black September Movement seized nine Israeli members of the Olympic team as hostages, was the first dramatic terrorist event on German soil. Its importance was two-fold: it emphasised that the West German authorities were unprepared for this kind of large-scale public operation, and it underlined the restrictions on government manoeuvrability because of dependence on international coordination, not to mention cooperation with the *Land* authorities in Bavaria. Because of the international interest in the Games and the prestigious importance of this event for West Germany, special precautions had been taken beforehand with international security consultations and restrictions placed on Arabs living in the Federal Republic. According to the later official report on the event,[61] massive security forces (such as 7600 from the Federal Border Guard) were deployed, even though this occasioned some unfavourable references to the militaristic atmosphere of the 1936 Berlin Olympics. Nevertheless, the handling of the affair went drastically wrong. Genscher, the Interior Minister, together with his Bavarian opposite number attempted to negotiate with the terrorists, but the need for speed inhibited full consultations between Bonn and Munich and the event climaxed at Fürstenfeldbruck airport when the Munich police chief ordered the police to open fire on the terrorists in a forlorn attempt to save the hostages, with a total of seventeen deaths. The German authorities had sought during the brief affair to play for time by delaying tactics, but the decision to meet the terrorist demands lay in Israeli not German hands. So far as German involvement went, it became clear that while the police were armed they were not trained to deal with political fanatics. In a newspaper interview afterwards, Chancellor Brandt stressed the future need for 'mobile units, who are trained for such cases, and would probably have a higher likelihood of success'.[62] As a result of the Munich affair the new anti-terrorist force GSG 9 was formed.

The novel feature of the Lorenz kidnapping in 1975 was that it was the first time a prominent public figure had been kidnapped, although von Drenkmann had been assassinated a few months before, and the first time that the West German authorities were fully responsible for dealing with a major terrorist crisis. The occasion had been selected by 2nd June Movement for its potential drama coming as it did in the final stage of the West Berlin state election — Peter Lorenz was the CDU's top candidate. The crisis, which lasted five days, ended with the government's decision to accede to terrorist demands and release five prisoners. There are various aspects of the affair worth noting. Even though the government decided on a 'soft' course, the principle of inter-linkage was accepted in that the authorities recognised at once that a further terrorist attack was probable and the public was repeatedly warned in those stark terms.[63] The handling of the affair was conducted within the new framework of a 'grand-crisis committee' (officially called the *grosser Politischer Beratungskreis*), with participation from not only the Chancellor and government ministers but also opposition leaders and *Land* government representatives.[64] This form of consensus-building became a practice during later major terrorist crises. Finally, the Lorenz affair saw the first serious stirrings of a fundamentalist interpretation of the terrorist challenge to the state. The government itself spoke of 'a massive blow against the constitutional state and democracy', while some opposition politicians did not resist the temptation to exploit the government's 'lack of foresight' and criticisms of the 'weak' German state were voiced in the press.[65] Altogether, the government was made painfully aware of the problems of merging tactics and strategy *vis-à-vis* the terrorists with party-political pressures and public relations.

The Stockholm embassy attack, in which four terrorists calling themselves the 'Holger Meins Commando' (named after one of the Baader—Meinhof leaders who had died from hunger strike in prison some months before) broke into the building and threatened to blow it up with their hostages, could be bracketed with the Lorenz affair, since it turned out to be the awaited ensuing event. Strategic lessons were drawn from the earlier occasion, and the situation was more tactically advantageous for the authorities, e.g. this time the location of the terrorists and hostages was known. Cooperation with the Swedish government proceeded efficiently, and the Bonn cabinet, using once again the mechanism of the grand-crisis committee, refused to meet the terrorist demands for the release of twenty-six prisoners including the Baader—Meinhof leaders. This 'hard' line apparently took the terrorists by surprise and the affair ended abruptly when an explosion occurred in the embassy, the terrorists were caught and the hostages freed. On 25 April Schmidt made a firm speech to the Bundestag in which he asserted that this had been 'the gravest challenge our constitutional state has faced in its 26 years of history', that the release of prisoners would have led to further crimes and tested security too much and that anti-terrorist measures were now taking effect.[66] The government's swift — and successful — handling of the affair made a strong public impression.

The Schleyer kidnapping, the best-known case and the culmination of the 'year of terrorism' of 1977, was by contrast an extended crisis lasting seven weeks, so that strategic considerations had to be different. The length of the affair, which developed into something of a 'war of nerves', stimulated much public discussion of the meaning of terrorism with a tendency to cultural soul-searching. The challenge to the state was perceived quite visibly as now there was a different trend of attacks on establishment figures — judicial personalities, a politician, a prominent banker and now a top industrialist (an obvious symbol of the capitalist system and one with a Nazi past). The action of kidnapping Schleyer and killing his guards in Cologne in early September was carried out by one of the RAF successor groups called the 'Siegfried Hausner Commando' (named after a terrorist who had died from wounds in the Stockholm attack). This time the authorities adopted constant delaying tactics in their policy towards the terrorists, although as it later became clear from the government report on the affair there was never any serious thought of exchanging prisoners (once again the RAF leaders). A decision of principle not to meet the terrorist demands was taken in a combined session of the cabinet and the grand-crisis committee on 6 September, the day after the kidnapping.[67] This resolution was summarised by Schmidt as 'not endangering the state's capacity to act and confidence in it at home and abroad; that also means not setting free the prisoners whose release is extorted'.[68] This principle was adhered to throughout, while efforts were made to locate Schleyer and the terrorists. On 14 October a special meeting of the cabinet reviewed all political and tactical factors in the situation, including the effects of a hypothetical release of the RAF leaders, but the same firm line was confirmed although the prospects for Schleyer's life were now very slim.[69] By then a new twist in the situation had occurred to put further pressure on the government, with the Palestinian hijacking of a Lufthansa plane with eighty-seven hostages. This additional problem was erased dramatically in an Entebbe-style freeing of the hostages by the anti-terrorist unit GSG 9 at Mogadishu in Somalia, this being hailed as a German triumph in which the figure of Schmidt clearly emerged overnight as a national hero. The whole affair ended tragically soon afterwards with the suicide of the Baader—Meinhof leaders in prison and the discovery of Schleyer's body.

Although the outcome was not an unqualified success for the government, political leadership was conspicuously on show. Schmidt personally orchestrated the official handling of the affair from start to finish, as he did the two cases in 1975, and was almost the exclusive beneficiary in terms of popularity of the widespread sense of public relief that flowed from the Mogadishu success. This action allowed him to overcome at a stroke the popularity doldrums with which he had been contending over the preceding year because of unemployment and slow economic growth. The Schleyer affair more than any other terrorist crisis provided an opportunity for a demonstration of Chancellor authority (although there were signs of this during the Stockholm attack). During the affair itself public nervousness had been revealed in a trend of letters to newspapers on the theme of the need for a 'strong man';[70] Schmidt eventually managed to satisfy this through a combination of living up to his image of effective performer in a crisis ('Schmidt the *Macher*') and calculated luck (Mogadishu might have gone wrong). Such catchphrases as 'the all-party Chancellor' and 'Chancellor of the crisis team' were applied to him, and the final publicity accolade came with the *Spiegel* cover story after the event with a stern but thoughtful looking Schmidt on the front with the caption: 'After Mogadishu: the admired German'.[71] One crucial aspect of Schmidt's handling of the affair had been his control of the grand-crisis committee, which became a household name during these weeks, for this guaranteed him party-political neutrality as well as serving to reassure public feeling. The committee operated effectively despite Schleyer family pressure on some opposition politicians.

There were, however, other less unambiguous sides to government policy during these crises. The first concerned official publicity about terrorism and terrorists. Beginning with the Munich massacre of 1972, this policy had come to rest on the belief that 'systematic publicity efforts' were essential not only because of the authorities' reliance on members of the public for recognising terrorists but also to put psychological pressure on the terrorists and to inform the public of old and new security procedures so as to avoid misunderstanding about their nature.[72] This was carried into effect despite a certain bureaucratic reluctance to supply details. But such a policy was more easily stated than practised. The fact is the media have different functions and purposes from the government notwithstanding the weight of public solidarity behind the government during a terrorist crisis. For instance, one authority on security precautions commented in 1976: 'The media in reporting convey to the population the comforting feeling that something will be done in Bonn to increase their security'.[73] Not only do the media place an exacting onus on government 'success', but it follows as well that their extensive coverage during terrorist events might not always suit official circles. The Springer press's habit of fanning public emotions and exploiting 'defeats' for the state (under left—liberal leadership) was an extreme case in point.

There was a further complication in the deliberate use of the media by the terrorists as part of their 'scare' strategy. The view that publicity is all sometimes seemed to mark the behaviour of the terrorists, and was underlined by their frustration in prison with their 'isolation'. One of the stipulations of the embassy attackers during the Stockholm affair was that following the release of terrorist prisoners 'the air take-off of our comrades will be broadcast directly by West German television and Swedish television'.[74] The question of the media role came to a head during the Schleyer affair when the government asked for their cooperation in restricting news coverage during the crisis — the so-called *Nachrichtensperre*. This unprecedented request was presented as a temporary necessity as otherwise efforts to locate the captive might be inhibited and 'the terrorists would acquire that public resonance which they regularly plan as part of their criminal actions'.[75] Despite this justification and the media's co-operation, this matter became an issue of some controversy with historical undertones about the principles of informing the public.[76] The main conclusion arising from this problem was that public approval of government performance during a terrorist crisis was inevitably conditioned by the media's interpretation.

A second controversial side to government action arose over the deficiencies of security officials in the field. Criticisms of their mistakes in failing to track down terrorists in the autumn of 1977 did not surface until several months after the Schleyer affair, especially once the Höcherl report revealed the neglect of a vital tip-off that might have saved Schleyer. On the opposition's initiative, these mistakes became a political dispute and rebounded on the government, specifically the Minister of the Interior Maihofer, who combined with long-term doubts about his political authority was eventually unhorsed by the issue. Resignation over anti-terrorist policy was not unique, for two West Berlin justice senators resigned in 1976 and again in 1978 over jail-breaks by terrorists. Only a few months after Mogadishu, Schmidt's government was subject to fears for its durability when the Defence Minister was forced to retire in early 1978 over a security tapping scandal. Schmidt had then acted to prevent an erosion of his government's authority by a lightning cabinet reshuffle, but this and further revelations later in the year about police bungling in failing to spot terrorists' reconnaissance of politicians' homes under their very noses caused public alarm. Reactions to the inefficiencies of anti-terrorist methods illustrated how sensitive opinion could be to the level of performance by authorities in this area.

Party-political and public reactions

It is already evident that, despite the government attempt to the contrary, terrorism as an issue was not kept entirely free from party-political exchanges and polemics. Schmidt had cultivated an above-party stance and tried to make a virtue of broad consensus, as was clear in his speech introducing the debate on anti-terrorist legislation on 13 March 1975 in the aftermath of the Lorenz affair:

> Because we wanted to establish political co-responsibility, we brought to one table the four appropriate *Land* governments, the chairmen of the four large democratic parties and the chairmen of the three Bundestag party groups, and discussed and took together the decisions in common.[77]

Schmidt went on to quote Helmut Kohl with approval (for the Chancellor a highly unusual gesture in the Bundestag) for a remark he had made in the grand-crisis committee: 'Either we all pull on one rope, or we might as well say good-bye to the state'. This initial emphasis on consensus soon became forgotten in one of the most traumatic debates the parliament had seen for years, interpolated with historically coloured and suggestive allusions. Schmidt warned against new 'stab-in-the-back myths' arising from attempts to implicate Social Democrats in 'the deeds of these criminal groups'; Dregger lived up to his strong law-and-order reputation with a highly polemical speech countering Schmidt's plea and painting a picture of 'political gangsters' on the loose; while Kohl, taking Brandt to task for an 'accusatory' speech, later found it necessary to point out that he (born 1930) was too young to have been involved in the Third Reich. In reference again to Brandt's earlier speech (see above, p. 21). Kohl attacked the SPD chairman's rejection of his party having any ideological sympathy with the terrorists with the following remarks:

> Look, Herr colleague Brandt, that is what I meant just now by hubris: You determine ex cathedra who is an old Nazi and who is not. That is a simple distinction you are taking on yourself. He who in the Third Reich held the Brown party membership-card and then took the Red party-card, who, Ladies and Gentlemc и, purified himself and has in your view the right to heavenly and earthly bliss. It is this you are determining . . . None of us has the right to lay down and say that one story suits me and not another. For me — I say this to you — Auschwitz, Maidanek and Treblinka belong just as much as 20 July and Count Stauffenberg to German history . . .[78]

The highlight of the debate came when Herbert Wehner accused Franz-Josef Strauss, his perennial adversary, of being 'spiritually a terrorist' for his controversial Sonthofen speech of 1974,[79] at which the opposition deputies left the chamber.[80] Without doubt terrorism had a potentially strong emotive content as an issue, so that the government exercise in consensus formation must be seen in this context.

While the grand-crisis committee did in fact function reasonably during major terrorist crises, there were difficulties in keeping the issue out of party politics when national solidarity was no longer emphatically required. During the first such crisis over the Munich massacre in 1972 there had been an apparent desire by both Chancellor Brandt and CDU politicians to play down party differences,[81] not surprisingly in view of the painful spectacle of the murder of Jews on German soil in the full gaze of international opinion. The grand-crisis committee was of course justified as expressing the 'solidarity of all democrats', but party-political pressures proved too strong for the spirit of reconciliation to outlast its temporary usage. In the immediate aftermath of the Schleyer affair the mood in the Bundestag was one of wanting to maintain the unity between the parties over terrorism,[82] as expressed in better personal relations between some leading politicians like Schmidt and Kohl; but within several months Kohl himself was devaluing the importance of the crisis committee at the time of the Maihofer resignation and the publicity surrounding the mistakes of security forces.[83] The vagaries of opposition behaviour towards the government were not unconnected with the fact that the CSU under Strauss sought to make political capital out of the issue, either to embarrass the government or to use it as leverage against the CDU leadership. A classic example of this technique was Strauss's breaking ranks just after the end of the Schleyer crisis by disclosing the contents of a tape sent to Kohl by Schleyer, in which the latter (maybe speaking under duress) attacked the government's mistakes after his kidnapping and said he was not prepared to 'depart from this life silently' in order to cover them up.[84] At other times, the *Bayernkurier* conducted a campaign about the SPD's inability or unwillingness to defend the *Rechtsstaat*.[85]

There was nevertheless a general reason behind the brittle political consensus over terrorism: relations between government and opposition had for years been either openly or latently antagonistic. It was not just a matter of party-political calculation and polemical tactics. Being an emotive and historically loaded issue, terrorism tended to touch on the parties' different 'philosophies'. This was all the more likely as terrorism had emerged as an issue under left—liberal governments in Bonn, a combination of developments that opposition leaders chose to exploit with the aggressive manner of fundamentalist debate typical of the polarisation since 1969. This recourse to fundamentalist interpretations appeared in a number of ways, as is evident from looking at the arguments adopted by both main parties in the sometimes intensive public discussion over terrorism.

On the CDU/CSU side, the party's traditional concern with all matters of law and order came to the fore. Convinced of its own special competence in the area, the CDU/CSU produced its 'Offensive concept for fighting anarchistic terrorism' in the summer of 1975, frequently presented its own legislative proposals, which were usually harsher than those of the government, and in late 1977 the CDU was the first political party to hold a special conference on the subject of terrorism. The 'Offensive concept' among other things promoted the view that the left—liberal coalition was not offering enough to protect the public and society from this threat, and combined an overview of the terrorist problem with specific suggestions for changes in security regulations.[86] The special conference on 'The road to violence: spiritual and social origins of terrorism and its consequences' brought together mainly professors with some senior administrators to discuss broader aspects of the terrorist issue and was considered by some liberal observers as quite informative despite a tendency towards moralistic judgements.[87] Very often, however, a fundamentally conservative view prevailed in the line taken by the party leadership in political debate (e.g. the speeches by Dregger, Carstens and Strauss) arguing that terrorism derived *directly* from 1968 and 'leftism' in general, and that any form of *Gesellschaftskritik* or challenge to established social norms had only encouraged the terrorists on their path of violence. The polemical impulse became most vitriolic when attention turned to a discussion of the 'spiritual' roots of terrorism.

With the SPD the 'philosophical' problems in meeting the terrorist challenge were markedly different. Generally, as a party of the left, it was less inclined to assume a simplistic or straightforward position on the issue because of the complexities of overall left ideological tendencies as discussed above (see pp. 21-2). Furthermore, there was the related question that its own electoral supporters ranged from moderate left to radical left, so that the adoption of an overly intransigent line in combating terrorism might alienate some of the latter. Of course, through its chairman Willy Brandt, the party gave the necessary backing to the decisions of Chancellor Schmidt, but Brandt also performed his cherished function of keeper of the SPD's conscience. For historical reasons this could acquire a defensive tone. In the March 1975 debate in the Bundestag, Brandt proclaimed that the SPD was the 'main enemy of extremists' and that nobody could give Social Democrats lessons on defending democracy, a statement he supported with reference to the famous stand by the SPD deputy Otto Wels in the Reichstag in March 1933 against Hitler's bill for emergency powers.[88] Then at the SPD congress in November 1977 a resolution was passed emphasising the need to differentiate between legitimate democratic radical debate and the destructive strategy of the terrorists, and rejecting the attempt by conservatives to associate Social Democrats ideologically with terrorism. Yet some sections of the party, particularly on its left wing, were not always comfortable with the government's policies. This feeling became most apparent in the early months when the government's new package of anti-terrorist laws (including restrictions on terrorists' dependants and further police powers in terrorist searches) provoked dissent among a small group of SPD deputies whose stand on the question of individual conscience caused a delay in the passage of the laws. These were eventually adopted with a majority of only one in April, but only after strong pressures had been exerted in the interests of government solidarity. On other occasions, ill-feeling had surfaced among SPD deputies because the government's close majority necessitated potential or actual dependence on opposition consent. One of them commented bitterly: 'One swallows what the CDU demands, then strikes out half of it and that is Social Democratic policy'.[89] Indeed, the law passed rapidly during the Schleyer crisis isolating terrorist prisoners where the state required it received an overwhelming majority because of opposition support, but there were four votes against (all SPD) and seventeen abstentions (twelve SPD, five FDP). It was clear that the line taken by the SPD could also easily develop into polemical argumentation, but from a very different angle from that of the CDU/CSU.

This political—ideological divergence between the two parties became most evident in the emotive controversy over terrorist 'sympathisers' that swept the country in the autumn of 1977, as a culmination of the 'year of terrorism' and as an accompanying feature of the Schleyer affair. This controversy very swiftly acquired McCarthyite tones when the CDU produced a 'black list' of public figures alleged in different ways to entertain ideas analogous to some of those voiced by the terrorists. It included left-inclined writers, progressive professors, enlightened priests and some leading SPD and FDP politicians, and became linked to the highly charged issue of the *Berufsverbot* (or Radicals Decree of 1972, which excluded political extremists from employment by the state and was applied controversially) with its implications for political tolerance. Günter Grass, one of the chief targets of this list, responded publicly by calling it 'a throw-back to the Middle Ages: I grew up as a Catholic and acquainted myself with the practices and the whole scholastic teaching on the trials of witches and the inquisition'.[90] Heinrich Böll, the novelist and another listed 'sympathiser', similarly went on record as saying that all reasoned discussion was impossible as 'nobody will talk about the origins of terrorism'.[91] In essence, the attitude taken by the opposition expressed the anti-intellectualism of its predominant conservative circles, but its lack of political differentiation and the loosely employed concept of 'sympathiser' only contributed to the 'scare' atmosphere that pervaded the Federal Republic in these months. Accordingly, discussion of the issue (which in a reasoned context was significant for explaining the phenomenon of terrorism) devolved only too easily to the level of crude debate. Points of view rapidly became distorted, as in reaction to the semantic but superficial remark of Bernhard Vogel (CDU minister-president of the Rhineland-Palatinate) that he was a 'sympathiser' who referred to the Baader—Meinhof as a 'group' instead of 'gang'. Hans Filbinger, CDU minister—president of Baden-Württemberg and a prominent conservative figure, also urged that 'the quagmire of terrorism' at German universities be rooted out.[92] What followed paralleled the then extreme rightward trend among German students in the later years of the Weimar Republic, so that any open discussion of the genuinely critical though also negative viewpoints of many student circles towards the Federal Republic was out of the question. The one advantage the opposition possessed in its onslaught on 'sympathisers' was that general public opinion, incensed by the Schleyer kidnapping and later murder, was not prepared to give waverers over anti-terrorism anything but hard treatment. The silent majority thus made itself felt.

It is worthwhile at this juncture to diverge from party-political approaches to the terrorist issue and focus more specifically on public attitudes. Mass opinion was undoubtedly disturbed by the major terrorist crises. In this sense, the terrorists achieved one of their aims although with the opposite consequences they had predicted, for far from undermining the popular base of the Federal Republic the attacks on prominent figures produced a feeling of outrage in which one could perceive a certain attribution to the state of a sacrosanct quality. Was there nevertheless a chance that the terrorists might be right about their other assumption that in provoking a political over-reaction and forcing the state to 'drop its constitutional mask' public opinion might swerve in another direction? While public moods especially in terrorist crises seemed to move in swirls and eddies (usually according to the performance of the authorities), were there any visible long-term trends that might indicate a change in public attitudes as a result of the terrorist phenomenon?

By and large, any decipherable trends of opinion in the latter half of the 1970s could be read as indicating a reactivation of the old desire for 'security'. While this may be regarded as a blanket predilection, there were however different ways of judging it on specific questions. It goes without saying that the 'war of nerves' produced by terrorist crises would have some political effects, though how much these were temporary or maybe permanent was a matter for discussion. One fairly reasoned assessment during the Schleyer affair compared the effects to shock waves in water: 'As when one throws a stone into a lake the vibrations spread out from the centre to the periphery and touch those parts of the surface which are far from the scene of the throw — so it is with terror.'[93]

The picture presented by the media, especially the press, was often one of unmitigated hysteria. This impression could be gained by following the detailed reporting and sometimes obsessive editorials of the German newspapers, both popular and quality ones, but the most blatant promotion of this picture came in the more abbreviated reports in the foreign press. Thus, at the time of the early Baader—Meinhof activities one Bonn foreign correspondent gave as one reason for the prominence of this group 'a rising hysteria in West Germany about criminal violence'.[94] A few months later another British paper projected a 'Reds-under-the-bed' scenario by reporting that 'an anxious German public tended in moments of alarm to see agents of Baader and Meinhof behind every holdup'.[95] Perhaps more to the point was the commentary several years afterwards (in fact during the Schleyer affair) that 'the authorities, by giving them [the terrorists] such special treatment, aided by the sensation-loving media, have largely created' the situation where the RAF, 'never within the remotest reach of political power, has actually been allowed to acquire a special kind of power over the whole West German scene'.[96] Certainly, the party-political polemics described above could only serve to arouse public feeling to a higher pitch of disquiet. This in turn multiplied public pressures on the government during a crisis to demonstrate its 'success' and in the aftermath to follow up with yet further legislation. The onus on 'success', sometimes an elusive concept, was encouraged by the German press, with *Bild* painting the unnerving picture of the Federal Republic speeding down the road towards a 'banana republic' state of affairs and the more elitist but non-left *Frankfurter Allgemeine* featuring such headlines as: 'Cowardly murderers, cowardly state?'[97] — a reference to the authorities' failure to track down Schleyer.

What direct evidence has there been on what the public really thought, as distinct from their interpreted or projected moods? Here, opinion surveys provide some clues, though as with all polls their results must be qualified as pointers to long-term trends. It was to be expected that during a terrorist crisis the effect on opinion would produce an increased demand for firm measures. At the height of the Schleyer affair, one poll indicated that 67 per cent of the population favoured a return to the death penalty (which was banned by the Basic Law).[98] Also during the same crisis the results of a 'flash-poll' (*Blitzumfrage*) commissioned by *Stern* from Allensbach showed that whereas in mid-September 60 per cent of West Germans opposed granting the terrorists' wishes (only 22 per cent were in favour of doing so), views on the subject changed substantially a month later after the hijacking of the Lufthansa aircraft with eighty-seven holiday-makers on board: 42 per cent for giving in to the terrorists, 42 per cent against.[99] The difference was explained on human grounds, for on the earlier occasion only one life was at stake over the question of freeing ten dangerous terrorists, while later there were eighty-seven additional lives endangered and these were persons with whom ordinary people could identify. (This of course suggests that had the Mogadishu action gone wrong with severe casualties among the hostages, then the government would have suffered a 'defeat' in the eyes of the public and the outcome of the Schleyer affair would have been considered more negatively despite official firmness on freeing the terrorists.) On the government's performance, the same poll for October showed that 50 per cent (59 per cent for SPD/FDP supporters; 42 per cent for CDU/CSU supporters) considered this 'resolute and well-considered', 35 per cent not so (30 per cent SPD/FDP; 44 per cent CDU/CSU) and 15 per cent undecided.

During the year 1978, with no major terrorist crises, other survey evidence suggested that the experience of terrorism had certainly made an impact. In February, admittedly still under the shadow of the Schleyer affair, one much disputed poll revealed that three out of five (62 per cent) West Germans were prepared to accept curbs on their personal freedom for the sake of combating terrorism:[100] 62 per cent among SPD supporters, 72 per cent among CDU/CSU supporters and only 40 per cent among FDP supporters.[101] What was ignored in the dispute over this poll was an earlier Allensbach poll of May 1975 (after Lorenz and Stockholm), which showed as many as 69 per cent favouring personal restrictions. In March 1978, Allensbach published a further poll based on February figures showing that nine out of ten members of the public saw the state threatened by terrorism, thus representing no great change from the same questions put during the Schleyer affair four months before — inversely, in October 1977 only 5 per cent thought the state was 'hardly threatened', in November 13 per cent and the following February 7 per cent.[102] Finally, towards the end of 1978 an Infas poll reflected continuing public concern over the problem with a higher proportion (63 per cent) placing internal security as a priority over economic security (54 per cent), although social security received more with 69 per cent; 83 per cent feared an increase in terrorist actions, and only 51 per cent thought present security measures satisfactory.[103] Nevertheless, alongside this continuity of public concern there was a lessened intensity of attitude outside crisis periods.

There emerged therefore a clear and decisive majority concerned about defending the state against the terrorist threat, notwithstanding the volatility of opinion during a major crisis. This was not so surprising considering the politically sensitive outlook of the West German public, which owed much to the recent historical past; but all the same did the trend of public reaction to terrorism signify the authoritarian potential that some commentators feared would be provoked? Some press interpretation during 1977 expounded the alternative view that with the Ponto murder and the Schleyer affair the West Germans became for the first time emotionally rather than merely intellectually committed to the form of democracy represented by the Federal Republic. This question is difficult to answer simply in the light of the terrorist experience of the late 1970s, because many other issues and factors outside the scope of this study are involved. However, the problem does relate to the introductory distinction between the 'objective' and 'subjective' dimensions of West German democracy. In this context, the general discussion over democratic values that resulted from terrorism and the ensuing legislation bore some relevance, and this leads us back to the political debate over the issue in Bonn.

It is proposed here to identify the main leitmotivs of that discussion over democracy at the cost of some repetition, as several features have already been mentioned in this study so far. It was commonly stated during the debate over terrorism that attention concentrated exclusively on its effects rather than its causes.[104] This was not strictly true, as is already evident, but it is more apt to say that in searching for the causes political debate was very much more *geistig-politisch* than *sozialpolitisch* orientated — that is, it was characterised by a moralistic and often abstract cultural—historical approach to the problem rather than one that followed a 'social—scientific' mode of enquiry and would have allowed a more differentiating approach. Hence, the historically coloured insistence on defending the *Rechtsstaat* at all costs and the accusations levelled against the liberal press of trying to 'understand' the terrorists.

The pervasion of references to the Weimar Republic and the Third Reich in the debate about terrorism and its significance for democratic values hardly needs any emphasis here. One is reminded of Peter Merkl's telling comment on the Parliamentary Council of 1948—49 that the Basic Law was framed by those who were 'guarding against a recurrence of the nightmarish mistakes of the past' and were 'motivated by a deep distrust of the common man'.[105] As a 'subjective' factor in West German politics, the continuing memory of Germany's unhappy past, although less poignant than it had been immediately after the war, was in itself a reality that helped to condition or determine perception of the terrorist issue. Such historical parallels with the events of 1977 as the stringent Law for the Protection of the Republic passed after Rathenau's assassination in 1922, evocative references to 'Weimar conditions' (e.g. by Kohl after the Lorenz kidnapping) and the pensive comment of one respected liberal publicist that 'we Germans — and Democracy — have had a narrow escape'[106] were all made despite the obvious contrast between Bonn and Weimar in the former's record of political stability. In short, terrorism could not just be treated in West Germany pragmatically as perhaps befitted Helmut Schmidt's image and preferred method of policy-making.

The political discussion over terrorism in the Federal Republic seemed to confirm one German academic's comments: 'What comes to the fore in the 'terrorism shock' of the Federal Republic — in spite of the call for vengeance and retaliation — is not "Fascism"; however there are symptoms of its not being overcome'.[107] The need to come to terms with and master the recent historical past in all senses — political and psychological in particular — was of course no new theme in postwar Germany, but it received a new and uneasy airing in the terrorist crises. In the midst of the heated debate over new anti-terrorist legislation in early 1978, Alfred Dregger pinpointed this problem:

> . . . We who are responsible for the present and future of the Federal Republic of Germany must absolve ourselves from the shadow of Hitler. Neither the imitation of Hitler — which nobody in their right minds would wish to repeat — nor the antitype of Hitler can provide the yardsticks of our action. We must orientate ourselves to experiences which take us beyond Hitler and to basic values, which Hitler indeed misused but which he could not abolish.[108]

There emerged in connection with this a sense that the Federal Republic was lacking something of an historical identity. Although time had nullified its original 'provisional' character and the division of Germany was largely healed, its established legitimacy did not in the view of some arouse affective as well as functional support. One CDU official introduced a study of terrorism by remarking:

> It is clear to any attentive observer that the Federal Republic is again and again exposed to a remarkable absence of history and is made insecure by terrorism to an extraordinary degree, also in relation to the fundamental questions and principles of its system which manifestly have stood the test since 1949.[109]

At the same time, restrained criticism from the moderate left of the limited form of political development in the 1950s and 1960s focussed on such aspects as the preoccupation with material welfare and a consequent 'political immobilism' that excluded open political debate and broader political participation, thus implicitly granting that the authors of the 1968 protest had had some valid arguments. Helmut Schmidt contributed to this line of discussion by emphasising that during the reconstruction period 'too little was done to apply the values and conceptions of the Basic Law to society in practice'.[110] This critique did not endear itself to the CDU/CSU, for whom Adenauer was a sacrosanct figure and Erhard the 'father of the economic miracle'.

A more specific classification of the leitmotivs that accompanied the debate over democratic values would delineate the following. Despite the polarisation of discussion three commonly recognised theses were present. First, terrorism was regarded by both sides of the political spectrum as involving a challenge to West Germany's constitutional order or *Rechtsstaat*. This has already been discussed and was expressed again by such statements as Willy Brandt's that with the Schleyer affair 'our democracy has learnt how to maintain itself'. Second, the concept of 'active democrats' or the requirement of not merely passive loyalty to the Federal Republic as elaborated in the first section of the Basic Law became a touchstone of the need to counter terrorism. In the Basic Law West German citizens are acknowledged as possessing a range of basic rights but these are always hedged with communitarian norms,[111] e.g. article 2 recognises everyone as having the right to 'the free development of his personality' so long as he does not 'offend against the constitutional order or the moral code'. This mixture of individual freedoms and qualifying norms has of course become in recent years a controversial matter concerning those employed by the state, where the *Berufsverbot* of 1972 had insisted that they should be 'prepared at all times to uphold the free democratic basic order and to defend actively this basic order'. On the terrorist issue the general view prevailed that democracy should not be an unarmed society (ghosts of Weimar again), as when the Interior Minister specified that internal security was 'the necessary reverse side' of a liberal democracy.[112] However, this view was taken to the level of an absolute norm with assertions like that of the *Frankfurter Allgemeine* that the security authorities 'require solidarity . . . inner identification and external visible and audible identification from us all'.[113] Third, the nature of West German democracy was raised in the context of the balance between individual rights of the citizen as the criterion of a liberal state and the need for further security measures. Although commonly agreed as a point of discussion, this theme was also the most divisive of the three because of differences between the main political forces about how far to pursue security at a possible cost to individual freedom. Such catchphrases as 'better a helpless than a heartless state' coloured the discussion so that clearly the matter was not straightforward, as was evident during legislative debate in Bonn to which we now turn.

Institutional Procedures and Responses

The main guidelines of the political discussion of terrorism having been examined, it remains to consider the legal—institutional as well as political—institutional aspect of the state's response to the terrorist threat. It has already been noted that some legislation was carried with bipartisan support and some on the basis of the government's own majority, which was not always secure because of internal SPD dissent over the question of individual rights in a liberal state. The following analysis will therefore confine itself to an outline of the main legislative acts and then their significance in the context of West Germany's security structure.

One major problem in dealing with terrorism through constitutional means was that the Basic Law, with the Weimar anti-model clearly in mind, made no real provision for an emergency situation, so that action had to be limited to the use of criminal law. Moreover, the novelty of the terrorist issue and the unexpectedness of it in the early 1970s meant that there was something of a legal *lacuna* for facing its challenge. Indeed, the law on demonstrations had been liberalised by the new social—liberal coalition in March 1970, shortly before the recognised founding of the Baader—Meinhof group. The first measure against the new form of violence was passed in December 1971, allowing for strict sentences against hijacking and kidnapping. Two other measures followed in June 1972 enlarging the powers of the Federal Office for Protection of the Constitution (to include observation of politically motivated anti-constitutional activities) and permitting the Federal Border Guard to act in support of *Land* police when public security was threatened. This concluded the first phase of anti-terrorist legislation, for the main body of such legislation was approved during the period from the end of 1974 to early 1978. This included the following new provisions: the tightening-up in December 1974 of criminal procedure to expedite trials, which could under certain circumstances, e.g. hunger strikes, take place in the absence of the accused; the Anti-Constitutional Advocacy Act of January 1976 which inserted a new paragraph in the criminal code directed against those who publicly advocated or encouraged others to 'commit an offence against the stability and security of the Federal Republic'; the Anti-Terror Law (June 1976) which made the 'formation of terrorist associations' a criminal offence and provided for the supervision of written contact between terrorists in prison and their defending counsels (because of the mediative role played by some so-called 'terrorist lawyers' between terrorists in prison and those at large); the 'contact ban' of September 1977 whereby imprisoned terrorists could be placed under temporary isolation from each other and from their defence lawyers in the event of a threat to civilian lives or freedom; and the package of laws passed in April 1978 with further restrictions on terrorist defence counsels and considerable provisions to facilitate police searches.

An attempt will not be made here to engage in the niceties of German criminal law to estimate whether or not this legislation amounts to an infringement of individual rights,[114] for in accordance with the focus of this study on the political dimension attention will be drawn to several points that help to set this legislation in a general context. In doing so, it is worth bearing in mind that the caption 'more state but hardly more security', critical of the rush to legislate, sounded plausible in the light of the particular conditions in the Federal Republic surrounding the discussion over terrorism, but that security depended as much on its intrinsic efficiency or effectiveness as it did on legal provisions. Moreover, contrary to some contemporary views, the purpose of legislation was not to end terror but to reduce its dangerous effects in certain respects. Terrorism simply could not be legislated out of existence, an assumption that owed something to a traditional belief that political conflicts could be solved with administrative means and that quite ignored the sociological roots of this new phenomenon.

(1) West Germany's internal security system was relatively undeveloped come the advent of terrorism in the early 1970s. The growth of security forces during the decade may be easily measured by recording the increases in expenditure and staff at the federal level. Already in early 1972 the government was forced to allot almost 20 per cent more expenditure to combat the increasing threat to internal security, above all because of Baader—Meinhof activities.[115] The Federal Criminal Office in particular has increased its facilities considerably since 1969, with its total of staff rising from 818 in 1965 and 933 in 1969 to 1211 in 1970, 1585 in 1972, 2062 in 1973, 2237 in 1975 and 3122 in 1978.[116] Its expenditure during the same period rose from DM 16 million in 1965 and DM 22.4 million in 1969 to DM 122 million in 1973 and DM 149 million in 1976.[117] Similarly, expenditure on the Federal Office for Protection of the Constitution rose from DM 22.2 million in 1965 and DM 29.9 million in 1969 to DM 80.8 million in 1976.[118] Overall federal expenditure on internal security rose from DM 384.7 million in 1969 to DM 1,318.9 million in 1978.[119] In the autumn of 1977 the government agreed on an increase in the budget of nearly DM 1000 million for the two above-mentioned federal agencies over a period of 5—10 years.[120] There was also a concurrent strengthening of security forces in the *Länder*. Altogether, this development represented a dramatic departure quantitatively from the security system of the 1950s and 1960s, though whether it also amounted to the qualitative change in the pejorative sense feared by some critical observers, alarmed at the steep rate of its growth in only a few years, depended on other factors.

(2) One of these must be a comparison with the security systems in other West European countries. Here there has been a contemporaneous strengthening of security provisions, not surprising in the face of international terrorism. During the 1970s France introduced a series of new laws on fire-arms, police searches and prison sentences with similar trends in Italy, such as the introduction of new police powers over suspects and in the use of telephone tapping, while West Germany is no exception in placing restrictions on defendants' lawyers if abusing their duties — there are similar measures in Belgium, Denmark, Italy and the Netherlands. This comparative angle, while providing some contextual perspective, cannot however be decisive. It omits for instance the 'subjective' factor with regard to Germany, just as neo-fascism in that country is watched far more circumspectly than anywhere else in Western Europe including Italy. Obviously, there would be concern about the possible political misuse of the new powers in the event of

an authoritarian personality being elected at the head of a government in Bonn by the normal democratic procedure. Most West Germans are very aware of the need for internal restraint to buttress these security powers, but their instinctive pessimism may itself be regarded as an important counteractive agent.

(3) The same period of the Federal Republic has witnessed an evolving subordination of the *Länder* to the Federation especially in the economic and financial fields. While this process of economic concentration is common to other countries, the special problem in West Germany has been to adapt the federal system to changing realities from the 1960s and modify the autonomy of the *Länder* on the grounds of economic efficiency.[121] Although a separate development from that of internal security, it again helps to place the latter in a relative context. What is significant is that proposals to make the federal structure more uniform, as by the Ernst Commission of 1973, have been resisted. The essential maintenance of the federal nature of the state structure must be considered a crucial feature when discussing institutional constraints on any possible authoritarian potential arising at the political level.

It is therefore relevant to examine the federal/*Länder* aspect of internal security operations. Law and order are primarily a *Land* responsibility, but the principle of 'cooperative federalism' applies — as article 73, section 10, of the Basic Law specifies — 'in matters of criminal police and of protection of the constitution, establishment of a Federal Criminal Police Office, as well as international control of crime'. As a result of terrorism, improvements and changes have occurred in the methods of this cooperation, but the two levels of the state structure have not always worked harmoniously together. According to Heinz Schwarz, a former interior minister in the Rhineland-Palatinate:

> Disputes over competences do not occur at least on the operational level, neither between the *Länder* nor between the Federation and the *Länder*. They arise again and again when certain matters become politically spectacular because when things go wrong those who fail blame the others for the lack of success.[122]

This problem came to the fore with the first major terrorist crisis of the Olympic massacre in 1972, when recriminations between Bonn and Munich were eventually toned down by a mollifying statement from Chancellor Brandt.[123] Genscher as Interior Minister also notified the *Länder* that any new anti-terrorist unit as envisaged as a result of Munich would only be used on their request.[124] The root of this problem has been the need to coordinate central information with decentralised action and the factor of *Land* suspicions of federal intrusion. Even the CDU/CSU, with all its intransigence on law and order, has been adamant on preserving the federal structure, but *Land* administrations under SPD/FDP control have also been very wary of losing too much autonomy. This caution appeared for example early in 1978 over the question of extending the role of the Federal Criminal Office at the expense of the *Land* police authorities. Strong opposition came from the FDP interior minister in North-Rhine Westphalia, Hirsch, who was in fact a close party colleague of Maihofer, his federal opposite number and responsible for this proposal.[125] Despite this institutional rivalry, several useful steps have been taken to facilitate cooperation in the fight against terrorism, especially through the channel of the standing conference of interior ministers and various common working groups to promote anti-terrorist publicity policy and further investigation into terrorist activities. Following the Schleyer affair there was also some restructuring of *Land* police departments in the interests of better efficiency.[126]

Some brief mention should be made of the various federal agencies employed in anti-terrorism. These comprise primarily the Federal Criminal Office (BKA) and the Federal Border Guard (BGS), with the creation of special anti-terrorist departments in various other federal institutions. Established in 1951, the BKA has played a subordinate role as auxiliary to the *Länder* police and has been concerned with immediate tasks in anti-terrorist activity, above all with providing central information in police searches through its electronic data system at Wiesbaden.[127] In 1969 its competences were slightly enlarged, and in 1975 an agreement of the *Land* interior ministers committed them to following up initiatives of the BKA. Its role therefore is strictly limited in the context of the federal structure. The BGS, also operational since 1951, was principally required to patrol border areas, especially with the DDR, but following two laws of 1968 and 1972 it has had internal security functions and is now specifically used for some anti-terrorist duties. At the same time, the Federal Ministry of the Interior has adapted to the dictates of anti-terrorism by setting up a special commission with BKA officials and enlarging a department concerned with publicity about terrorism. The Federal Office for Protection of the Constitution, through its new terrorism department set up in 1972, has been involved in the long-term task of gathering information material through such means as infiltrating terrorist circles; while the Federal Prosecutor's Office has extended its own terrorism department. One might finally add the GSG 9, a special anti-terrorist task force of trained sharp-shooters set up after the Munich affair of 1972. For some time this was an object of satire, comparisons being made with the army of Formosa, which trains and trains and simply gets older, but it suddenly made the headlines with its successful Mogadishu action in 1977, this time earning the label of 'The desert foxes' in the British press. On a more regular basis, the *Länder* have been reluctant to employ its services because of a sense of rivalry with their own police forces.[128]

By the end of the 1970s, therefore, West Germany had developed an elaborate and fairly sophisticated internal security system but one that nonetheless had to mould itself around the country's federal structure. It clearly has had an impact in helping to reduce terrorist activities in the Federal Republic despite the well-publicised cases of inefficiency and in some respects rigidity. This system has evolved considerably from its relatively elementary character at the start of the 1970s, although in some ways — notably international cooperation — there is still much room for improvement, but this is not unique to the Federal Republic.

This process of extending and elaborating the internal security system in West Germany has been controversial because of the growth in the powers of the state (both federal and *Land*) and consequently its scope for personal intrusion. This is an undeniable feature of such a system, though much depends on how it is implemented. However, the Federal Republic cannot by any basic political—institutional and legal—institutional criteria be regarded as a 'police state', even if it may have certain superficial resemblances with armoured cars patrolling official buildings around Bonn and the massive and sometimes heavy-handed police searches, which may make the liberal flesh creep. In similar fashion, the *Berufsverbot* became a disputed issue not so much because of the principle behind its introduction in 1972 as its form of implementation and sometimes the exploitation of its letter.

Ultimately, the question returns to the problem of the Federal Republic as a form of liberal democracy. Here two criteria may apply. The political— institutional one relates to the constitutional structure and its modes of political conduct. In this respect, West Germany emerges as a strictly contoured liberal democracy, defined and conditioned by the Basic Law, with elements of imposed restraint with regard to popular participation. With the political right, a somewhat narrow definition of the *Rechtsstaat* has become such a fundamental value that this itself has sometimes acquired reactionary features, especially in the area of political tolerance. There is obviously scope for possible change here, now that the political system has stood the test of a generation and refuted the worst uncertainties of its founders, but the central directing role of competing political parties has all the while remained a cardinal feature of the West German parliamentary system. The second criterion is the political—cultural. This is where most complications arise, for a principal determinant is the imprint of history on political attitudes. In this way the Federal Republic has differed markedly from other West European democracies because of the profound and persistent shadow of Weimar and the Nazi past. This provides the basic element in the 'subjective' dimension of West German democracy as presented in the introduction to this study. For this reason, although itself politically marginal, terrorism had a strong political impact simply as it became closely interwoven with the 'subjective' dimension. This in turn enhanced the importance of terrorism as a 'crisis', because the perception of one may owe as much to subjective factors as to the reality of a particular threat. At the same time, the West Germans' capacity for worrying about their country's democratic credentials does underline another broad difference from the Weimar experience in addition to the record of political stability. This concern reached a new height during the major terrorist crises, especially the Schleyer affair, all the more because of highly critical foreign reactions — never an entirely peripheral matter for West Germans — in some neighbouring European states. Yet, the debate over the effects of terrorism on the political scene has revealed an evident and often passionate interest in the *quality* of the democratic system and not merely its stability.

Two effects have been popularly attributed to the rise of terrorism in the Federal Republic: promotion of a strong internal security system and encouragement of a trend to the right. The first is without doubt, but the second demands some qualification. Other left-wing circles accused the Baader—Meinhof and later groups of provoking a right-wing reaction, but in conventional political terms this is difficult to establish. The Social and Free Democrats were in power in Bonn throughout the course of terrorism in the 1970s, but despite some political setbacks and security failures they have by and large managed to contain the issue in the party-political sense, this being confirmed by their image of competence in the area of law and order. Nevertheless, there is always the possibility of severe political repercussions in the event of disaster in another major terrorist attack, particularly in view of the widespread West German obsession with all matters of security.

This study has been able to concentrate conveniently on the 1970s for examining a decade of the terrorist issue, and it makes no pretence to estimating future developments. There have been changes in both the operation of German terrorists over the decade and the methods employed to counter their activities. Some of the original factors behind the rise of terrorism, such as the Vietnam issue and the 1968 protest movement, now seem distant history. On the other hand, there are other new factors that may or may not engender further forms of terrorism: the illegal acquisition of highly destructive weapons would suit the terrorists' theatrical motives; the anti-nuclear movement might turn sour in a more pungent way than the 1968 protest and provide some ideological refugees for terrorism; and of course the more conventional approach of a major political assassination would at least in West Germany set in motion a mood of profound despair. The future course of terrorism in West Germany is therefore an open question, not least because of its unpredictable nature.

Notes and References

1. P. Lösche, 'Terrorismus und Anarchismus', in M. Funke (ed.), *Extremismus im demokratischen Rechtsstaat* (Düsseldorf: Droste Verlag, 1978), pp. 83—4.
2. See W. Laqueur, 'Terrorism today', in *Terrorism* (London: Weidenfeld and Nicolson, 1977).
3. H. Schueler, Der Staat muss Leben Schützen. *Die Zeit*, 7 March 1975.
4. Laqueur, *op. cit.*, ch. 4.
5. For a German discussion of this definition, see Funke, *op. cit.*, pp. 82—3; and M. Funke in *Aus Politik und Zeitgeschichte*, 15 October 1977, pp. 31—2.
6. According to one sociological-psychological report on German terrorists, Vietnam for them 'broke the unity between power and morality'; see *Die Zeit*, 9 June 1978.
7. J. Becker, *Hitler's Children: The story of the Baader—Meinhof Gang* (London: Granada, 1978), pp. 79, 105.
8. Quoted in *ibid.*, p. 185.
9. Quoted in *ibid.*, p. 173.
10. *Der Spiegel*, 20 January 1975, p. 55.
11. In Funke, *op. cit.*, p. 90.
12. K. Shell, 'Violence and the New Left', paper presented at annual conference of Association for Study of German Politics (1978), p. 4. See also his study of the APO: Extraparliamentary opposition in postwar Germany. *Comparative Politics* (July 1970), pp. 653—80.
13. Shell, 'Violence and the New Left', p. 8.
14. *Ibid.*, p. 12.
15. Becker, *op. cit.*, pp. 173, 191—2.
16. Quoted in *Die Zeit*, 9 September 1977.
17. Quoted in *Aus Politik und Zeitgeschichte*, 20 May 1978: 13.
18. See Shell, 'Extraparliamentary opposition'.
19. Quoted in Becker, *op. cit.*, p. 51.
20. *Der Spiegel*, 17 October 1977.
21. Quoted in obituary of Marcuse in *The Guardian*, 31 July 1979.
22. Laqueur, *op. cit.*, p. 4.
23. See annual security reports, *Verfassungsschutz*, published by the Federal Ministry of the Interior, Bonn.
24. *Die Anti-Terror-Debatten im Parlament: Protokolle 1974—1978* (ed. H. Vinke and G. Witt; Reinbeck bei Hamburg: Rowohlt, 1978), pp. 131—2.
25. For example, press statement of the Young Socialists, 14 September 1977: 'we oppose most strongly the attempts by conservative politicians and journalists to make the politics and social criticism of the Left responsible for terrorism or make them spiritual neighbours; the terrorists' ideology with its contempt for human nature and their criminal actions have nothing at all in common with left-wing or socialist theory.'
26. For example, see *Verfassungsschutz 1975* (Bonn: Federal Ministry of the Interior, 1976), pp. 96—7.
27. Funke, *op. cit.*, p. 149; Becker, *op. cit.*, pp. 200—1.
28. See Funke, *op. cit.*, pp. 106—9; Becker, *op. cit.*, pp. 265—6.
29. For example, H. Mahler in *Der Spiegel*, 24 January 1972, pp. 30—1; Meinhof with others in *Der Spiegel*, 20 January 1975, pp. 52—7; as well as Meinhof's tracts in prison, see *Verfassungsschutz 1976* (1977), pp. 115—16.
30. Quoted in Becker, *op. cit.*, p. 264.

31. Interview with Baader—Meinhof leaders in prison, *Der Spiegel,* 20 January 1975, p. 55.
32. For example, see Becker, *op. cit.,* pp. 50, 331, 338.
33. For example, the comment of *Frankfurter Allgemeine,* 12 November 1977 that 'psycho-analytical views frequently see in terrorist actions a compensation for the failures of their parents' in the Third Reich. Meinhof was apparently never able to forget the time when her aunt was taken to Auschwitz concentration camp; while H. Mahler remarked: 'If I were faced with having to tell how it all started for me, it would be fascism that would come to mind; outwardly, I had escaped it but even after that era everything was still overshadowed by it somehow . . . I wanted to become one of the "other Germans" '(*Die Zeit,* 9 September 1977).
34. In her early twenties Meinhof also read many books about the anti-Nazi resistance; see Becker, *op. cit.,* p. 159.
35. Interview with Baader—Meinhof leaders in *Der Spiegel,* 20 January 1975, p. 55.
36. This argument is treated at length by K. D. Bracher in H. Geissler (ed.), *Der Weg in die Gewalt: geistige und gesellschaftliche Ursachen des Terrorismus und seine Folgen* (Munich: Günter Olzog Verlag, 1978), pp. 201—16.
37. The term was of course taken from the title of Becker's book on the Baader—Meinhof group.
38. For critical discussion of terrorist views on consumer society, see C. Watrin in Geissler, *op. cit.,* pp. 147—62.
39. Bracher, for instance, emphasised the importance of terrorist language in his chapter in Geissler, *op. cit.*
40. Berlin correspondent in *The Times,* 15 December 1972.
41. This ideological rigidity is evident in the answered questionnaire from Baader—Meinhof leaders in *Der Spiegel,* 20 January 1975, pp. 52—7.
42. Becker, *op. cit.,* pp. 90, 94.
43. A full and detailed chronological list of German terrorist activities and events from 1967 to 1977 is provided by M. Funke, *Terrorismus: Untersuchungen zur Strategie und Struktur revolutionärer Gewaltpolitik* (Bonn: Bundeszentrale für politische Bildung, 1977), pp. 331—65.
44. *Die Zeit,* 9 June 1978.
45. Funke, *Terrorismus,* pp. 278—9.
46. Report in *Die Zeit,* 7 March 1975.
47. *Der Spiegel,* 3 March 1975, p. 22; *The Times,* 7 March 1975.
48. *Frankfurter Rundschau,* 12 September 1978.
49. See reports in *Frankfurter Allgemeine,* 11 May 1978 and *Die Zeit,* 2 June 1978.
50. See official research study on the social background of terrorists, full details of which were published in *Frankfurter Rundschau,* 9 August 1978.
51. On female terrorists in West Germany, see S. von Paczensky (ed.), *Frauen und Terror: Versuche, die Beteiligung von Frauen an Gewalttaten zu erklären* (Reinbek bei Hamburg: Rowohlt, 1978).
52. Quoted in Funke, *Terrorismus,* p. 285.
53. For a very informative discussion of the problem of 'sympathisers', see the five-part series in *Der Spiegel,* 3 October, 10 October, 17 October, 31 October and 7 November 1977.
54. G. Pridham, *Christian Democracy in Western Germany* (London: Croom Helm, 1977), pp. 340-1.
55. *Verfassungsschutz 1968* (1969), p. 3.
56. *Verfassungsschutz 1975* (1976), p. 3.

57. *CDU Wahlprogramm 1969/73*, p. 10.
58. *Regierungsprogramm der SPD, 1969*, p. 12.
59. J. W. Falter, Die Bundestagswahl vom 19. November 1972. *Zeitschrift für Parlamentsfragen* (March 1973), pp. 128—9. There was in fact a decline in public concern over terrorism between two polls in early October and early November with the former taken just after the Munich massacre.
60. *SPD Regierungsprogramm 1976—80: Weiter arbeiten am Modell Deutschland*, pp. 38—40.
61. See details of this report published in *Süddeutsche Zeitung*, 21 September 1972 and *Frankfurter Rundschau*, 22 September 1972.
62. *Süddeutsche Zeitung*, 9/10 September 1972.
63. *The Times*, 25 April 1975. Schmidt mentioned the inevitability of a further attack in his TV broadcast on 5 March.
64. *Frankfurter Allgemeine*, 14 March 1975.
65. *The Times*, 7 March 1975; *Frankfurter Allgemeine*, 14 March 1975; and *Die Zeit*, 7 March 1975.
66. *The Times*, 26 April 1975; *Frankfurter Allgemeine*, 26 April 1975.
67. Federal Press and Information Office, *Dokumentation zu den Ereignissen und Entscheidungen im Zusammenhang mit der Entführung von Hanns Martin Schleyer und der Lufthansa-Maschine 'Landshut'* (Bonn, November 1977), pp. 17—18.
68. *Ibid.*, p. 18.
69. *Ibid.*, p. 95.
70. *Die Zeit*, 17 February 1978.
71. *Der Spiegel*, 24 October 1977.
72. K. H. Krumm, 'Problems der Organisation und Koordination bei der Terrorismus-Bekämpfung in der Bundesrepublik' in Funke, *Terrorismus*, p. 324.
73. R. Wassermann 'Sicherung oder Aushöhlung des Rechtsstaats?' *Aus Politik und Zeitgeschichte*, 27 March 1976, p. 6.
74. *Die Zeit*, 2 May 1975.
75. K. Bölling, government press spokesman in *Schleyer-Dokumentation*, p. 5.
76. See complementary articles on the *Nachrichtensperre* by Bölling and a journalist in *Die Zeit*, 30 September 1977.
77. *Die Anti-Terror-Debatten im Parlament*, p. 82.
78. *Ibid.*, p. 148.
79. In this speech to CSU activists Strauss had rejected the idea of cooperation with the government because of the critical state of the country, and among other things accused the SPD and FDP of 'abandoning the state to criminals and political gangsters'.
80. *Die Anti-Terror-Debatten im Parlament*, pp. 208—9.
81. *Süddeutsche Zeitung*, 9/10 September 1972.
82. *Frankfurter Allgemeine*, 21 October 1977.
83. *Ibid.*, 16 June 1978.
84. *Frankfurter Rundschau*, 1 November 1977.
85. For example, 'The scandal of Moabit' (the prison break-out by terrorists) *Bayernkurier*, 3 June 1978, and 'From Bonn more words than deeds' (article on the influence of the SPD Left) *Bayernkurier*, 28 October 1978.
86. See the discussion of the CDU *Offensivkonzept* by W. Mensing in *Aus Politik und Zeitgeschichte*, 19 June 1976, pp. 17—29.
87. For example, M. Dönhoff in *Die Zeit*, 9 December 1977. The full text of the proceedings was published in Geissler, *op. cit.*

88. *Die Anti-Terror-Debatten im Parlament,* pp. 119, 121–2.
89. Quoted in *ibid., p.* 8.
90. In debate on ZDF television, 27 October 1977.
91. Interviewed on ZDF television, 18 December 1977.
92. *Die Zeit,* 7 October 1977.
93. Professor K. Lenk in *Frankfurter Rundschau,* 11 October 1977.
94. *The Times,* 14 April 1972.
95. *The Guardian,* 17 June 1972.
96. P. Oestreicher in *The Times,* 12 September 1977.
97. *Frankfurter Allgemeine,* 12 September 1977.
98. Quoted in Italian weekly *Panorama,* 27 September 1977.
99. *Stern,* 20 October 1977.
100. The precise question was: 'If the influence of the state and police must be strengthened for fighting the terrorists — would you accept or reject a limitation to your personal rights by such measures as surveillance and house searches?' The poll was in fact taken in November.
101. *Frankfurter Allgemeine,* 10 February 1978.
102. *Ibid.,* 10 March 1978.
103. *Frankfurter Rundschau,* 30 October 1978.
104. For example, K.-H. Krumm in Funke, *Terrorismus,* p. 317.
105. P. Merkl, *The Origin of the West German Republic* (New York: Oxford University Press, 1963), p. 176.
106. M. Dönhoff, The answer to terror. *The Observer,* 7 May 1978.
107. K Lenk, Bewährung oder blinder Wiederholungszwang? *Frankfurter Rundschau,* 11 October 1977.
108. *Die Anti-Terror-Debatten im Parlament,* pp. 330–1.
109. R. von Voss (ed.), *Von der Legitimation der Gewalt* (Stuttgart: Verlag Bonn Aktuell, 1978), pp. 7–8.
110. *Die Anti-Terror-Debatten im Parlament,* p. 93.
111. See the useful paper by D. Kommers, 'Expression and security in the Federal Republic of Germany: a constitutional analysis', presented to conference on German terrorism at University of Notre Dame, March 1979.
112. Werner Maihofer in introduction to *Verfassungsschutz 1976* (1977), p. 3.
113. *Frankfurter Allgemeine,* 26 April 1975.
114. See Kommers, 'Expression and security'.
115. *The Times,* 24 March 1972.
116. Federal Ministry of the Interior, *Innere Sicherheit im freiheitlichen Rechtsstaat — Leistungsbilanz* (Bonn, 1975), p. 107; Funke, *Terrorismus,* p. 315.
117. Federal Ministry of the Interior, *Innere Sicherheit,* p. 107.
118. *Ibid.,* p. 108.
119. Quoted in K. Porzner MdB, letter to SPD Bundestag deputies, 8 June 1978.
120. *Frankfurter Allgemeine,* 15 September 1977.
121. J. Holloway, 'Decentralisation of power in the Federal Republic of Germany', in J. Cornford (ed.), *The Failure of the State* (London: Croom Helm, 1975), esp. pp. 121–2.
122. Federal Press Office *Kommentarübersicht,* 2 November 1977.
123. *Süddeutsche Zeitung,* 9/10 September 1972.
124. *Frankfurter Rundschau,* 12 September 1972.
125. *Frankfurter Allgemeine,* 17 January 1978.
126. *Neue Zürcher Zeitung,* 31 August 1978.
127. Article on the Federal Criminal Office in *Das Parlament,* 17 January 1976, p. 4.
128. *Der Spiegel,* 9 July 1979, pp. 57–62.

CHAPTER 3

Political Terrorism in Italy: Responses, Reactions and Immobilism

Paul Furlong

INTRODUCTION

Routine business

'You're a boy,' I said, 'how has a boy like you come to this?'
    'The system forces us,' he answered, 'against this bourgeois power there is no other response.'
    'I suppose you're here to shoot me,' I said . . .[1]

The above quotation is taken from an interview with a management consultant named Filippo Peschiera, a member of the Italian Christian Democrat Party (DC), who on 19 January 1978 was attacked in his office in Genoa by an armed group apparently belonging to the Red Brigades, who took documents and shot Peschiera, wounding him with care. The episode is typical of much of the organised political violence against the state that has been a prominent feature of Italian politics since 1969. In the precision of its execution, the coolness of the operators and the obvious care that had attended its planning, the episode bore some of the characteristics usually associated with its perpetrators, the Brigate Rosse (BR). There is something of the impression of a well-trained but bureaucratic military organisation in this episode as in others, and not least might this impression be obtained from the banality of the language of the terrorists. Another salient feature was the target — a middle-ranking businessman with well-known political connections, not a personage of any great weight even in the local party, but both sufficiently well known and sufficiently ordinary for an attack on him to be highly symbolic. Operations such as these, which are relatively safe and low-level, serve several purposes for the terrorist organisation: the documents stolen provide it with information that may prove useful in the identification of other targets or that may in the eyes of the terrorist be incriminating and therefore suitable for propaganda; the operation itself may be a means of giving combat practice to new recruits and of keeping older hands in proper condition; and the attack occupies police resources for some time afterwards and perhaps distracts attention away from more sensitive and more important areas. The publicity attendant on such operations indicates the group's survival and might stimulate the flow of potential recruits, always important for clandestine groups under continual pressure from security forces. Yet these results do not really amount to much. Detailed calculations of the functional efficiency of organised political violence are hazardous and not often undertaken in public, for obvious reasons, but overall one might be left with the suspicion that the time, the manpower and the risks involved do not appear to be justified by the outcome of the operation. Yet operations such as these have been carried out with almost monotonous frequency by the BR and other groups over the last ten years, interspersed with the spectacular attempts on targets of national prominence, (in particular the kidnapping of Mario Sossi, the murder of Francesco Coco, and the kidnapping and murder of Aldo Moro — see below, pp. 00-0), and the clashes with the neo-fascists in which the left-wing terrorists appear to take on themselves the role of vengeance-seeker for the proletariat (as, for instance, during the week of 14—21 January 1979 after a neo-fascist raid on a private left-wing radio station in Rome).[2] The effort involved in the latter forms of terrorism is more easily understood but it is the Peschiera episode that is more typical of their workday routine. One may suppose that in the logic of the terrorists the outcome does indeed justify the effort and the risks, though in the phrase 'the system forces us' there is perhaps a certain implicit acknowledgement that the 'response' of the terrorists, if not futile, is at least not destined to bring about the rapid achievement of their ultimate aims. Though the results referred to above (information, training, diversion, recruitment) would undoubtedly be welcome to the terrorists, I would argue that they are not sufficient to explain this kind of operation. The outcome they are seeking, and by which these operations may be distinguished from the outcome of the attacks on 'the heart of the state' and the clashes with the neo-fascists, is found in the single word 'terror'. In this chapter I attempt to analyse how political terrorism has developed in Italy and what has been the response of the state to this assault on its authority.

Terrorism

There is not the space here to consider all the definitional problems inherent in the use of the term 'terrorism': the bibliography covers a wide variety of perspectives. The question of definition is undoubtedly beset with traps for the unwary researcher (and indeed for those wary as well). We must content ourselves here with merely enough preliminary clearing of the ground to enable us to use the term with a minimum of clarity. It may already be understood from my reference to the Peschiera episode that I intend to use the term 'terrorism' in a narrow sense,[3] in which the primary aim of terrorism is indeed to terrorise, that is, to induce terror in intended subjects. Intended subjects may be entire populations, specific sectors of society or isolated individuals. Terrorism therefore involves among other things the use of violence to induce compliance, where the victim of violence is of symbolic value to a wider community rather than of direct value. Political terrorism is terrorism used for political objectives, usually either by insurgents wishing to overthrow an existing government ('revolutionary') or by existing governments to maintain themselves in power or to enforce their policies ('governmental').

Hutchinson analyses the basic components of the concept of terrorism as including a revolutionary strategy, acts of politically and socially unacceptable violence, a pattern of representative selection of victims and the deliberate intention to change political behaviour and attitudes.[4] I have already indicated that I think the term 'terrorism' may also apply to nonpolitical strategies; here we are concerned only with political terrorism. The logical jump is often made from the arbitrariness and indiscriminate nature of the violence to its unacceptability. Hutchinson describes terrorism thus:

> Acts of terrorism are often particularly atrocious and psychologically shocking
> . . . It usually occurs within the civilian population, both the victims and the
> scene of violence are unaccustomed to it and it occurs unexpectedly. The act is
> not only unpredictable but often anonymous. This arbitrariness of terrorist
> violence makes it unacceptable and abnormal.[5]

But though terrorist violence may be unacceptable and abnormal, and indeed often does occur in environments not normally associated with violence, nevertheless it may not be unpredictable in its general selection of targets nor is it indiscriminate. If it were indiscriminate or arbitrary, the symbolic value or representativeness of its victims would be undermined. Even attacks on the general public, such as those of the Algerian National Liberation Front (FLN) described by Hutchinson, are carried out with due regard for the symbolic use of the attack on public opinion at large. One of the reasons for the emphasis commonly given to the supposed arbitrariness of terrorism is probably the intention of distinguishing the violence of terrorists from the coercive force of the liberal—democratic state, which is usually described as essentially predictable, regulated and uniform. The violence of terrorists differs from the coercive force of the liberal—democratic state in many ways, but arbitrariness is not necessarily one of them; if there is arbitrariness, it lies not in the lack of criteria for choice of target but in the fact that whereas the liberal—democratic state applies its coercive sanctions to all in an impartial and uniform manner, the violence of the terrorists does not have a uniform or impartial application over all those to whom its criteria for selection might apply. Terrorism relies for its effect not so much on any general unpredictability, but rather on its specific unexpectedness, as well as on the eruption of violence into environments normally free from it. If terrorism is not arbitrary it is not necessarily irrational either, except in the sense that it implies the production of panic or of unwarranted fear in the target groups. As Hutchinson argues, terrorism may indeed be an extremely economical instrument for insurgent organisa- tions, since the threat implicit in the act of violence may be imagined to be to a wider area possibly beyond the real capacities of the operators.

There will often be an element of terrorism in attacks on persons who occupy leading positions in the political system, in that such attacks, particularly if successful, also carry a threat against susceptible groups in the public at large; but this terroristic effect should not lead us to ignore or underestimate the fact that such attacks are also, and perhaps more importantly, directed against 'obstacles to be eliminated'[6] and may significantly impair the functioning of the system. If this is the case, they may be part of guerrilla warfare, civil war or an armed frontal attack on the political system, rather than part of an attack by way of public opinion. Insurgents engaged in these other forms of internal warfare may use terrorism among other strategies or may find it merely a welcome side-effect resulting from operations designed for different purposes. Not all the aggressive actions of terrorists are necessarily to be regarded as terroristic.

In practice, the strategy of those who wish to attack the state or to use violence to achieve political ends will often be to mix the common criminal activities — such as bank-robbing and kidnapping for pecuniary gain — with attacks on representative targets and with direct attacks on the state. As their capacity increases, such groups may also engage in a fourth category of operation, aimed at 'policing' or 'disciplining' their area of control, by the punishment of defectors or attacks on rival groups. All of these categories have in common the characteristic that they are expressions of organised political violence directed against the state. But only one of them is strictly political terrorism. In the Italian case, which we now come to consider, we find all these forms of organised political violence, combined in some cases with a high degree of sophistication in tactical flexibility. The combination of a variety of forms of organised political violence poses particular problems for the state, and is further complicated by the occurrence of a spontaneous disorganised political violence that follows no coherent strategy.

Social and political preconditions of political terrorism

Though political terrorism may be considered an international phenomenon, in individual countries it necessarily reflects local conditions, cultural and political no less than economic and social. In Italy, recent history certainly from the Risorgimento is scattered with minority groups committed to political activism that finally issued into organised violence and sometimes into terrorism. Left-wing political terrorism in Italy in its contemporary form is in its ideological expressions and organisation very much dependent on international models, in some cases with explicit rejection of indigenous theories of political violence; right-wing political terrorism on the other hand is ideologically close to the fascist traditions of 1920—22, though in its operations it differs somewhat from that model. Despite these differences, the traditions of violence in Italy are important for an understanding of its modern political terrorism.

Italy presents us with conflicting and confused strands of political culture that result in a wide variety both of forms of political violence and of attitudes towards political violence on the part of political actors. There is the traditional authoritarianism of the Liberal state that developed after the unification of Italy exaggerated and developed by the fascist state, which has residual survival in areas within the central administration, the judiciary and the armed forces. Second, the guerrilla warfare carried out with some success by the partisans against the occupying German forces is significant as a model for some modern terrorists, but not only for that. The idealism and tenacity of the resistance movement found only partial expression in the constitution of the Republic, but their tradition is claimed as a source of legitimacy by many contemporary political actors. Third, there is a specifically Italian tradition found in the violence, almost invariably unsuccessful, of those who opposed the Liberal state, whether in an organised form as anarcho-socialists or 'bourgeois patriots' or in a disorganised and spontaneous fashion as brigands and outlaws, particularly in the South. The modern Italian state is an amalgam of these strands. It has inherited both the tradition of centralised administration and the emphasis on the supremacy of the law that characterised the Liberal state, with its formalism, its authoritarianism and some of the practical failings, in particular its vulnerability to political pressure. The combination of this 'strong state' tradition with the relatively radical democratic and federalist state that appears in parts of the postwar constitution is uneasy, but it is these two together that influence in different directions both the development of organised political violence and the response to it by the state.

Against the 'redneck Marxism' of the left-wing terrorists and the grandiose operations of the neo-fascists, the Italian polity presents an ambiguous and polyvalent set of tactics, torn between its liberal—democratic constitution and origins and its authoritarian heavy-handed tradition. Political terrorism is implicitly an attack on the authority of the state, and may be closely connected with the development of a minority that believes itself to be permanently excluded from the political system; the questions that arise in the Italian case might therefore concern the authority of the Italian Republic and the economic, social and political conditions that have led to the emergence of a 'permanent minority'.

The social and political origins of Italian terrorism can be found in the contradictory influences that produced the Italian constitution and that resulted in the radical expectations engendered by the resistance movement; in the tempering of the populist democratic elements in the Constituent Assembly; and in the delays and lapses that accompanied the implementation of the constitution. The political system that has developed is characterised by the continuous occupation of power by one party, the Christian Democrats (DC), for over thirty years and the exclusion from ministerial posts since 1947 of the next largest party, the Italian Communist Party (PCI). The electorate, divided for much of this period into two hostile and exclusive blocs supporting one or other of these parties, is extremely stable in its voting patterns. The only major change in the formation of government coalitions since 1948 has been the inclusion in 1963 of the Italian Socialist Party (PSI) into the group of minor parties who are acceptable coalition partners to the DC. The continuous occupation of power by the DC has fostered the development of a system of government based on clientelism and petty compromise, known commonly as immobilism, in which unstable coalitions are cobbled together on the basis of distribution of ministerial posts with programmes nominally supported by the coalition parties rarely reaching the stage of implementation. The coalitions are beset by inter-party and intra-party wrangling, by personal feuds and ideological rigidities, by vacuous adherence to fine-sounding principles and by cynical opportunism.

At the same time the second-largest party, the PCI, has been slowly coming to terms with its revolutionary past and with the demands of providing sound administration in local government in a liberal democracy. Though the 'Italian road to socialism' developed by the PCI is certainly a complex and sophisticated approach to the strategic problems of a revolutionary party in a parlimentary democracy, it cannot be said that it possesses clarity and ease of comprehension; the PCI has undoubtedly found itself in an ambiguous position, attempting to reconcile revolutionary rhetoric with a practice that is often quite openly reformist. The effect of this both on its grassroots membership and on its electorate as a whole is difficult to assess, but the recent strategy of the PCI, in particular the proposed historic compromise with the DC, appears to have confused supporters and threatened its position as the party of protest and struggle as well as of government.

But if the revolutionary expectations of the socialist and communist area have been disappointed, so too have the expectations of rising standards of living produced in Italian society as a whole by the economic development of the postwar period. Instead of rising living standards, the last ten years have brought unemployment, recession, inflation, together with the emergence of severe strain on the resources of the large cities, unable to cope with the massive influx of workers who left the land, particularly in the South, during the period of very rapid economic growth in the 1950s and early 1960s. Thus an economic crisis of daunting proportions is exacerbated in its social consequences by the incapacity of the political system to provide urgently needed reforms in the fields of housing, education, health services, transport and public administration.

So the preconditions of political terrorism may be clearly perceived in Italy: an economic crisis producing unemployment particularly among the younger age-groups, political parties that are unable to agree on appropriate measures, a social fabric severely threatened by the industrial mobilisation of the immediate postwar period, and not least a political culture that supports radical expectations and gives legitimacy to the unsatisfied hopes and programmes of the postwar political reconstruction.

Traditions of political terrorism

The third strand of political culture mentioned above is that of violence not of the state but rather of groups in society opposed to the state, and it is as well to remember that this has been not only the violence of republican nationalists and anarcho-socialists but also the violence of the National Fascist Party (Partito Nazionale Fascista) after the First World War. This tradition is important for the veneer of ideological consistency it can give to such groups as well as for its strength as a persistent and valued theme in Italian politics: that against an arbitrary corrupt and authoritarian state, which often has recourse to violence, the recourse to violence by the subjects or victims is legitimate. Indeed it might be argued that contemporary Italian terrorism bears some similarity in its precepts to the 'propaganda of deeds'[7] of Carlo Pisacane and Enrico Malatesta. Pisacane was an early Italian socialist who died in an unsuccessful expedition into the Southern hinterland in an attempt to rouse peasantry against the Bourbon kingdom in 1857. In his Political Testament, written just before the expedition, he contrasted the 'propaganda of the idea' with the 'propaganda of deeds':

> The propaganda of the idea is a chimera . . . the education of the people is an absurdity. Ideas result from deeds, not the latter from the former, for the people will not be free when they are educated, but educated when they are free. The only work a citizen can undertake for the good of the country is that of cooperating with material revolution; therefore, conspiracies, plots and attempts are that series of deeds by which Italy proceeds to her goal.[8]

The significant element in Pisacane's writing and activities appears to be the emphasis on the spectacular blow with little regard for immediate success of

the operation. Bowyer Bell appears to have this tradition in mind when he
argues that:

> Brigate Rosse—NAP, [Nuclei Armati Proletari], however spectacular their
> operations, are quite irrelevant to Italian politics except as provocateurs. They
> have no general following and the adamant opposition of the Parliamentary
> left. They represent an anachronism — the brief comet arising in Paris 1968
> and snuffing out in various European prisons. They will age or also end in
> prison.[9]

The question of how effective and long-lasting terrorism in Italy may be
will be considered later; here I would disagree with the 'more spectacular
than significant' argument on the grounds that though the aim of the
clandestine violent groups is propagandist it is also something more than
that. Though others may describe their actions as terrorist, the clandestine
groups themselves appear to believe that they are engaged in incipient civil
war which bears little similarity to the propaganda of deeds. Unlike Pisacane,
who believed that granted the right conditions only a vigorous impulse such
as his expedition to Sanza was needed to inspire widespread popular revolt,
the terrorist groups have a much more long-term view of the revolutionary
struggle. A resolution of the Strategic Control of the BR dated February
1978 analyses in tortuous complexity the 'present crisis' and argues that the
class war is now engaged in the passage from armed peace to war.

> This passage appears as an extremely contradictory process which now shows
> itself as the restructuring of the State into the Imperialist State of the
> Multinationals. This is therefore an extremely important crisis whose duration
> and form depend on the relationship which is established between revolution
> and counter-revolution: this is not however a peaceful process, rather as it
> develops it assumes the form of war.
>   The principle tactic of the guerrilla in this crisis is the disarticulation of the
> enemy's forces . . . The length and in the final analysis the outcome of the war
> depend to a great extent on how the conflict is resolved in this phase.
>   The disarticulation of the forces of the enemy is therefore the last period of
> the phase of the armed group and introduces progressively that of the
> revolutionary civil war.[10]

Pisacane and to a lesser extent the anarcho-socialists who followed him
believed in the single revolutionary impulse that, even if unsuccessful in the
short term, would indicate to the masses that violent revolution was both
necessary and feasible. The documents available that originate from the BR
tend to the justification in the long term of their clandestinity and violence,
against the criticism voiced by the extreme left that the BR have set
themselves apart from the working class and have lost contact with its
struggle. One of the theoreticians of the extra-parliamentary left in Italy,
Antonio Negri, arguing in a recent book for a different sort of violence, that
of industrial sabotage, implicitly referred to the clandestine groups.

Proletarian opposition must consolidate itself in practical destruction, in subversion. But it is the entire [class] relationship which must be subverted, in its political aspects and its structural foundation. It is not possible to eliminate the complexity of the state-form of the organisation of exploitation by fleeing from the difficulties, the problems, the determinate results, which are produced in the face of that complexity — fleeing from them either by subjectivist voluntarism or by collective spontaneism. But this is what has been risked in the latest phase of the struggle.[11]

The 'subjectivist voluntarism' referred to by Negri can be interpreted as the strategy of organised clandestine violence against the state, while the 'collective spontaneism' is the indiscriminate and uncontrolled urban violence of the 'Autonomi', the autonomous groups who reject all organised forms of political activity not directly controlled by themselves. Since it is essentially symbolic, all terrorism may to some extent be seen as 'propaganda', but despite Negri's condemnation of the strategy of the clandestine groups as 'subjective voluntarism', there is little resemblance between the nineteenth-century anarchist strategy of 'propaganda by deed', which was highly voluntarist and spectacularly unsuccessful, and the 'redneck Marxist' strategy of terrorism as one of a set of instruments in the class war.

According to the analysis of the BR, terrorism in Italy is justified as part of an incipient civil war, guided by them.

In the last few years . . . the expressions of class antagonism have radicalised and extended themselves to such an extent that it does not appear to us improper to talk of a creeping civil war . . . Proletarian Offensive Movement of Resistance [MRPO] is the name we give to the area of the expressions of class antagonism produced by the harshening of the political and economic crisis, we call MRPO the area of the forces, of the groups and of the revolutionary cells which give a politico-military content to their anti-capitalist, anti-imperialist, anti-revisionist, communist struggle. It is clear that the concept of MRPO does not reflect a simple homogeneous movement but rather an area of struggle and of partial movements, very different from one another and yet tied together by a common denominator: the process of crisis-restructurisation brought about by the imperialist bourgeoisie.[12]

It is over this 'MRPO' that the BR aim to establish their control, and it includes not only the other terrorist groups but also the 'Autonomi'. But the 'Autonomi' on the whole are loth to accept control or leadership from any direction, and indeed tend to reject the idea of programmes and strategies as mystificatory attempts at rationalising the irrational; in Negri's terms, proletarian violence is the only rational response, but it must be a completely new violence operated directly by the working class. Negri argues:

In socialist tradition, violence, the use of violence, is attributed to the party. The socialist party is the institution of violence. But we are against this image of the party and against each and every one of its present revivals . . .: its monopoly of violence, its being the reciprocal and not the determinate antithesis of the state-form, has determined the functional possibility of the repression of proletarian violence, — the Gulag originates from this.[13]

Much of the activity of the BR can be explained in terms of the need to affirm the legitimacy of their strategy in the face of the confused anarchist violence of the extreme left. In implicit answer to the criticism of Negri and others, the BR 'resolution' argues the Third International case for party control of violence:

> To transform the process of creeping civil war, at present dispersed and disorganised, into a general offensive, directed by a unitary design, it is necessary to develop and unify the movement of proletarian resistance constructing the Communist Party of Combat.[14]

The organisation and operation of the BR therefore are associated with a particular vision of the 'class war' as already characterised by open violent conflict, to which they respond by organising and leading the armed struggle of the proletariat.

> The Red Brigades are not the Communist Party of Combat, but an armed vanguard which works inside the metropolitan proletariat for its construction.
> While we affirm that BR and Party of Combat are not identical, we affirm with equal clarity that the armed vanguard must 'act as a Party' from the very beginning.[15]

The BR in Italy have produced and 'published' large quantities of material in explanation and attempted justification of their strategy. In *a posteriori* rationalisation of a strategy whose increasing violence appears inevitable, they argue that violence is the legitimate and indeed necessary proletarian response to the Imperialist State of the Multinationals, that this violence should be directed and controlled by a Party of Combat or its vanguard, and that the target of the violence of the working class must be the state itself. From these premises follow the clandestinity, the selection of targets on terrorist criteria and the apparent obsession with self-justification and explanation to the working class. Whatever one may think of their justifications, it is clear that they are not operating in an arbitrary or wholly unpredictable manner, nor are they simply the frustrated remnants of the 'events' of May 1968; and while their commitment to violence is not unusual in the Italian tradition, its specific origins appear to be more dependent on non-Italian models of guerrilla warfare and violent political action.

THE DEVELOPMENT OF POLITICAL TERRORISM

Political terrorism and political culture

Political terrorism in Italy is not a subject on which the researcher will find a lack of material; Italian newspapers and magazines of all political leanings carry many columns devoted not only to the identifiable operations of terrorists but also to hearsay, gossip, rumour and speculation about their origins, scope and intentions. The Italian constitution provides for freedom of opinion and freedom from censorship; the prevailing political culture appears to tolerate even extreme expressions of dissent in published material, and much that elsewhere might never reach the public is readily available. This is where one might begin trying to analyse political terrorism, in that a more intolerant political system might much earlier identify extremes of dissent as 'intolerable' and be more ready to prevent their outward manifestation. It is one of the paradoxes of the Italian political system that the formal guarantees of a liberal democracy and a relatively open political culture should coexist with a state executive that can be arbitrary, partial and violent in its authoritarianism. But this is not a view of Italy that one finds frequently in the Italian mass media, where much ink has been spilt identifying and explaining what are seen as the particularly dogmatic and repressive ideological modes typical of the Italian political system. Thus a respected and widely read journalist referred to the ideological origins of the Red Brigades as 'Cathocommunism'; from the premiss that many of the BR began their political careers in subsidiary organisations controlled either by the Christian Democrat Party (DC) or by the Communist Party (PCI), the conclusion is reached that the brigatisti and other terrorists have acquired a particularly intolerant and anti-liberal approach to the ideals or values of others, as well as the propensity to adopt exclusive all-embracing world views.[16] Another way of interpreting the same premiss might be that the brigatisti and other terrorists usually have political experience within the legal framework before they become clandestine subversives. In the Italian political system, in which two mass parties dominate not only parliament but also much of organised political society outside the legislature, it is to be expected that of those who have any experience as political activists the majority will have had that experience under the Catholic or communist aegis. Perhaps the significance of their 'Cathocommunist' origins is that such origins indicate prior political experience, not that they indicate a dogmatic and intolerant cast of mind.

The theory that right-wing and left-wing political terrorism originate in some dark repressive corner of Italian political culture is denied by the practice of Italian politics in the postwar period, which has been characterised by the need to tolerate and bring within limits acceptable to constitutional practice two potentially revolutionary movements, the Marxist and the fascist, both of which have succeeded in attracting significant proportions of the electorate. The success of the postwar Italian Republic is that for over thirty years, with all its thirty-seven governments and twenty-four different kinds of coalition, despite the obvious centrifugal elements within the political system, the system has survived and managed to effect some integration of these elements.

In the case of the Marxist movement, it is relatively clear how this has been done: the size of the PCI vote (which has increased from 20 per cent in 1948 to 30 per cent in 1979, with a peak of 34 per cent in 1976), the essentially Italian traditions of the communist sub-culture, the capacity of successive PCI leaders to maintain the militant commitment of their grassroots membership while working within the constitutional framework, all of these factors made the integration of the PCI into the workings of parliamentary democracy both urgent and possible. But the price of that integration has been increased by the intransigence of a Catholic party that is founded on anti-communism, and that is encouraged in that stance by NATO allies. There is an ambiguity in the attempt to combine the revolutionary fervour and organisation of a Leninist communist party with the compromises enforced by close involvement in coalitions with non-Marxist parties, an ambiguity that is exacerbated by a hostile international environment and that has put considerable strain on the political skills of the PCI leadership and on the commitment of the party members.[17] Some of the early left-wing groups (for instance, 22 October Group in Genova) appear to have had a significant proportion of disillusioned or expelled ex-PCI members in their ranks, and it is clear that one source of recruits to the terrorist groups, not necessarily the largest, continues to be political activists who have passed through the PCI.

In the case of the fascist tradition, which was thoroughly discredited by defeat and economic collapse at the end of its 21-year dictatorship, the integration has been rather different. The supporters of the extreme right were significant in the immediate postwar period from the Allies' point of view, not as destabilising agents (as was the PCI) but rather as a source of stability. The most important contribution of the right wing to the new Italian Republic was vigorous anti-communism; suitably purified and sanitised, fascism delivered both a core of administrative personnel, trained under the fascist dictatorship, within the civil service, the judiciary and the armed forces, and the support of right-wing industrialists and landowners to the new regime. Associated with the integration of these potentially destabilising elements were the emergence and continued survival of an extreme right-wing party, the Italian Social Movement (MSI), which throughout the postwar period has been a parliamentary pariah, and whose policy towards the constitution and the political system has been clearly condemnatory. The significance of the 'sanitised' neo-fascists within the system has been that they have guaranteed the exclusion of the PCI from government by reason of the threat of extreme right-wing reaction that they were imagined to control. Under Giorgio Almirante, leader from 1968, this threat became more vocal with his dual strategy described as 'combining the double-breasted suit with the club'; in less hermetic terms, his strategy attempted both to reduce the isolation of the MSI in parliament by forming alliances and eventually merging with the moribund Monarchist Party, and at the same time to give political support to the more violent neo-fascist militants. It may be argued that the survival of a neo-fascist party that both denies the legitimacy of the state and encourages low-level violence as a form of political action is more destabilising in practice than the development of a communist party that does neither.

In their different ways both of these traditions have been integrated at least partially into the political system. At the parliamentary level one of the products of this integration was undoubtedly an increase in tolerance of the opinions of others, even if this tolerance meant no more than willingness to operate the same political machinery. The survival of the system over thirty years is an indication that parties with widely differing views have come to a *modus vivendi*. Though this tolerance may still be functioning among the political parties,[18] it can be argued that within society as a whole the strains are still felt strongly and are not so well absorbed. I would argue therefore that political terrorism in Italy is not the product of a dogmatic cast of mind peculiar to 'Cathocommunists' but rather that it is associated with the incomplete integration of potentially centrifugal elements into the accepted political framework[19] and that the emergence of both right-wing and left-wing terrorism, against the background of economic crisis and within an immobilist political system, is associated with the threats and opportunities perceived by the excluded elements. The threat was, to the neo-fascists, that of the eventual entry of the PCI into the government following the failure of the already unacceptable centre—left coalitions in the period 1963—68, while the opportunity was of course the possibility of imposing an authoritarian solution on a weak regime by coup d'etat using sympathetic elements in the armed forces. To the groups on the fringe of the extreme left, the threat was precisely that of the right-wing coup d'etat, while the opportunity could be held to have been demonstrated on an international scale by the May events in Paris, the failure of the American effort in Vietnam, Cuba, the Tupamaros and other events and figures of the time, which passed rapidly into the mythology of the left in Italy as elsewhere.

First phase: 1969—73

In the first years of terrorism post-1968, it was clearly the right-wing terrorists who dominated the scene with a series of spectacular gestures. On 12 December 1969 a bomb exploded in the Piazza della Fontana in Milan. There were fourteen deaths and eighty people injured. Three days later the police arrested Pietro Valpreda, a known anarchist, and the mass media loudly proclaimed his guilt.[20] But it was nearly nine years before the case was to be closed with Valpreda acquitted on all charges, two neo-fascists convicted for the attack after having fled from house arrest, and damaging revelations made both in court and out concerning the involvement of security services in the manipulation of right-wing terrorism. In the five years from 1969 to the end of 1973 there also occurred a series of bomb attacks against political targets, an abortive coup d'etat in December 1970, the long drawn out riots in Reggio Calabria fomented by the MSI, and the development of the so-called strategy of tension. This was the period of mass political terrorism operated by the neo-fascists in which the victims were indiscriminately selected from the target group — the general public — with the aim of producing panic prior to the armed takeover of power. The MSI and neo-fascist groups outside parliament attempted also to establish themselves as the spokesmen for and protectors of the armed forces and the police, using expressions of public sympathy for policemen injured or killed on duty to foment riots and create tension within the police forces. (For instance, after the accidental death of a carabiniere during a riot on 19 September 1969 in Milan, the funeral was the occasion of violent 'reprisals' for his death by neo-fascist groups.)

At the same time there was the steady growth of a more selective form of political terrorism, in which the target group was narrower and the victims therefore more limited: this was the terrorism of the Red Brigades, in this period overshadowed by the terrorism of the right, but later to come into its own. A major difference between the two forms of terrorism, which indicates their differing objectives, is the frequency with which the neo-fascist groups use bombs in crowded places, while the BR rarely use bombs and do not appear to have aimed any operations directly against the public at large. Table 3.1 indicates clearly the disparity in style and frequency of terrorist attempts between the period 1969—73, dominated by the right, and 1974—79, dominated by the left.

The activity of the BR began in August 1970 in Milan.[21] They were a development of the Collettivo Politico Metropolitano (Metropolitan Political Collective), later termed Sinistra Proletaria (Proletarian Left), a group restricted to Milan some of whose leading members, in particular Renato Curcio and Margherita Cagol, had been together at the University of Trento and had their first known taste of political activity in left-wing Catholic groups there. Others who joined the BR at this stage or soon after, such as Alberto Franceschini and Roberto Ognibene, came from the PCI-dominated area of Reggio Emilia. Though the BR appear to have chosen clandestinity early in 1971, the terrorist attacks mounted by them were high in symbolic content and low on physical injury for a considerable period. Arson against cars belonging to managers of large firms or against known neo-fascists appears to have been their trademark, with occasional well-planned and well-publicised kidnappings that inevitably resulted in a 'proletarian trial' and the release of the prisoner. Throughout this period the BR showed a gradual increase both in expertise and in ambition. The arson attacks constituted bread-and-butter operations undertaken against representative targets with the aim both of inducing terror among the 'ruling class' and of stimulating the working class to take up arms. The BR also showed at this stage a great interest in and knowledge of factory conditions and organisation. Many of their 'proletarian trials' were little more than interrogations to extract information about suitable targets. Their purpose appeared to be to establish themselves as 'vigilantes of the workers', and their operations were usually explained in the inevitable leaflets as actions on behalf of particular groups of workers. The last of these factory-oriented operations, and the most ambitious, was the kidnapping on 10 December 1973 in Turin of Ettore Amerio, the personnel director of FIAT Cars. Amerio was released unharmed after eight days, with no ransom having been paid. This was virtually the last time that the BR would engage in kidnapping such a figure, though it was not the last time that a kidnap of theirs failed to produce the ransom demanded.

The experiences of those years, though not marked by any obvious success in achieving their overall objectives, may paradoxically have confirmed the BR and other left-wing groups in the validity of their strategy. Clandestinity and 'proletarian justice' may have begun as a reaction to the heady days of 1968 and the labour struggles of the 'hot autumn' of 1969 in the belief that the intensification of the class struggle was both desirable and necessary. The heavy-handed violence of the police in dealing with demonstrations and with the intermittent civil unrest throughout 1968 and 1969 appears also to have drawn some members of the extreme left, Curcio included, to the conclusion that violence was an appropriate reaction.[22] (But it was five years before one of their operations resulted directly in loss of life. On 17 June 1974 two MSI militants were killed outside party branch offices in Padua. The long build-up resulting finally in hardened terrorism is indicative not only of the ineffectiveness of symbolic terrorism but also of the worsening of the political environment over those five years.) Whereas others, particularly those in the heterogeneous Lotta Continua (Continuous Struggle) emphasised the importance of mass violence (strikes, pickets, sabotage, demonstration, self-defence against the police) as one revolutionary instrument among many, the violence of Sinistra Proletaria and its offshoot BR was a violence of the revolutionary elite — exemplary, selective and organised. It was therefore clandestine from the beginning; and because clandestine, it was the violence of an isolated group, unable to achieve any direct relationship with the masses it was supposed to be serving. Though to some extent BR has been able to overcome this isolation in recent years, the pattern of its activity is still characterised by reliance on clandestine violence as the single valid instrument of revolutionary activity. In this also it is to be distinguished from the revolutionary groups on the extreme left that have not chosen clandestinity, whose view of the BR is well summarised in the description of them as 'compagni che sbagliano' — comrades who are in error.

Both the failure of the strategy of terror to induce the desired responses in the working class and the repeated spectacular mass terrorism of the right would have been interpreted as indicating the need for further intensification. To reinforce this reaction there was the example of the death in obscure circumstances of Giangiacomo Feltrinelli on 15 March 1972. Feltrinelli, a millionaire left-wing publisher, had founded the Partisan Action Groups (GAP) against the possibility (or as he appears to have seen it, the probability) of a radical authoritarian swing to the right. He died in an explosion underneath an electricity pylon in the countryside outside Milan, and though it later transpired that his death resulted from inexperience in handling explosives and that he was in fact on a 'training exercise',[23] the obscurity of the circumstances lent credibility to the beliefs of heightened imaginations that it was all part of a 'strategy of tension' — of right-wing terrorism manipulated and controlled by the security forces with the aim of discrediting the left.

Throughout this period, while the MSI was providing a cover of respectability for the extreme right, political groups to the left of the PCI were undergoing an intense and chaotic series of splits, mergers and dissolutions. After over twenty years of almost unchallenged hegemony over the Italian Marxist left, the capacity of the PCI to control and absorb fringe movements on the left was finally weakening. Indeed among the reasons both for the deliberate choice of clandestinity and for the slowness with which that strategy developed into hard shoot-to-kill terrorism, the policy of the PCI towards liberal—democratic politics and the difficulties of finding a convincing alternative to that policy are influential. Groups such as Potere Operaio (Worker Power), Lotta Continua (Continuous Struggle), and Avanguardia Operaia (Workers' Vanguard) all attempted to formulate that alternative strategy and in so doing provided the forum for the debate over the armed struggle, which has reappeared at frequent intervals in the extreme left in Italy since 1969.

Second phase: 1974—79

Periodisations, particularly of relatively recent history, are notoriously problematic. Yet, granted that any division of the decade of terrorism 1969—79 must to some extent obscure the continuity of trends that clearly covered the entire decade, the year of 1974 is particularly apt as the dividing-point. It saw the maturity of the strategy of the BR into the objective of striking at the heart of the state; it also saw the demotion of the efforts of the neo-fascists, who in this year lost their most important links with the security services; and it saw the emergence of a variety of left-wing groups committed, like the BR, to political terrorism, though lacking the expertise and discipline of that group.

As Table 3.1 indicates, from 1974 onwards there was a major increase in the numbers of terrorist attacks. The Parthian shots of the neo-fascists were a bomb attack in Brescia at an anti-fascist rally on 28 May 1974 that killed 8 and injured 102, and on 4 August 1974 a bomb that exploded on the Italicus express between Bologna and Florence and resulted in the deaths of 13 and injuries to over 100. But right-wing terrorists in Italy appear more vulnerable than those of the left to changes in political direction in the country as a whole, and it was this vulnerability as well as their more haphazard organisation and spectacular propensities that weakened their position. Though somewhat simplistic in its approach compared with the terrorism of the left, right-wing terrorism was capable of inflicting considerable physical injury and contributed much to the political tension of the period. Its figurehead, Prince Valerio Borghese, is now dead and many of its known leading activists are abroad or in prison.

TABLE 3.1   *Terrorist Attacks*

	With explosive devices	With incendiary devices	Others	Total
1969	145	69	—	214
1970	112	144	55	311
1971	146	197	—	343
1972	175	275	24	474
1973	117	190	3	310
1974	145	317	20	482
1975	130	436	62	628
1976	238	805	158	1201
1977	459	1532	136	2127
1978	749	1460	186	2395
1979*	275	512	89	876

*January—March.
Source: Ministry of the Interior.

With the breaking of the links between the right-wing groups and the administration, the capacity of the neo-fascists seemed much reduced, and though such groups continued to be active, their efforts were somewhat overshadowed. Their major operation in the period 1974—79 was the murder on 10 July 1976 of a well-known magistrate, D'Occorsio, responsible for several judicial enquiries into neo-fascist groups. MSI sectional offices continue to be 'base camps' for groups of violent youths who wander the streets in search of likely looking left-wingers, but such street violence, though provocative to the extreme left and intimidatory to the local public, must be distinguished from political terrorism because of its haphazard occurrence and limited effect.

In this period there has been a rapid increase in the number of left-wing groups claiming responsibility for acts of terrorism. Detailed statistics prior to 1977 are not available, but according to data published by the PCI, the number of such groups was 67 in 1977 and 181 in 1978, with a corresponding increase in the number of attacks and in the number of deaths following terrorist attacks (176 attacks, 31 deaths in 1977, 674 attacks and 37 deaths in 1978).[24] Many of the groups are ephemeral, lack organisation and support, and make little real attempt to explain what they are doing. For this reason the groups that persevere, that can strike in more than one city and that can attempt to produce some theoretical justification of what they are doing tend to command the most attention. The most successful groups so far are BR, NAP, and Prima Linea (Front Line). NAP have been severely hit by the security forces and are now in decline. They depended heavily on the example and theoretical framework of the BR, and in late 1977 virtually merged with BR. Prima Linea are the main rivals to BR both in organisation and in strategic thinking. Though their attacks have not been numerous, their targets are carefully selected and their operations well planned. Their major operation so far was the murder on 30 January 1979 of the magistrate, Alessandrini.

The years 1974—79 were the boom years for BR with several major operations against their name and the clear assertion of their leadership over the pullulating left-wing terrorist groups. As well as the regular attacks on representative figures, the declared strategy of the BR was to strike at the heart of the state. This they attempted to do with the kidnap of Mario Sossi, a public prosecutor in Genova, on 18 April 1974, three weeks before the divorce referendum; the murder of Francesco Coco, chief magistrate in Genova, on 8 June 1976; and the kidnap of Aldo Moro, president of the DC, on 16 March 1978, who was murdered (presumably on 8 or 9 May) and whose body was found in the centre of Rome on 9 May. These grand manoeuvres appear to have been expressly designed to have the maximum political impact, since they invariably occurred either during election campaigns or at times of government crisis. Sossi was kidnapped during an extremely divisive referendum campaign, which pitched the DC against its governmental allies and the PCI and in which the issues raised spread wider than the single question of the divorce law to cover the fundamental political direction of the country. Coco, who had been responsible for the rejection of the terms previously agreed with the BR for Sossi's release, was murdered exactly a fortnight before the parliamentary elections of 20 June 1976 in which the PCI were expected to make large gains. Moro was kidnapped on the day that Prime Minister Andreotti, after a prolonged government crisis resolved with the considerable help of Moro's negotiating skills, was presenting his new government's programme to parliament, with the support of the PCI. But the dual strategy of the BR, comprising persistent attacks on middle-ranking officials, industrialists and police with the occasional grand attack, has so far failed to incite the working class to civil war or even to mobilise them against the state and the parties. Indeed, as I discuss in the next section, the state and the parties have survived intact though not unharmed, while the control of the BR over their 'working class' is even now insignificant and seems to be diminishing.

The universities and the overcrowded cities provide the BR and the terrorist groups with a recruiting-ground for full-time terrorists and for the 'irregulars' — those who support, inform, provide accommodation.[25] But the anarchy of the extreme left in the universities escapes even the direction of the terrorists; the groups known as the 'Autonomi', to which I referred earlier, are united only by their rejection of all forms of political organisation not directly and immediately under the control of each individual. Though no doubt many in these groups are sympathetic to the terrorists, the reaction of the anarcho-socialist groups to the strategy of the BR and in particular to the murder of Moro, in so far as the *mélange* of voices can be reduced, appears to have been typically ambivalent: 'Ne con lo Stato ne con le BR' (neither with the state nor with the BR) was a slogan that appeared to synthesise the perspective of the extreme left.

The BR now have an articulated organisation with established groups — 'columns' — of full-time clandestine terrorists in at least four major cities and probably elsewhere. Each column consists of about six members, one of whom is in touch with the central control; the columns are kept strictly separate from one another. The BR are directed by a national executive known as the 'Strategic Control' (Direzione Strategica). Though the organisation is well able to preserve clandestinity, the isolation of the columns appears to have led to problems for the Strategic Control of keeping the operations of the individual columns under central direction. The BR are well equipped, well trained, thorough and determined. They are extremely careful in their recruiting and appear successfully to have resisted significant infiltration since 1975. They are not short of finance, which they obtain by robbing banks and from kidnappings. Unusually for groups of the extreme left they have survived for nine years under difficult circumstances apparently without major defections or divisions, and have not been deterred from their operations either by the overall failure of their strategy or by the increasing frequency of arrests of their members.

In an effort to avoid the isolation from which the BR suffer, their main rival group, Prima Linea, operate on part-time clandestinity. The members of PL are expected to hold ordinary full-time jobs and as far as possible live the lives of normal members of society, though any involvement in 'mainstream' politics is not feasible. PL operates therefore like a traditional 'secret society'. This 'part-time' clandestinity probably explains the restricted quantity of PL's operations; it does not appear to have increased their capacity to establish direct relationships with working-class organisations.

Despite the continued success of the anti-terrorist group led by General Dalla Chiesa (see below, p. 81-2), it is not a hazardous speculation that the operations of BR and PL will continue for some time to come and that they will be increasingly determined and ruthless. In January 1979 for the first time the BR murdered a member of the PCI who had notified the police of the presence of a BR informant in the factory where he worked.[26] This operation could only be necessary if the BR had failed to win the argument with the PCI and other organised groups over the political direction of the Marxist left, and may be interpreted as indicating the reliance of the BR on terrorist tactics to achieve some control over the area they claim to be organising and leading.

At the same time, it must be acknowledged that left-wing terrorism attracts significant consent in certain sectors of society and sympathy in others. BR and PL both rely on the support and cover provided by 'irregulars', and both appear to have good contacts in some of the major industrial complexes in the North, as well as in the larger universities (in particular, Rome, Bologna, Turin and Milan). BR appear to recruit mainly from the universities, among the urban unemployed and in the prisons; PL, because of their different strategy, cannot be so reliant on the urban unemployed. These sources are likely to continue to supply the groups both with permanent activists and with irregulars. Administrative rearrangements have produced some change in the prisons, where the policy of establishing top-security prisons preferably on outlying islands, such as the Asinara, for long-term and dangerous prisoners appears to be having some success both in keeping captured terrorists behind bars and in preventing their proselytising activities in the ordinary prisons.[27] The left-wing terrorists appear able at present to retain these links with limited sectors of society while the overwhelming majority of the population appear either to reject them completely or to prefer to ignore them. This is perhaps more a function of the failure of the political system adequately to cope with chronic social problems than a result of any great success of the BR in winning support for their strategy. The sympathy of the unemployed and the anarchic student groups is ambivalent and unstable. Political terrorism of both left and right is likely to lose sympathy and consent because of the increasing intensity of their methods; combined with the increased efficiency of the security services who now appear to be taking terrorism seriously, this means a bleak future for the terrorists, though the short-term prospects for the Italian citizen are not good either.

THE STATE AND POLITICAL TERRORISM

Decision-making and political terrorism

The responses of the state to political terrorism have been conditioned most obviously by the specific development of terrorism in this period. But other determinants are the structures of decision-making in the political system and the development of those structures. The most important political issue throughout this period has been the entry of the PCI into the government, which has already fundamentally affected decision-making in the Italian political system, even though in 1979 the PCI had still not provided ministers for any government since 1947. The increasing importance for the DC of reaching agreement with the PCI has, in concert with other factors, removed real decision-making from parliament and from the cabinet and placed it in the hands of the governing bodies of the major parties. Major policy decisions now tend to be reached by agreement between the party secretaries, who usually come to the inter-secretarial joint meetings of the government parties under clear and relatively narrow mandates from the governing bodies of the parties. So at the time of the Moro kidnapping, the crucial decisions over whether or not to negotiate and what other measures to undertake were not made by parliament or by the cabinet. In particular, the decision not to negotiate was made by a small group of leading members of the national executive of the DC, in conjunction with the prime minister. That decision was supported by the secretaries of the parties in coalition with the DC, with the sole dissentient voice of Craxi, secretary of the PSI. There were indeed other groups and institutions urging negotiation on the government, and that the government did not move from its declared policy was at least partly due to the firm refusal of the PCI to countenance any move that might imply recognition of the political legitimacy of the BR. The PCI view of the terrorism of the BR and similar groups is that it is not to be regarded as of the left at all, and that it is in fact part of the same strategic design as the violence of the neo-fascists.[28] Terrorism is itself in part a response to the prospect of closer collaboration between the PCI and the other 'constitutional' parties. Its effect has been to reinforce that collaboration, and to enable the PCI to present itself as a legitimate party of the constitution — and one of the effects of that has been the greater efficiency of the political responses to political terrorism.

Early responses: 1969–73

But it cannot be said that those effects showed themselves immediately. It took the Italian political classes at least five years to alert themselves seriously to the problem of terrorism, in the sense that their initial reactions to it were immobilist, using the events for short-term political gains and leaving their sources untouched. Initially, successive governments appeared disposed to use terrorism to reinforce the position of the DC and to a lesser extent of the minor lay parties as bulwarks of democracy. The term 'the strategy of tension' was coined to refer to the apparent coincidence of increases in terrorist activity with critical political events such as elections or the formation of new governments. The use of the phrase particularly on the left was intended to imply that terrorism was in fact being directed in a strategic manner to favour the short-term aims of the government parties, as if somewhere a 'mastermind', probably an established politician, was in control. Though a lot of evidence has come to light on the close relationship between the security services and the right-wing terrorist groups, there is no evidence to indicate that there is or was a 'mastermind' of terrorism, inside or outside the DC. There were undoubtedly neo-fascist sympathisers occupying senior positions in the security services, and some left-wing terrorist groups appear to have sympathisers at a lower level in the police and civil service. The links with the security services probably helped the right-wing groups sustain a certain level of activity, and the secret intelligence services appear to have known in advance of some of their major operations, in particular of the attempted occupation of the Ministry of the Interior in 1970 and the similar operation in August 1974. But it is not necessary to find a 'mastermind' to explain the apparent strategy of tension, for the operations of terrorists must surely be most effective when political awareness is already heightened, and it would be surprising if terrorists did not attempt to plan their activity to take account of this. To say that successive governments used terrorism reflects not 'strategy of tension' conspiracy theories but the rather less contentious observation that governments did not react vigorously against terrorism in this period and that leading politicians (of the DC in particular) took the opportunity to attack communists and socialists and to affirm their own centrality to the political system.

To the public at large the official explanation was that of 'opposed extremes': Italian democracy was threatened equally from the right and from the left. In fact, as is now clear from the trials of neo-fascists held responsible for the major terrorist attacks from 1969 to 1974, successive ministers of the interior, ministers of defence and prime ministers allowed and in some cases encouraged the Italian security services (SID and ŚdS, at the time) to infiltrate both right-wing and left-wing groups with their agents and to develop close relationships particularly with the right-wing groups Ordine Nuovo (New Order — later banned as a revival of the Fascist Party) and the clandestine Rosa dei Venti (Compass). This relationship, supervised by General Vito Miceli, then head of SID and later parliamentary deputy for the extreme right-wing Italian Social Movement, remains obscure, and attempts by magistrates to have Miceli's parliamentary immunity lifted have failed. It is clear however that the leader of Ordine Nuovo, a freelance journalist named Giannettini, was on the payroll of SID and was used by the security services to carry out anti-communist propaganda in the armed forces. In June 1974 he was also said by Andreotti, Minister of Defence, to have benefited from the protection of SID at crucial points in the investigations of right-wing terrorists. At the same time, as is clear from

Prefects' reports leaked to the press, the Ministry of the Interior was well aware of the existence of the Red Brigades and their activities in Milan and Turin, though as far as can be ascertained the ministry did little to keep them in view individually when they went 'underground'.[29] In this sense, just as the terrorists could be described as not having taken seriously the capacity of the political system to absorb and neutralise the effects of violent dissent, so the state may be described as having failed to take seriously the intentions of the terrorists to pursue to the bitter end their choice of clandestinity and terrorist violence. The political value of active left-wing terrorists in this period perhaps outweighed the need for control of what was at this stage a relatively minor if persistent threat to internal security.

The political background to the 'controlled' terrorism of this period is that after the disappointment and disillusion of the centre—left coalitions between 1963 and 1968, there followed a series of weak, unstable governments marked by inter-party policy disputes. Increasingly, granted the instability and incapacity of other governmental formulas, the choice seemed to rest between the 'authoritarian solution' and the acceptance of the PCI as a legitimate governmental party.[30] Since the PCI were not acceptable either internally to the DC or externally to Italy's NATO allies, the threat of the 'authoritarian solution' in the shape of neo-fascist terrorism and attempted coups d'etat served the purpose of impressing on the minor parties the urgency of not depriving the country of a government at certain times as well as of reinforcing the centrality of the DC. At the same time, the existence of left-wing terrorists, described by themselves as 'communist', 'red' and 'Marxist', enabled the DC to lay suspicion on the attachment of the PCI to liberal democracy, and therefore its suitability for government. This strategy paid off most notably in the parliamentary elections of 1972, which produced a relatively decisive swing to the right with an increase in the MSI vote and in the DC vote. While the DC complacently used the terrorist threat to attack the parties of the left, those parties, particularly the PCI but also to some extent the PSI, found themselves unable to escape from an essentially defensive posture on problems of internal security, and it was not until the escalation of violence in 1974, the revelation of links between the security services and the neo-fascists and the swing of the electorate to the left that it became possible for agreement to be reached between the major parties over the strategy to be pursued against terrorism. This change in attitudes can be explained predominantly by the emergence of terrorism as a major and persistent problem not readily manipulated or kept within controllable limits. In this process the steady development of the violence of the BR was probably a crucial factor. Before the autumn of 1974, the major parties were clearly divided over terrorism, with the DC in favour of strengthening police powers and imposing stiffer sentences, while the PCI and PSI called for the reform and democratisation of the police and the armed forces. But the former line of policy was at the time unlikely to be

Political Terrorism in Italy

forced through parliament by the DC alone, and the latter line would have required a fundamental change in the use and structure of the police and security forces that to many would have smacked dangerously of weakening the defences of the state. As such it was not the sort of policy that the left-wing parties could safely put over, without rendering themselves vulnerable to right-wing and DC criticism.

To talk of 'crisis management' in this period would be something of a misnomer, since the state was faced on the whole with a steady escalation of violence that required not short-term 'management' but long-term strategy. Crises of relatively lengthy duration occasioned by terrorist activity did not occur while the neo-fascist strategy predominated. In practice, as I have indicated, little was done to halt the increase in frequency and seriousness of terrorist incidents.

Learning to live with terrorism: 1974—79

By 1974, however, internal and external pressures were developing to make the strategy less feasible. In the first place, the foreign policy of Italy's guide in international affairs, the USA, had already swung towards detente; the international climate was easing and the strident anti-communism that characterised the DC for much of its early history was disappearing, to be replaced by a greater willingness to recognise the PCI as a 'constitutional' party, though not as a suitable government partner. Internally, the major neo-fascist groups had been severely weakened both by the arrests of their leaders for implication in the bomb attacks of the early 1970s and by the revelation of the links with the security services. After the right-wing electoral successes of the early 1970s, the electorate appeared to have acquired an increased volatility; the divorce referendum of May 1974 produced a clear victory for the pro-divorce lobby supported mainly by the parties of the left, and subsequent local elections appeared to confirm that the electorate had swung markedly to the left. With regional elections due in June 1975, the DC was in need of allies, and internal security was one issue on which agreement could now be reached readily.

But the traditional immobilism of the Italian state is not easily changed, and the major failings of the response to terrorism remain. The overall inadequacy of the state's responses to terrorism has been clearly indicated by the development of the BR over ten years to a formidable level of efficiency, and the rapid increase in recent years in the number of smaller groups. The security services have failed in the preventative functions, in that the terrorists continue successfully to attack figures who might be considered as politically significant targets. They have also failed in their investigative functions, most notoriously in the Moro and Sossi kidnappings. The police are under-equipped and under-trained,[31] the judicial system is so slow as to make a mockery of the judicial process on occasions, and the prisons are overcrowded and disorganised. But behind the failure of the coercive instruments of the state are more significant political failures. The incompetence of the security forces in these matters may be seen as one of the results of deliberate policy choices and in some cases non-choices in the field of internal security. The refusal of DC ministers in 1949 to demilitarise the police reflected the view that the major function of the police was that of internal security of the state — the preservation of public order — rather than the prevention and investigation of crime, and in these latter fields the police corps (corpo delle guardie di publica sicurezza) has remained underdeveloped, lacking both expertise and equipment. The emphasis on public order is supported by the complicated lines of authority that make the police subject not only to the local Prefects, who are responsible to the Minister of the Interior, but also to the investigative magistrates and therefore ultimately to the Ministry of Justice.

A notable source of inefficiency in security is the rivalry and competition between the several forces who have police functions, in particular between the carabinieri and the police corps. The former are part of the army, and are subject formally to the Minister of Defence. In 1975 both of these bodies had about 80,000 men each, including officers. The division of functions between them is confused both in theory and in practice, except that the carabinieri have exclusive competence over the armed forces as military police, and for historical reasons have a more complete coverage of rural areas than does the police corps. Otherwise, their functions are identical, and at the practical level the two bodies tend to operate without coordination, with the result that police functions of all sorts are uselessly repeated.

After the bomb attacks in Brescia and Bologna in 1974, the government attempted to enforce greater coordination on the carabinieri and the police by instituting the General Inspectorate for Action against Terrorism; though at the national level this appears to have operated with some success, repeated criticisms were made by opposition parties that at the regional and local level the lack of coordination was as bad as ever. This problem was only partly resolved by the creation by administrative decree in June 1978 of a special anti-terrorist group with agents taken from both bodies, from the other major police force (the Finance Guards — Guardie di Finanza) and from the secret services and responsible through its head, General Dalla Chiesa, to the Ministry of the Interior and the prime minister. Dalla Chiesa, a member of the carabinieri, had previously been in charge of prisons and was responsible, after the escape of several leading brigatisti, for the creation of the special security prisons. General Dalla Chiesa appears to have had considerable success in finding and arresting known terrorists, and despite criticisms that he was virtually independent from political control and more concerned with demonstrable results than with the rights of suspects, his reappointment in August 1979 was supported by all the major parties.

In 1974 the intelligence services had been able to infiltrate the BR with informers, as a result of which the two first-generation leaders, Renato Curcio and Alberto Franceschini, were captured. Curcio later escaped, was recaptured, and sent to one of the special island prisons instituted by Dalla Chiesa. It was partly as a result of his experience with the BR in prisons that Dalla Chiesa was able to achieve the rapid success that made his position safe. In October 1978 his anti-terrorist group descended on three bases in Rome, capturing nine brigatisti and a wealth of documents. Further arrests followed in April and June 1979, with what might be described as a 'strategy of reassurance'. One week after the dissolution of parliament and the declaration of parliamentary elections, the anti-terrorist police mounted a large operation centred on Padua and arrested leading members of the 'Autonomi' including Antonio Negri, Professor of Political Theory at the University of Padua, Oreste Scalzone and Guiseppe Nicotri, a journalist based in Padua. Others sought included Franco Piperno, Professor of Physics at the University of Calabria. Negri and others were charged with being the national organisers of BR. Later, the Rome magistrates investigating the Moro kidnapping charged Negri and Scalzone with direct complicity in the Moro affair, accusing Negri of having made the final telephone call to the Moro family before Moro's murder. Nicotri has since been released for lack of evidence. In June, three days before the elections, the anti-terrorist police in Rome arrested Morucci, said to be a leading clandestine brigatista, and discovered considerable evidence relating to the recent activities of the BR, in particular material connected with the attack on the DC offices in Rome during the election campaign.

One of the problems facing the judiciary is the professionalism of the major terrorist groups in leaving little that might incriminate them individually at the scene of the crime. Many of the major terrorist crimes remain unsolved, in the sense that the individual terrorists involved are not sufficiently identified to be brought to trial. The charges against those terrorists who are captured tend to be generic — that of belonging to an armed band held responsible for attacks against the state. On 1 April 1979, according to figures released by the Ministry of the Interior, a total of 259 left-wing terrorists were convicted or awaiting trial in prison; of these, 172 were claimed to be members of the BR. A further 49 left-wing terrorists were sought by the police, of whom 29 were said to belong to the BR. Again according to the Ministry of the Interior, between 1974 and 1979, 1812 right-wing 'extremists' had been arrested; no figures were available on the number sought.

Though there have been some successes, the overall response of the state has been lethargic, dilatory and unbalanced. Directly political responsibility for the incapacity of the state may be found in the failure of the parliamentary parties to exercise any real control over the police forces or over the secret services. The intelligence services in Italy in the postwar period have traditionally operated through the Ministry of Defence and the prime minister, though the President of the Republic, who has the right to be informed on matters of state security and may have reserve functions as yet untried, has also been involved in this area in the past. It appears that throughout the postwar period their operations have been characterised first by lack of accountability to parliament, second by dependence on the policy decisions and resources of Italy's NATO allies, in particular of the United States, and third by a vigorous anti-communism. The activities of the intelligence services came to light most conspicuously in 1964 when the head of military intelligence, General De Lorenzo, was accused of using his position to establish the opportunity for a coup d'etat. General De Lorenzo resigned and later became a parliamentary deputy for the right-wing Monarchist Party.[32] The fear of uncovering further skeletons in the cupboard is probably one of the reasons for parliament's lack of enthusiasm on the subject of the intelligence services. Though a reform of the intelligence services was carried out, how little it achieved became clear in 1974 and 1975 with the judicial implication of the services in terrorist groups. A more thoroughgoing reform of the security services was demanded by the communists and socialists after the parliamentary elections of June 1976, and this was indeed undertaken, with the dissolution of SID and SdS and their replacement by the Democratic Security Information Service (SISDE) and the Military Security Information Service (SISMI), the former to deal with internal security and the latter with espionage and counter-espionage. Lines of communication with parliament were tightened and clear terms of reference established for the services. However, it proved extremely difficult to fill the post of head of SISDE, which remained vacant for some time; indeed, the secret intelligence services were in the middle of reorganisation and were reported to be barely operational at the time of the Moro kidnapping.

Apart from the reform of the anti-terrorist agencies, the major indication of the new-found seriousness with which governments are responding to terrorism came with the Reale Law passed in May 1975, with amendments made in July 1977 and April 1978.[33] The main thrust of the law was against revivals of the Fascist Party, but its provisions applied to all forms of clandestine organised violence against the state. The law made sentences for terrorist crimes much more severe, placed restrictions on bail and gave the security forces powers to search and arrest without a formal warrant on suspicion, and to hold suspects for forty-eight hours. The law also gave the police more freedom to use firearms. It did not grant the most contentious demand of the security forces, the right to interrogate without the presence of the defence lawyer. Later amendments controlled the use of firearms and explosives. Finally, after the Moro kidnapping, a decree of 21 March 1978 granted the long-held wish of the security forces to be able to interrogate legally in the absence of a defence lawyer; the same decree, which passed into law with some amendments on 18 May 1978, also increased the sentences for kidnapping and made telephone tapping easier for the security forces.

The declarations by leading figures in the DC in 1974 to the effect that terrorism was predominantly a right-wing phenomenon enabled the left-wing parliamentary parties to rally to the support of the Reale Law. The dissentient voices were those of the smaller left-wing parties at that time outside parliament, and the most vocal of these in the field of civil liberties, the Radical Party, began to collect signatures in 1977 for a referendum against the Reale Law and against seven other laws. They collected the necessary 500,000 signatures, but most of the laws concerned were declared by the Constitutional Court not to be open to abrogation by referendum. The referendums that were held jointly on 11 June 1978, a little more than a month after the finding of Moro's body, referred to the Reale Law and to a law passed in 1973 providing for the state financing of political parties. Referendums notoriously provide a misleading simplicity of answers to complex questions, and are difficult to analyse. In what might be interpreted as implicit corroboration of this, the joint referendums provided a clearly ambivalent response to the mobilising efforts of the government and the supporting parties (Table 3.2). Both laws remained on the statute books, but the wide variation between the two results and the inter-regional differences gave the parties little scope for claiming unquestioned national authority.

TABLE 3.2 *Referendum 'Reale' and Referendum on Party Financing*[1]

Area	Reale		Party financing		Abstention, and spoilt or blank votes[2]	
	Yes	No	Yes	No	Reale	Party financing
North	20.4	79.6	39.8	60.2	17.7	17.8
Centre	21.3	78.7	40.8	59.2	18.8	18.8
South	29.9	70.1	51.4	48.6	34.9	35.0
Islands	32.6	67.4	54.7	45.3	36.0	36.1
Total	23.5	76.5	43.6	56.4	23.8	23.9

Notes: (1) The question on the ballot paper asks the voter whether he or she wishes the law in question to be abrogated. A 'Yes' vote is therefore a vote against that law. A majority of valid votes cast is required.
(2) Results in the first four columns are percentages of the valid votes cast. Results in the last two columns are percentages of the total electorates.

Source: Ministry of the Interior

I have argued that one of the effects of terrorism has been to encourage the development of the 'constitutional area' and of coordination among the parties that inhabit that area — Christian Democrats (DC), Communists (PCI), Socialists (PSI), Democratic Socialists (PSDI), Republicans (PRI) and Liberals (PLI). The government led by Andreotti that was presented to parliament on the day of Moro's kidnapping was composed entirely of DC ministers, with the support in parliament of all the 'constitutional' parties except the PLI. This was consecrated in the wake of the Moro crisis as a 'government of national unity'. In the sense that this government represented the unity of the parties supporting the constitution and the state, the Moro crisis could therefore be said to have reinforced the legitimacy of the PCI as a governmental party. In attempting to 'strike at the heart of the state', the terrorists have tended to choose as direct objects of assault persons or places closely associated with the DC. Despite this, it may not appear unreasonable to suggest that the targets of the left-wing terrorists ('target' in the sense of 'group whom they wish to influence by terrorism') are the sectors of society directed by the PCI. It is a major part of the strategy of the terrorists to undermine the hegemony of the PCI, and to prevent the occurrence of the 'historic compromise'. But the capacity of the PCI to mobilise the support of the industrialised workers of the North and Centre appears not to have been affected more than marginally by the terrorists, and the strategy of the terrorists appears in fact to have accelerated the march towards respectability of the PCI.

The threat to the capacity of mass mobilisation of the PCI comes rather from the failure of the terrorist organisations to achieve any durable connection with the Autonomia Operaia. As we have indicated, it is from these groups that the terrorists draw recruits and material support. The riots in Rome University in March 1977 and the occupation of the centre of Bologna shortly after were both carried out by directionless mobs of students and unemployed given to spontaneous yet persistent violence against all symbols of external control. For them, the PCI just as much as the state is an oppressive, unresponsive institution. It is in groups belonging to the 'Autonomi' that one finds the most equivocal attitudes to the violence of the BR. Though the state may be able to neutralise and absorb the terrorism of the BR, it is not yet able to absorb, control or even manipulate the disorganised political violence of the extreme left-wing groups.[34]

CONCLUSION

The responses of the state to political terrorism in Italy provide an instructive example of how the modern industrialised state may both foster terrorism and learn to survive with it. The inefficiency of the administration, of the police and of the judicial system make it unlikely that in the immediate future political terrorism can be significantly weakened by a strategy dependent on administrative efficiency in the carrying out of policy directives from elected politicians. At the same time, though some agreement has been reached over short-term measures, it is not clear that elected politicians are united either over the appropriate strategy to be followed against terrorism or over the administrative reforms that would be a necessary precondition of any long-term approach to the problem.

I have argued that the major failings in the response to terrorism have been the deliberate manipulation of organised political violence to satisfy short-term goals — goals that have been predominantly electoral but that have also been concerned with the formation of alliances within and between the parties — and, more broadly, the continued underestimation by politicians and senior civil servants of the capacity of clandestine groups to strike politically significant targets and of their intention to do so. This applies both to left-wing and to right-wing terrorism. These failings are intricately connected. The Italian state has been attempting to 'ride the tiger'. The continued support given to General Dalla Chiesa by all the major parliamentary parties is perhaps an acknowledgement of their own incapacity to produce consistent policy direction, but it is also very much a traditional solution for this political system to give a non-elected figure large amounts of free rein and to pay little attention to the less satisfactory aspects of his approach.

I have attempted in this short case study to understand political terrorism within a fragmented yet highly developed political system. If the response of the state has been less than adequate, it may be argued that the inadequacy results from the disparity between a dynamic and open political culture, based on a radical constitution and populist traditions, and the stultifying immobilism of the governmental system. The dangers for the political system are not, as may be elsewhere, that civil liberties will be snuffed out at the behest of an oppressive and authoritarian political culture but that in the face of the inefficiency and indecisiveness of the formal institutions individual actors may operate outside formal controls. The continued tendency of sectors of state administration to seek and indeed to achieve autonomy from political control is to some extent a function of the survival within the state of residues from the fascist dictatorship and from the Liberal state that preceded it. The personnel and institutions that carry these residues constitute a would-be alternative elite to the unchanging political elite of the postwar republic, just as do the terrorist groups on the left. The growth of terrorism and the responses of the state may thus both be related to the unbalanced economic development and incomplete political development of the postwar period.

But the failure of the terrorists and particularly of the BR is more tragic and more complete. As Leonardo Sciascia has commented:

> The central error of the Red Brigade consists precisely in believing that they can succeed in striking at the heart of the State. The heart of the Italian State does not exist. Neither, any longer, does its brain. And it is that which paradoxically is its strength or at least its capacity to resist.[35]

The Italian state is not susceptible to the sort of attack that the BR and most other groups wish to mount. When the youth told Peschiera 'the system forces us', there was an ironic truth in his words. The terrorists chose clandestinity and 'hit and run' tactics in Italy as an instrument of political activity, and developed around their choice a considerable volume of strategic theorising aimed at justifying *a posteriori* a choice made for quite other reasons. The world they appear to move in is inhabited by symbols, not by people. Within the terrorist groups there is, as in other exclusive homogeneous institutions, a large element of cognitive dissonance. As their violence is unsuccessful, they are drawn not to a reconsideration of their initial choice but to an exacerbation of the violence. In this sense, the system 'forces' them; granted their initial choice against other more conventional forms of political activity, the failure of their strategy leads them further into violence, and further into exclusivity and isolation.

One of the reasons for their lack of success and for the inevitable spiral of violence in which they find themselves is that the instruments they have chosen are simply not sufficient for the task. I would not argue complacently that terrorism is necessarily unsuccessful because 'pathological' or 'irrational'; but it does seem to me that where it is successful it is because, whatever the long-term strategic aims of the terrorists, between them and their goal there is a series of negotiable demands or intermediate goals which may under certain circumstances be met by the opponent with less harm than is threatened directly by terrorist action. In some cases one of the intermediate goals most useful to terrorists and most readily obtainable is the publicity given to them and their action. But to take on the authority of the state with hit and run terrorism or with bomb attacks against civilians is to overestimate the effectiveness of the symbol, and in such cases publicity is of little value. There is little the Italian state can give the terrorists other than its own dissolution; the liberation of prisoners demanded by the BR during the Sossi and Moro kidnappings was invested with such symbolic significance that to have granted it would have been to give the BR the legitimacy of the title of 'guerrilla fighters' that they are seeking. They have succeeded in criminalising dissent, in rendering large sectors of the left, including some members of the PCI, vulnerable to the suspicion of being 'pro-terrorist'. Their actions have certainly made the task of government by consensus more difficult, and they have amply demonstrated the vulnerability of politically significant individuals to terrorist attack. But the fragmentation of the Italian state and the dispersion of authority within it make symbolic attacks against it by clandestine terrorists a particularly inefficient form of warfare.

Notes and References

1. G. Bocca, Viaggio nelle citta della nuova violenza/Genova. *La Repubblica,* 5 April 1979, p. 5. All translations in this chapter are those of the author, unless otherwise stated.
2. On these incidents, see *L'Espresso* 22 January 1979, pp. 14—18.
3. On narrow and wide definitions of terrorism, see A. Arblaster, Terrorism — myths meanings and morals. *Political Studies, 25,* no. 3 (September 1977) pp. 413—24. A useful discussion of definitions of terrorism may also be found in M.C. Hutchinson, The concept of revolutionary terrorism. *Journal of Conflict Resolution, 16,* no. 3 (September 1972) pp. 383—97.
4. Hutchinson, *op. cit.,* pp. 384—5. Hutchinson's analysis is explicitly restricted to 'revolutionary terrorism' as opposed to 'governmental terrorism'.
5. *ibid.,* p. 385.
6. *ibid.,* p. 385.
7. On 'propaganda of deeds' see W. Laqueur, *Terrorism* (London: Weidenfeld and Nicolson, 1977), pp. 49—53.
8. Translated and quoted by R. Hostetter, *The Italian Socialist Movement,* Vol 1: Origins 1860—1882 (Princeton, NJ: Van Nostrand, 1958), p. 23.
9. J. Bowyer Bell, Violence and Italian politics. *Conflict, 1,* nos 1 and 2 (1978), pp. 49—69.
10. Brigate Rosse, Risoluzione della Direzione Strategica, February 1978; published in *CONTROinformazione, 5,* no. 11—12 (July 1978), pp. 76—95, p. 89.
11. A. Negri, *Il dominio e il sabotaggio* (Milan: Feltrinelli, 1978), p. 14.
12. Brigate Rosse, *op. cit.,* pp. 89—90.
13. Negri, *op. cit.,* p. 67, but see below, p. 82. This section was written before Professor Negri's arrest on charges connected with the BR, and of course cannot constitute any expression of opinion on those charges.
14. Brigate Rosse, *op. cit.,* p. 93.
15. Brigate Rosse, *op. cit.,* p. 93.
16. G. Bocca, *Il terrorismo italiano* (Milan: Rizzoli editore, 1979), pp. 7—21; see also S.S. Acquaviva, *Guerrigha e guerra rivoluzionaria in Italia* (Milan: Rizzoli editore, 1979), pp. 51—9.
17. For a discussion of the development of the PCI, see S. Tarrow, Le Parti Communiste e la société italienne (pp. 1—54 in *Sociologie du communisme en Italie,* no author, but edited in the Fondation Nationale des Sciences Politiques, Paris: Armand Colin, 1974). The significance of external pressures on Italian politics is analysed from differing perspectives in N. Kogan, *The Politics of Italian Foreign Policy* (New York: Praeger, 1963) and D.L.M. Blackmer, *Unity in Diversity, Italian Communism and the Communist World* (Cambridge, Mass.: MIT Press, 1968).
18. The functioning of the Italian parties in parliament is now relatively well documented, and there is considerable evidence relating to the long-standing and pervasive cooperation between the DC and the PCI. See G. Di Palma, *Surviving without Governing, the Italian Parties in Parliament* (Berkeley, Calif.: University of California Press, 1977). Sartori argues that such cooperation

on the whole relates to trivial issues and that the destabilising effects of the PCI follow from the decisions that they block — G. Sartori, 'Rivisitando il "pluralismo polarizzato" ', in F.L. Cavazza and S.R. Graubard, *Il caso italiano* (Milan: Garzanti, 1975), pp. 196—223.

19. The best-known analysis of centrifugality in the Italian political system dates from 1966 (G. Sartori, 'Italy — the case of polarised pluralism', in J. La Palombara and M. Weiner, *Political Parties and Political Development* Princeton, NJ: Princeton University Press, 1966), though it is reiterated in the later work by the same author — *Parties and Party Systems* (Cambridge: Cambridge University Press, 1976). For a contrasting model of the system see G. Galli and A. Prandi, *Patterns of Political Participation in Italy* (New Haven, Conn.: Yale University Press, 1970). An attempt to combine the two models is made in L. Pellicani, Verso il superamento del pluralismo polarizzato? *Rivista Italiana di Scienza Politica, 4,* no. 3 (December 1974), pp. 345—74, an amalgamation repudiated by Sartori in the same issue in G. Sartori, Il caso italiano — salvare il pluralismo e superare la polarizzazione. pp. 675—8.

20. See M. Fini and A. Barberi, *Valpreda — Processo al processo* (Milan: Feltrinelli, 1972).

21. A chronological description of the activities of the BR up to 1977 is given in V. Tessandori, *Br, imputazione: banda armata* (Milan: Aldo Garzanti Editore, 1977). See also A. Silj, *'Mai piu senza fucile!' alle origini dei NAP e dei BR* (Florence: Vallecchi Editore, 1979); A. Bolaffi, Ideologia e tecnica del nuovo terrorismo. *Rinascita 35,* no. 12 (24 March 1978) pp. 4—5; B. Bertini, La mappa del 'partito armato'. *Rinascita 35,* no. 19 (12 March 1978) p. 26.

22. See A. Silj, *op. cit.,* pp. 79—93.

23. See *Corriere della Sera,* 15 February 1979, p. 1. Also Tessandori, *op. cit.,* pp. 79—90.

24. Direzione PCI, 'Attentati e violenze nel 1978', cyclostyled MS. edited by the Sezione Problemi dello Stato of the PCI, no date, but 1979. The statistics on terrorist groups produced by the Ministry of the Interior are marginally different, usually giving slightly larger total numbers in the various categories. As the figures released to me by the Ministry of the Interior were far less detailed than those of the PCI, I have chosen to use those of the PCI. The differences between the two sets of data appear to result from a wider definition of terrorism used by the Ministry of the Interior.

25. On educational policy in Italy, see G. Ruffolo, The Italian education crisis. *Review of Economic Conditions in Italy, 29,* no. 1 (January 1975) pp. 24—74, and P. Pridham, The problems of educational reform in Italy — the case of the decreti delegati. *Comparative Education, 13,* no. 3 (October 1978) pp. 223—41.

26. On this episode and its aftermath, see M. Scialoja, Un omicidio suicido. *L'Espresso,* 4 February 1979, pp. 12—15.

27. Detailed accounts of conditions in the prisons are given in: Carceri speciali, documenti e testimonianze. *CONTROinformazione, 5,* nos 11—12, (July 1978) pp. 46—65 and 128.

28. Representative examples of PCI analysis of terrorism may be found in E. Roggi, P. Gambescia and L. Gruppi (eds) *Terrorismo, come opera, a che cose mira, come sconfiggerlo* (Rome: PCI, n.d. but probably 1978); F. D'Agostini, L'uso politico del caso Moro e la crisi d'oggi — intervista con Alessandro Natta. *Rinascita, 36,* no. 3 (16 February 1979) pp. 3—5.

29. See Tessandori, *op. cit.,* pp. 36—7.

30. On the 'authoritarian solution' see P.A. Allum, *Italy — Republic without Government?* (New York: W. W. Norton, 1973) pp. 239—51; also L. Magri,

Spazio e ruolo del riformismo, in V. Parloto, *Spazio e ruolo del riformismo* (Bologna: Il Mulino, 1974) pp. 15—41.

31. See S. Flamigni *et al.* (eds), *Sicurezza democratica e lotta alla criminalita. Atti del convegno organizzato dal Centro Studi per la riforma dello Stato, 25—6 febbraio 1975* (Rome: Editore Riuniti, 1975); also O. Rossani, *Intervista sui rapimenti* (Milan: Edizione Elle, 1978).

32. On the 'De Lorenzo affair' see R. Collin, *The De Lorenzo gambit: the Italian coup manqué of 1964* (London: Sage, 1976).

33. *Gazzetta Ufficiale* 24 May 1975, no. 136, pp. 3274—9, law of 22 May 1975 no. 152, 'Disposizioni a tutela dell'ordine pubblico'; *Gazzetta Ufficiale* 20 August 1977, no. 226, pp. 6096—8, law of 8 August 1977, no. 533, Disposizioni in materia di ordine pubblico; and *Gazzetta Ufficiale* 19 May 1978, no. 137, pp. 3571—2, law of 18 May 1978, no. 191, Conversione in legge del decreto-legge 21 marzo 1978 n. 59.

34. It has not been possible here to do more than indicate the existence of these multifarious and unpredictable groups. The interested reader might make a start to the voluminous outpourings by and on the Autonomi with S. Bologna, *La tribu delle talpe* (Milan: Feltrinelli, 1978) and G. Martignoni and S. Morandini, *Il diritto al odio* (Verona: Bertani, 1977).

35. In J. Binde, Entretien avec Leonardo Sciascia, *Le Monde,* 4—5 February 1979, p. 16.

CHAPTER 4

France: Non-Terrorism and the Politics of Repressive Tolerance

Philip G. Cerny

Terrorism as a political phenomenon lies at the margin of the modern social order. Defined by the norms of the liberal—democratic state, it appears as a form of deviance, an extreme form of political pressure that threatens to subvert the fragile balance of cross-cutting interests upon which the stability of politics in a pluralist society rests. Seen thus in a pathological perspective, it is treated by the state as a 'law-and-order problem' — and the methods of law and order, always problematic in a liberal—democratic context, inevitably mean the recourse to measures of a repressive nature. However, the widely internalised pathological image, far from evoking a mass outcry or protest, not only carries public opinion along with greater repression but also creates public — 'democratic' — pressure for tougher measures still. For terrorism, as communicated by contemporary mass media, has become the eschatological myth of capitalist society, evoking an existential dread, the fear of the collapse of the social order itself.

The reason for this is not simply the 'revolutionary' ideology of certain terrorist groups. Rather, it is their own self-definition of their position as outside, rather than inside, the social order itself, and the definition of their stance as that of war. Far from seeking 'legitimate' ends within the political bounds of pluralism, they threaten the social contract with a new state of nature by attempting to force the authorities to break their own contract, to reveal the underlying authoritarianism of the political bond, and thereby to demystify 'democratic' capitalist society and catalyse a popular search for alternatives. The potential power of these groups seems to lie not in their

*I should like to express my gratitude to the British Academy and the Maison des Sciences de l'Homme (Paris) for their financial support during a research visit to France in April 1979 in connection with the preparation of this chapter, and to the Institut d'Etudes Politiques for the use of its research facilities.

91

threat to overthrow society by force of arms *per se,* but in their ability to symbolise the fragility and vulnerability of the social order and to force that order to subvert itself by eroding the liberal and democratic values upon which its own legitimacy is based.

The evidence of the 1970s suggests that such a confrontation leads to a two-fold trap. In the first place, the terrorist groups themselves are caught in a trap of escalation. Although their symbolic threat is felt as a deadly broadside by the guardians of society, the material resources of such groups in money, arms and troops are circumscribed and vulnerable. In a pitched battle with the army and the police, they will succumb, unless they have a territorial base (as nationalist or ethnic guerrilla groups sometimes have) that is relatively defensible. Only where the old social order is so unjust and inherently unpopular that to speak of 'terrorists' is wholly misleading (and may more aptly be applied to the authorities themselves), and where a true guerrilla movement can take root, do 'terrorist' methods really threaten society — and only then as part of a larger strategic picture. In contrast, terrorist methods employed in a society where systemic norms are widely internalised will lead to strong popular support for increased repression. Terrorism is thus firstly a trap for the terrorists themselves.

The second trap, however, is set for the social order. For while the terrorists may fail to spark a popular insurrection, the reaction to their threat does put the value of liberal democracy at risk, all the more because public opinion has been anaesthetised by the fear of the collapse of society itself. Repression in this context takes many forms. On the one hand, censorship, increased police and military coerciveness, the erosion of the rights of defendants, psychological torture and the political manipulation of the judicial process all affect the individual in his relationship with the state. On the other hand, the identification of 'sympathisers', the association of terrorism with radicalism of any kind, the generalisation of the notion of 'violence' to include political demonstrations, the blacklisting of groups and individuals, and the like, threaten the rationale of the pluralist state itself by interfering with the interaction of groups and are often aimed at the suppression of free political and ideological opposition. When both of these forms of repression are used *in tandem,* as in the Federal Republic of Germany today, society falls headlong into the trap set by the terrorists, although the terrorists themselves are in no position to exploit the situation (if they still exist at all).[1]

In this context, terrorism itself becomes a myth that can be used for purposes of social control. It becomes embedded in the catch-phrases of the media and the rhetoric of politicians. In an age of limited wars in far-away places, it fulfils the function of a war-in-microcosm, increasing social solidarity. In this era of international communications and the increasingly interlocking interests of the developed capitalist countries, it does not merely evoke the image of defending a nation, but raises the spectre of a threat to Western civilisation not seen since 'international communism' was deactivated by polycentrism and peaceful coexistence. But it goes even deeper into the heart of social mores, providing visible and frightening bogeymen and pirates to reawaken the dark and mystical fears that still lie latent in a culture that demands a modern and empirically verifiable veneer for its superstitions.

The political significance of terrorism, then, lies less in its organisational or violent manifestations than in its interaction with the social formation and political system in which it occurs. If a strong authoritarian potential is latent in a society with a liberal—democratic political order, then the danger to liberal democracy is that it will be subverted through its own forms and institutions as the objective of social survival takes priority. This danger exists most strongly where the process of modernisation has been controlled, overtly or covertly, by a coherent set of elite groups whose position derived originally from a pre-modern — feudal or dynastic — social order, but who have been able to transform and reinforce that position in the context of industrial capitalism. In contrast, if the democratic political revolution, based on social pluralism and the peaceful competition of elites, antedates the economic modernisation process, and if the idea of progress is culturally associated more strongly with the former, then the threat of terrorism — like the threat of foreign war — is less likely to subvert liberal democracy. Indeed, it might be hypothesised that terrorism is less likely to occur, less likely to lead to public paranoia where it does occur and less likely to provoke systematic repression from a state that not only fears the undermining of its democratic legitimacy but may also contain within itself countervailing elites who will resist the temptation to fall into the trap.

To all appearances, France fits the second stereotype fairly well. She has not experienced the appearance of an archetypal terrorist organisation comparable to the Red Army Faction in Germany or the Red Brigades in Italy. There has certainly been no full-scale urban guerrilla movement comparable to the Tupamaros in Uruguay, nor any guerrilla-cum-terrorist group with a strong territorial base like the Provisional Irish Republican Army or the various Palestinian guerrilla organisations. Although violence has become an issue in France, its ideological overtones have always been overt rather than covert, and the plurality not only of French political parties and groups but also of the French press has kept it in perspective. And the state, while making minor symbolic moves, has relied primarily upon ordinary criminal law and enforcement methods and has eschewed emergency measures and extraordinary powers. The democratic tradition appears to have stood firm. However, the picture is far more complex than this favourable generalisation admits, and an analysis is required of the tangled skein of French political culture, the development of the French state and the French experience of terrorism if we are to explain the balance of non-terrorism and repressive tolerance that characterises French society today.

TERRORISM AND NON-TERRORISM: THE FRENCH EXPERIENCE

Terrorism and the French Political Tradition

The concept of terrorism is deeply embedded in French culture — but it is a different form of terror from that with which the world has become familiar in the 1970s. To the French, the state terror of Robespierre and the Jacobins in the wake of the French Revolution remains the touchstone of terrorism, whether carried out by the state or by a self-appointed revolutionary 'counter-state'.[2] Just as the Revolution of 1789 is still seen by all groups in French society — whether approvingly or pejoratively — as the first truly modern revolution, foreshadowing the collapse of feudalism and absolutism every-where, so the three periods of terror between August 1792 and the *Grande Terreur* of 1794 (culminating in the fall of Robespierre) are seen as the forerunners of the modern terrorist state (culminating in Stalin's Russia and Hitler's Germany but ever-present in Chile, Argentina, Kampuchea and many other places) and of the small groups of revolutionary terrorists whose victory, it is feared, will simply transform anti-system terror into new manifestations of state terror.

Paradoxically, however, this entrenched concern with terror and terrorism, rather than exacerbating public reactions to contemporary terrorism, demystifies it, making it somehow less terrifying. At the same time, it provides a form of expiation, reflecting as it does the most extreme excesses of that most revered of traditions, the Revolution, and thus appearing as a form of catharsis, a purging of the guilt for those excesses, symbolised in the death of Robespierre himself. Seen as a ritual bloodletting, an anachronism yet hallowed in tradition, terror still frightens, it still evokes outrage and protest, but it ceases to strike so deeply into the heart; it has a certain air of *déjà vu*. At another level, the romanticism of the revolutionary tradition, so strong even among some conservative groups in France, creates a certain emotional sympathy with the aims, if not the methods, of many so-called 'terrorist' groups, whether ideological revolutionaries or national irredentists. After all, France was the crucible of revolutionary nationalism of the left; it was only towards the end of the nineteenth century that the right donned the mantle of French nationalism. Indeed, it is sometimes asked, what was the French resistance during the Second World War if not a form of terrorism? Thus the revolutionary (and nationalist) tradition provides a frame of reference that explains terrorism in a manner that mutes its pathological connotations and thus mitigates the cultural perception of its potential threat.

At the same time, the democratic tradition in France, rooted in other revolutionary values — especially the Declaration of the Rights of Man and Citizen — and experienced in the various forms of liberal—democratic constitution that have been dominant since 1870, has established a greater confidence in democratic political processes *per se,* which are valued for their moral qualities and not merely as a means to material prosperity. (In contrast, Almond and Verba suggest that cultural support for democratic institutions in West Germany is derived from their coincidence with postwar prosperity and might be undermined if prosperity collapsed.[3]) However, it is not merely the forms and institutions of French democracy that give it its resilience; indeed, governmental instability and political immobilism have until quite recently been its most salient and visible characteristics, and much ink has been spilled in describing its flaws.[4] Rather, it has been the deep social roots of defensive pluralism — a distrust of others and of the state itself, combined with a recognition that no one group is strong enough to dominate, leading to social and political strategies based not on dominating but on preventing others from dominating — that has given the democratic tradition in France its stubborn durability.[5]

This resilience is found at many levels. It has been seen in the forms of political leadership characteristic of France — a weak, shifting form of routine authority, dependent upon the grudging acquiescence of coalition partners and vulnerable to the appearance of new problems, tempered by the occasional resort to an exceptional form of crisis authority, based on a specifically delegated set of tasks and limited to their successful discharge.[6] It has characterised the political party system, wherein old 'families' or 'tendencies' continually reappear in new guises,[7] readjusting their blocking strategies to new circumstances and constraints.[8] It is found in the particular forms of French bureaucracy and administration, where the fear of face-to-face relations and the compartmentalisation of offices creates strong internal vested interests and poor communication except on a highly formalised routine basis of rituals and red tape, short-circuited only by the old-boy network of the *grandes écoles.*[9] And it forms the sociological basis of political behaviour itself, as class and religion intersect to form distinct sub-cultures in permanent but uneasy coexistence and competition.[10] Therefore, despite the modernisation of French capitalism since 1945[11] or that of French political institutions since 1958,[12] the structures that underlie French political culture reflect the specifically French process of political development over a much longer historical period.[13]

The significance of the French democratic tradition for the development (or non-development) of terrorism is two-fold. The first consequence is that

France has never developed a pure authoritarian tradition comparable to fascist or totalitarian regimes in other parts of Europe. Even Napoleon sought to spread the French ideals of *liberté, égalité, fraternité* in a Europe still dominated by dynastic regimes. The July Monarchy nursed the development of a liberal bourgeoisie. And the Second Empire sought to establish a supervised form of democratic process in the 1860s. In the 1930s, fascism never progressed beyond the organised street-gang stage underpinned by a conservative vision of the social order represented by Maurras and the Action française (French Action), while even under the German tutelage of 1940—45 the Vichy regime concerned itself primarily with strengthening the traditional values of *travail, famille, patrie* (work, family, country) through social conservatism and a mild form of corporatist economic decision-making that actually had a decentralising effect.[14] Maurice Duverger has written that France would not have turned to a leader like Hitler, as this was not in her political temperament;[15] and de Gaulle, the closest France has come to a dictator, had no desire to be one even when, in 1945, it was within his grasp.[16]

Without such an authoritarian tradition, the various groups in French society have seen fascism as an external phenomenon, foreign to the nature of France. It is significant in this context that some of the most virulent revolutionary terrorist groups in the 1970s have developed in societies characterised prior to 1945 by various forms of fascism — Germany, Italy and Japan — where the two-fold issue of whether 'fascism', as a form of socio-economic structure (as distinct from its façade of political authoritarianism), was ever really defeated from within after the Second World War, and of whether new forms of fascism are taking over the façade of the liberal—democratic state today, will always be at the back of people's minds both at home and abroad. In France, in contrast, the enemy is kept at arm's length. Each group has its stake in the maintenance of the equilibrium, and thus fascism faces a huge credibility gap. In this context, the resort to terrorism appears to be out of proportion, a distorted form of political response in a society that provides many other channels for political opposition, even revolutionary opposition — which retains its own rather abstract, intellectual romanticism in a culture that has traditionally prized critical intellectualism.

The second consequence, then, is the reverse of the token — the continual effervescence and ferment of French politics itself. In a society with as diverse a political culture as that of France, despite the appearances of a developing dominant 'consensus',[17] opportunities for ideological assertion and political activity are widespread. Furthermore, such activities are usually regarded, even by conservative circles, as creative and culturally legitimate. The vacillation of large sections of the bourgeoisie during the complex and intense events of May 1968, with even the centre—left and sections of the liberal right being swept along in the revolutionary tide for a time, is merely an extreme manifestation of this ambivalence. Trotskyists stand for the presidency and get their share of free television time. A large section of French trade unionism retains its nostalgia for syndicalism. The Socialist Party ceaselessly debates the more abstruse aspects of defining and achieving the *rupture* with capitalism, and the Communist Party vacillates between a social—democratic Eurocommunism, obeisance to its Leninist (some would say Stalinist) traditions and a kind of nationalist worker populism. The party of the President, Giscard d'Estaing, is a hotch-potch of liberals, conservatives, social christians and progressives in an uneasy alliance, and the Gaullist Party, the most authoritarian party of them all, is committed to a welfare state and economic planning. Defining one's political stance in such a way as to inject a dose of originality, and expressing that stance in a polished and intellectualised rhetorical form, is a key element in the hallowed political ritual of the Republic. And the debates and discussions — and polemics — that take place within and between the multifarious intellectual groups and ideological factions provide a kaleidoscopic backcloth for political activity, especially in the centre around which much of that activity revolves, Paris.

An admirer of French political life might say that these legitimate forms of activity provide sufficient variety and choice to accommodate almost the entire spectrum of political taste and opinion, ostracising none and offering opportunities to all to pursue their own viewpoints. A sceptic would argue that they provide a safety valve through which potentially dysfunctional activity can discharge itself harmlessly. In either case, opposition groups are not forced to choose between tame consensual politics and extra-systemic opposition, even though, in the long run, radical groups may not have a very great impact upon macropolitical processes. Nonetheless, the impact of regional and ecological pressure groups, along with the more innovative sections of the trade union movement such as the French Democratic Confederation of Labour (CFDT), have been identified as the source of political innovation in the Fifth Republic,[18] and the political will of the Communist Party to innovate in local politics has been the source of a variety of significant concrete initiatives in public policy.[19] Thus the direct frustrations that often lead to revolutionary terrorism in other societies are less salient in France, and a variety of more or less efficacious forms of substitute political behaviour exists for radical activists.

Reactionary Terrorism in the Twentieth Century: the OAS

Favourable conditions for the development of classic revolutionary terrorism are significantly lacking in the French scene. But this does not mean that terrorism has been totally absent from France. In the course of the twentieth century, however, indigenous terrorism has been primarily a reactionary terrorism of the right and not a revolutionary terrorism of the left. In the late

1930s, after the dissolution of the quasi-fascist leagues and the electoral victory of the Popular Front coalition of Radicals, Socialists and Communists, some of the more extreme ex-members of the leagues allied with some of the more reactionary middle-ranking officers within the army (supposedly with the approval of certain senior officers and, it was claimed, the tacit indulgence of Marshal Pétain) to form a secret society known as the 'Cagoule' (a hooded robe or cloak, copied from the Ku Klux Klan). They set up a clandestine organisation, collected arms and made plans to take over the state in the event of an attack from the communists. They even attempted to trick army leaders into a preventive coup d'état in October—November 1937. Their time, however, did not come.

In the period after the Second World War, certain right-wing elements, some with connections with the Cagoule or the Vichy regime, attached themselves to General de Gaulle, whom they saw as the best hope for a right-wing authoritarian regime. They, too, organised clandestine networks, and in the period following de Gaulle's resignation in January 1946 until his return to power in 1958 they were ostensibly prepared to attempt a coup, especially during the depths of the Cold War, when the Communist Party, having accepted the Cominform line in 1947, was ousted from the government in the summer of that year and thereafter attempted to exert extra-parliamentary pressure, especially by means of a series of damaging strikes in the winter of 1947—8. De Gaulle, however, merely made use of this group for political intelligence, keeping order at the meetings of the Gaullist party (the RPF) and occasional strong-arm tactics and 'dirty tricks' during election campaigns, etc.; he never gave the call for an uprising. The 'barbouzes' (bearded ones), as they were called, did, however, play an important clandestine role in the internecine right-wing terrorist battle between the Gaullists and the OAS — the Secret Army Organisation.[20]

The OAS was the closest one can come in the history of twentieth-century France to identifying a genuine terrorist movement. Yet, unlike the somewhat more hypothetical terrorists of the Cagoule or the barbouzes, the alliance of hard-line French settlers in Algeria, right-wing groups within the army and certain reactionary elements within France that comprised the OAS engaged in a real terrorist war lasting nearly two years. The background to their campaign was, of course, the bloody and traumatic Algerian War. With one-tenth of Algeria's population of European origin, some of several generations' standing, this was no ordinary colonial war. Regarding themselves as French Algerians rather than as colonial occupiers, the *pieds-noirs* opposed any move to loosen ties with the mainland or to give greater rights to the native Muslim population — other than those who had been assimilated into the dominant French culture and socio-economic system. The uprising by the Algerian National Liberation Front (FLNA), which broke out in 1954 and which in its guerrilla campaign employed terrorist methods, was seen even by high-ranking members of the French government, such as the then Minister of the Interior, François Mitterrand, as an attack upon the integrity of France herself. Successive Governors-General, the Socialist Robert Lacoste and the Gaullist Jacques Soustelle, had been sent to Algeria to promote incremental reforms, but had been converted to the hard-line stance of the colonists. The Socialist Prime Minister, Guy Mollet, also adopted a tough stance towards the FLNA, refusing to open negotiations before the declaration of a cease-fire.

The French army's role in this situation was crucial. Torn apart by the conflict between de Gaulle's Free French and the Vichy regime during the Second World War, its traditional acceptance of subordination to the civil power had come into question. After a long, losing struggle with the Viet Minh in Indochina, a defeat that was attributed to Mao's and Giap's doctrines of guerrilla warfare, the officer corps was more than ever loath to be defeated again. They developed the first coherent experiment in counter-insurgency, using irregular groups, hostage-taking, torture and the like, in their attempt to prevent the FLNA fish from swimming in the water of the Muslim population; they even claimed, by 1960, to have defeated the guerrillas. But along with new methods came new attitudes. The war against the FLNA was seen as a holy war for Western civilisation against the communistic barbarians, and the cause of the colonists themselves was espoused with missionary fervour. In 1958, a coup in Algiers led by the army commander there, General Raoul Salan, threatened Paris with an airborne invasion if a government were elected there that was not hard-line enough on Algeria; it was by manipulating the conditions created by this uprising that de Gaulle himself returned to power, and for a time he was thus at least partially dependent upon the forces of Algérie française (French Algeria), led by the high-ranking Gaullist Jacques Soustelle.

In 1959, however, de Gaulle began to change his line on Algeria, calling for a greater degree of self-determination and proposing a referendum in Algeria itself to choose between three options — integration with France, independence, and a form of association the details of which were never laid out. In January 1960, hard-line elements in Algiers, at first with some tacit support from the army, set up barricades and tried to take over government offices, in order to force de Gaulle to ensure the victory of the first alternative. De Gaulle, having ensured the purging of his party, the Union for the New Republic (UNR), of the most hardline supporters of Algérie française during 1959, did not budge, and the army did not rebel — this time. A year later, in place of the local referendum, came a national one, proposing self-determination for Algeria and a provisional government for an eventual Algerian Republic. This received the support of 75 per cent of those who voted, but it also brought to a head the crisis in the army; three months later, in April 1961, four high-ranking generals, Challe, Salan, Jouhaud and Zeller, staged a putsch in Algiers, which failed because the authorities in Paris did not crumble and because the largely conscript ranks, ordered by de Gaulle over the radio not to follow the orders of rebellious officers, were listening in on their transistor sets. From the failure of the 'generals' putsch' came the birth of the OAS.[21]

The aim of the OAS was to ensure French control of Algeria despite the 'abandonment' of the country by the French government. Its members terrorised Muslim neighbourhoods, assassinated Muslim leaders, bombed public places and threatened French officials who were too compliant with their government's policy. Growing out of earlier Algérie française movements, such as the Front national français (French National Front), it was led by the retired General Salan, who had been in exile in Madrid since 1960, and the official headquarters were set up there. The operational leadership came mainly from Jean-Jacques Susini, an Algiers student leader who had succeeded Pierre Lagaillarde, the leader of the 1960 barricades revolt, as leader of the student movement that had provided the organisational underpinning for the early Algérie française protests. Many in the army were sympathetic to the OAS, as was much of the administration within Algeria; sympathy was, of course, also widespread in metropolitan France. The violence of the FLNA,[22] which had been raging for more than six years, matched by the counter-terror of the army, had inured the conflicting groups in the province to violence, and a peaceful solution did not appear to be viable to any of the participants. Only the French government, with a realism that, with hindsight, appears all the more remarkable in view of the pressure it encountered within the French right as well as within the intensely committed Algerian crucible, was able to sever the Gordian knot. Unlike the British government after the First World War, which in comparable circumstances surrendered to the blackmail of the Ulster Volunteer Force and partitioned Ireland (partition was considered as an alternative in Algeria too), de Gaulle realised that anything less than complete independence would do nothing more than create a permanent sore that would plague French and Algerian politics for many decades to come. So negotiations with the FLNA continued, despite disputes, delays and adjournments, and on 19 March 1962 a cease-fire agreement was signed at Evian along with agreements setting out the terms of Algerian independence.[23]

In the meantime, the OAS had been active. Its original programme, which appealed to Christian, corporatist and anti-parliamentary values, revealed shades of the Cagoule and of Vichy. But it was far too disparate an organisation for its programme to do more than reflect a mood within a particular context of action. That action context was the dedication to keeping the French presence in Algeria, and, if that failed, to maintaining European control by force within Algeria itself, even if this meant merely the coastal enclaves around the major cities where the vast majority of the European population lived. In 1960, with the tacit support of much of the army, with the FLNA hard-pressed militarily in much of the country, and with much sympathy within official circles, the objectives of the OAS seemed credible. Its downfall was due to three factors: the determination of the French government, both legally and clandestinely, to prevail; the long-term position of strength of the FLNA; and the political and military weaknesses of the OAS itself.

De Gaulle had seen the writing on the wall for Algeria well before his return to power, but the manner of his ascendancy — on the back of the army revolt in Algiers in May 1958, and seemingly at the behest of General Salan himself, the leader of that revolt — forced him to dissimulate his intentions until he was firmly enough in the saddle to control opposition to his plans.[24] The purging of the UNR, the policy switch from a referendum on three options (one of which — integration — would have satisfied the hard-liners) to a vote simply on self-determination and the setting up of a provisional government, the barricades trial of a cross-section of civilian and military participants, and the dogged pursuit of negotiations with the FLNA, were mere prelude. The attempted 'generals' putsch' provided the basis for more severe action. For the only time in the history of the Fifth Republic, the President invoked the emergency powers provided in Article 16 of the constitution, reasserting control of the army and the administration and establishing special military tribunals to try the rebels. He also unleashed the barbouzes, who fought the OAS in a war of clandestine terror and counter-terror, infiltrating its networks and eliminating its activists. In the meantime it became obvious that the FLNA had not been pushed out of its positions of strength, whether in the countryside or in the Muslim quarters of the European-dominated cities. Furthermore, its political strength was continually increasing because of recognition from abroad (the late 1950s and early 1960s were the great era of anti-colonial victories in terms of both the rate of colonies becoming independent and the influence that these 'new states' were coming to wield internationally, in the UN, for example) as well as *de facto* recognition by the French government itself, which insisted on bargaining solely with the FLNA as the representatives of the Algerian people.

The OAS itself, despite its network of sympathisers and its position of strength within the European quarters of Algerian cities, was in no position to hold out in these conditions. Its ability to acquire arms did not compensate for its lack of organisation and the enormity of its task. In the first place, the official headquarters were in Madrid, and although Salan and Susini were able to enter and leave Algiers relatively easily, communications between the leadership and the ranks were weak and intermittent. The relative isolation of the leadership, who, even when in Algeria, had to communicate orders and receive information through a tortuous clandestine structure, led them to envisage plans far beyond the material and human resources, not to mention the possibilities of coordination, of the organisation itself. Most of the action undertaken by the OAS, then, was envisaged and carried out by fairly isolated operatives in the field, and consisted mainly of attacks on local Communist Party offices and FLNA networks. In the second place, the OAS had to fight on two fronts if it was to succeed — in Algeria itself and in metropolitan France. Whereas in Algeria it represented a strongly committed section of the population — the mass of Europeans — in France it faced the hostility of the great majority, symbolised in the huge majorities for de Gaulle's proposals in January 1961 and April 1962 (ratification of the Evian Agreements, which gained a 'yes' vote of over 90 per cent!), as well as a much more closely controlled police and legal system — not to mention the barbouzes.

But the problems of Algeria did not penetrate the surface of life in the *métropôle,* concerned with economic prosperity, the political competition of the new Fifth Republic, the Cold War, and the like. Even the referendums on Algeria were seen more as tests of confidence in de Gaulle's overall political leadership than in terms of the detailed policy questions involved. And the state broadcasting monopoly, the ORTF, presented only the government's line; television was not yet ready to play the role that it was later to do in Vietnam at the height of American involvement. In any case, most of the attacks in metropolitan France were the work of unconnected *groupuscules* using the OAS label. Hard as it might try, the OAS was never able to rally and control these movements; and competition between Madrid and Algiers exacerbated matters. Most operations were diversionary tactics, and the attacks on the Communist Party failed to achieve their aim of exacerbating the contradictions of the French party system.[25] The most spectacular operations were the various attempts on de Gaulle's life — their number is estimated at thirty-one, some of which failed only because of the most extraordinarily lucky escapes for the President[26] — but these were usually the work of isolated individuals and groups, occasionally acting against OAS policy. And after the signing of the Evian Agreements and the eventual transfer of power to the new government of the Republic of Algeria, the massive exodus of the European population to France destroyed the last foundation for the OAS. General Jouhaud had been arrested in March 1962 and Salan in April; Jouhaud was to be sentenced to death, Salan merely to life imprisonment (after which de Gaulle, in disgust, dissolved the High Military Tribunal). However, Jouhaud was later reprieved on the intercession of the Prime Minister, Pompidou, and both were released in the amnesty declared during the election campaign of 1968, after the Events of May. Susini went underground, later appearing briefly in bank raids and in an attack on the former treasurer of the OAS.

But as the Algerian War faded into French history, it became clearer that the OAS represented the exception that proved the rule. As Alfred Grosser has pointed out, France was the only major Western country in the postwar period to experience both of the great international conflicts of the age directly in her domestic politics — the opposition between communism and anti-communism and the mammoth task of decolonisation.[27] The army, the colonial administration and the European population of Algeria saw these conflicts in a different light than did the inhabitants of the *métropôle*. The anti-communist fanaticism of the officers, disillusioned by 1940 and by Dienbienphu, and determined to compensate for those failures despite lukewarm support from the French government, allied with a desperate settler population faced with the loss of its recognised world. Although the long-term causes of the problem lay with French colonial policies in the nineteenth century and with the failure of the French Empire and the French Union in the twentieth, the Algerian War was a parenthesis in the development of postwar French politics and society, and the futility of the desperate rearguard actions of the OAS neither reflected the situation in France nor affected it in any profound way — except possibly further to isolate and immunise French society against the recrudescence of terrorism in the world of the 1970s.

The Problem of Terrorism

I have already observed that in the 1970s France was relatively free from the kind of classic terrorism that predominates elsewhere in this book. But the analyst is once again caught in the dilemma of definitions. The first of these is the definition of terrorism itself. 'Terrorism' is first and foremost a pejorative term. It denotes something evil and dangerous. Any conscientious anti-fascist will have little trouble in identifying the Cagoule, the OAS and even the barbouzes (although the last may have been on the 'right side' in historical perspective) as terrorists or proto-terrorists. It is not even very hard to denounce the Red Army Faction in Germany, the Red Army in Japan and the Red Brigades in Italy as essentially 'terrorist', possibly even in their own definition — despite a permissible sympathy with the underlying *cri du coeur* that motivated them and a distaste for the repressive measures taken as a result of the reaction to their activities. National irredentist movements with an anti-colonial rationale, like the Palestinians or the Provisional IRA, are somewhat more problematic, although the random threat to non-combatants offends both political and moral sensibilities; however, one can approve their aims and denounce their methods as terroristic. In contrast, to denounce as 'terrorists' a full-scale national liberation movement fighting a guerrilla war against colonial or authoritarian settler repression — as in Southern Africa or Southeast Asia — or to apply the term to broadly based revolutionary movements fighting against the state terrorism of cruel dictatorships — as in pre-revolutionary Cuba or Nicaragua, Argentina or Chile — implies that the speaker is committed strongly to supporting the forces of repression in those places — even if, in a technical sense, 'terror tactics' are used as part of a wider guerrilla strategy.

This problem also appears on another, interdependent level — a level that is particularly significant to a study of the situation in France. This is the scope of the concept of terrorism. If we see pure terror tactics — anonymous attacks by clandestine groups on either symbolic or random individual targets with the intention of spreading a generalised and abstract fear and anomie among the mass of the target population — as a core of the concept of terrorism, then how far can we move towards the periphery of the notion before it becomes analytically absurd? (Of course, to use such a term in an analytically absurd way implies either an unintentional misuse of the term or an intentional distortion for specific political motives.) Other terms that are often associated in journalistic, political and everyday speech with terrorism include violence, subversion and extremism. Furthermore, if the notion of 'sympathising' is added to the brew, then anybody who dissents from the social order or who frightens 'peaceful, law-abiding citizens' can be ostracised by association with terrorism. Are left-wing political movements somehow essentially terroristic? Are political demonstrations or trade union picketing somehow part of this wider phenomenon? What about juvenile delinquency and football hooliganism? Throw in a reference to terrorism, and the image is reinforced of a world seized by a contagion of violence, with civilisation in danger of collapsing, and with all dissenters from this view categorised as either active or passive sympathisers with the apocalypse.[28]

This mixture is especially potent in a world where terrorism makes the most effective media impact of almost any event short of war. An airplane hijacking or the taking of a hostage, even where no one is killed or there is no intention of killing anyone, is the ultimate media event. A drama of fictional intensity is played out in full view of the public, with the event stretching over hours or days, and with all of the suspense provided by a dramatic, visible yet unpredictable outcome. The pain of the non-combatant civilians such as airplane, train or bus passengers, or the isolation and humiliation of individual hostages, is intensely felt by the audience, and so a limited threat is perceived as a mass threat. The normal credibility gap faced by car accident or lung cancer statistics, not to mention the shadowy outlines of real but distant small wars — the feeling that 'it can't happen to me' — is eliminated. The experience is felt as real and imminent.[29] Therefore the power to tar groups and ideas with the brush of terrorism is one of the most potent symbolic weapons in the armoury of contemporary politics.

Terrorist Activity in Contemporary France

Although France escaped the direct impact of a domestic terrorist movement in the 1970s, terrorism as a phenomenon nonetheless had a strong impact in terms of these wider questions I have been posing. Four sorts of phenomena were associated, in a more or less relevant way, with terrorism, and an examination of these will highlight the problematic nature of the notion of terrorism today, in ways both specific to France and more widely applicable across national frontiers.

The first category is the most directly linked with terrorism in the broader contemporary sense, and consists of the various ways in which foreign terrorist groups have used France either as a base or as a battleground. The tradition of France as a *terre d'asile*, a country that freely accepts political refugees and exiles from abroad, has meant not only that the intellectual life of the country has been continuously leavened by international contacts and ideas, but also that clandestine political activity among foreign groups based in France is not infrequent (refraining from political activity is a normal condition of asylum, but it is hard to enforce).[30] *Sunday Telegraph* journalists Christopher Dobson and Ronald Payne have claimed that 'Paris has become the world capital of terrorism':

> It is ideally placed by geography and circumstances to fulfil this role. It has excellent rail, road and air communications with the rest of Europe and the Middle East; it connects with five land frontiers, which, because of the volume of traffic crossing them, are difficult to police; it is, moreover, traditionally a haven for political refugees and a magnet for young people, still full of romantic notions about its charms.

The Japanese Red Army submerged itself in the 'most numerous colony of Japanese students in Europe'; the members of the Red Army Faction spent long periods there; and the Palestinians swam in the sea of Paris's Arab population of half a million, the legacy of France's lost North African and Near Eastern colonies. Paris provided the base for the establishment of the international terrorist network led by Ilich Ramirez Sanchez, nicknamed Carlos, until his cover was blown in June 1975 and he fled to Algiers and later to Libya.[31] The hard-line former Minister of the Interior, Raymond Marcellin, claimed in an article in *Le Figaro* in August 1978[32] that ten years earlier the French police had listed forty-four terrorist organisations in the world, of which twenty included elements living in France, but that present legal provisions, combined with the lack of a preventive capability on the part of the police, stymied any attempt to counteract this menace. Indeed, between April 1973 and July 1977, a leader of the Popular Front for the Liberation of Palestine (PFLP), Basil Al Kubaisi, was shot; Mohamed Boudia, a Fatah activist (and predecessor to Carlos), was blown up by a car bomb; a Chadian opposition leader was shot; five Saudis were taken hostage at the Saudi Arabian embassy by the Palestinian Liberation Organisation (PLO) and flown to Kuwait; the Uruguayan military attaché was assassinated; the Spanish deputy military attaché was seriously wounded; the Turkish ambassador was shot dead; the Bolivian ambassador was shot dead; the former PLO representative in Paris, Mahmoud Ould Saleh, who ran an Arab bookshop there, was shot dead; and the Mauritanian ambassador was seriously wounded.[33]

A more serious incident occurred at the Iraqi embassy on 31 July 1978, when a terrorist (thought at the time to be the brother of Saïd Hammami — the PLO representative in London who had recently been assassinated), having taken hostages at the embassy but later surrendered to the French police, was shot by snipers within the embassy as he was being taken to a police wagon. In the fusillade, a policeman was also killed, and the police claimed that at least fifteen snipers were shooting from the embassy windows at the man who had taken the hostages. The police demonstrated in protest against the lack of recourse against the snipers, who had diplomatic immunity, although three Iraqi 'diplomats' were expelled by the French government for carrying arms.[34] The war between the PLO and the Iraqi hard-liners of the Rejection Front did not spare Paris. Indeed, three terrorists who had planned to massacre passengers (not hijack an airliner) were killed in an Orly Airport lounge. The operation was claimed by a group (unknown to the PLO and presumably linked with the Rejection Front) that called itself the 'Sons of South Lebanon', presumably in reference to the French presence among United Nations forces patrolling the supposed buffer zone in that country torn by civil war and foreign interventions; it had already threatened a series of attacks in France to protest against French neo-colonialism in the Middle East and Africa (Zaïre, Chad). The group was thought to be an offshoot of the PFLP. In addition to the three terrorists killed, a brigadier of the French CRS riot police also died, and six people were wounded.[35] The Orly attack brought back memories of earlier attacks at Orly: in October 1972, when a bomb near the El Al desk was defused; and the two attacks in January 1975, attributed to Carlos, involving a rocket attack on a full El Al plane (it missed and hit an empty Yugoslav plane) and another attempt to blow up an El Al plane, which also failed but led to an attack on passengers in a departure lounge, the taking of hostages, and a negotiated escape flight.[36] Indeed, the attacks by supporters of the Rejection Front continue unabated. In March 1979 a Jewish student restaurant in the rue de Médicis, catering in fact for a mixed clientele with even some Muslim students frequenting it, was hit by a large bomb during the lunch hour on the day following the signing of the Egyptian—Israeli peace treaty.[37] And another PLO representative was assassinated at the beginning of August.[38]

It is not only the Palestinians who choose France as a haven or a battleground. The Red Army Faction held the German industrialist Hans-Martin Schleyer hostage somewhere in France, and his body was found in Mulhouse on 16 October 1977. The Basque organisation ETA has an extensive network in France, which was left alone so long as Franco was in power; however, in January 1979 the French government removed the status of political refugee from the Basques, ostensibly because Spain had become a democratic state (including adhering to the Geneva Convention, declaring a general amnesty and introducing a new democratic constitution).[39] Seventeen Basques were removed to forced residence in the

Alpes-de-Haute-Provence in February 1979, and seven were expelled from the country and returned to Spain at the beginning of March.[40] A Croat nationalist leader, Bruno Busic, was assassinated in Paris in October 1978.[41] In May 1978 Henri Curiel, the founder of the Egyptian Communist Party and accused by many — including the weekly news magazine *Le Point* and Dobson and Payne — of being the centre of an international terrorist network (his supporters regarded him as a retiring — and retired — radical intellectual), was assassinated by an unknown right-wing group that took the name the Delta Organisation, referring to an affiliate of the OAS that undertook various assassinations, including attempts on de Gaulle, in 1960—62.[42] And in addition, Professor Antonio Negri, accused by the Italian police of being the 'brains' behind the Red Brigades, was said to have directed the kidnapping of Aldo Moro while giving a course of lectures in Paris.

This sporadic terrorist activity on French soil by foreign-based groups does not contain much to strike terror into the heart of the average Frenchman. Of the mere eleven deaths from terrorist incidents in the five years 1972—77, eight were those of foreigners and only three of French citizens.[43] Calls for tougher measures by hard-liners like Marcellin fall on deaf ears. The evidence would seem to indicate that indigenous violence has been even less menacing. However, it is the domestic brand of violence — especially when labelled 'terrorism' — that arouses the political passions, and the other three categories we are considering here are all varieties of this sort. They are, first, the violence pursued by single-issue pressure groups; second, violence that occurs in the course of political conflict and the vague sense of political and social malaise; and, third, attempts to establish straightforward terrorist groups.

Of these, the most violent activity occurs in the first category, carried out particularly by the regional autonomist movements led by those in Brittany and Corsica. The Breton Liberation Front (FLB), sometimes supplemented by the Breton Revolutionary Army (ARB), is merely the most recent of a number of movements that fall somewhere between the IRA and ETA, on the one hand, and a nationalist party on the other. With no territorial hinterland in which to hide and organise, and with the efficient and centralised French state always close behind, the Breton nationalists generally stick to highly symbolic targets for their small bombs. Symbols of central domination such as small gendarmerie headquarters, telephone exchanges and television transmitters tend to be attacked in the middle of the night, when there is no one around to be injured.[44] Attacks in 1975 and again in January 1979 on the Brennilis nuclear power station actually earned the FLB the fury of Breton environmental and anti-nuclear groups, because it allowed the French Electricity Board (EDF) to claim that anti-nuclear groups were terrorists![45] Occasionally a more spectacular target is chosen, such as the Versailles Palace in June 1978. The two bombers wanted to leave their package in the Hall of Mirrors, but they could not find a hiding place; their six kilogramme bomb was eventually left in recently renovated rooms from the Napoleonic period, and mainly destroyed large canvasses showing Napoleon's victories.[46] All was repairable. But the cost to the FLB was high, as the police response hit the organisation hard and the movement was divided over the action. Nonetheless, the eight charged with the offence admitted twenty-six attacks on television stations, the prefecture at Rennes, the rector's office of the Academy in Brittany, tax offices, an officers' mess, EDF offices, banks, Shell offices, customs offices, etc.[47] Indeed, the FLB/ARB was credited with 206 attacks over the three years prior to the Versailles bombing.[48]

Corsican nationalist groups have been busy, too, but the combination of the geographical isolation of the island from mainland France and the intricate socio-political structure of the area has meant that the autonomist groups are as concerned with defending their separate vested interests within Corsica as they are with attacking the central government. Family feuds, banditry, opposition to the influx of *pieds-noirs* into the island economy and the maintenance of Mafia-like business activities and political patronage are as important in understanding the politics of Corsican nationalism as is the defiance of central authority.[49] The example of the clandestine regionalist groups has spread to other parts of the country as well. In the Clermont-Ferrand area, a group calling itself the Inter-urban Narcissist Intervention Group (GINI) claimed responsibility for three attacks in 1978 and threatened to bomb mail planes.[50] A Lyon Self-Defence Group threw two Molotov cocktails against the doors of Lyon city hall in September 1978 as 'a warning to all the services of state coercion. This is a response to the only kind of violence we recognise — that of the state.'[51] And a Savoy Nationalist Front bombed a cable-car station of the Aiguille du Midi at Chamonix, symbol of the tourist development of the region.[52]

The low-level symbolic violence of the nationalist groups is probably the closest approximation to indigenous 'terrorism' in France, but there is little terroristic or terrifying about it. In the context of contemporary society, however, some of the mud is bound to stick. The fact that some small ecological groups have been known to attack motorway toll stations, holiday centres, construction sites and even beach-cleaning machines in Brittany[53] has meant that the ecological movement as a whole, especially when gathered in large demonstrations (such as the attempt to prevent the army from extending its practice ranges at Larzac or the anti-nuclear demonstration on the site of the proposed nuclear power station at Créys-Malville in 1977), is regarded as a potentially terroristic element and treated as such, and the public association of environmentalism with regionalism further confuses the issue.

Broader social and political violence, our next category, seems to draw the most fire from government and police. We can briefly identify three subtypes. The first arises out of the confrontation of the more radical political parties and trade unions with the police during demonstrations and strikes. The fear of another May 1968 is strong among the forces of order in France, and the French police are not known to be gentle. Recently, however, a new phenomenon has exacerbated the situation — the appearance of the 'autonomists'. Not to be confused with the movements for regional autonomy, these are anarchists with new and devastating tactics. Wearing helmets and scarves over their faces, they wait in the wings until a major political rally or demonstration (such as the annual May Day march of trade unionists and leftist parties and groups from the Place de la République to the Place de la Bastille) has very nearly passed off peacefully. As the tail end of the march is about to enter the area where it is due to disband, and where many marchers and bystanders are milling around under the watchful eye of the police, they appear. They start breaking shop windows and building fires in the street. They half-loot some shops, throwing the goods around in the street rather than claiming them for themselves. They throw missiles at the police.

The police in France have still not worked out effective tactics to deal with this sort of attack. Socialised to fear all 'extremists', their first reaction, after a period of vacillation, is to attempt to clear the streets. They bring out the tear gas, and charge marchers, bystanders and autonomists alike. During the demonstration of 23 March 1979, called by the trade unions and parties of the left to protest against the government's rationalisation plan for the steel industry and against unemployment in general, the police were accused of provoking violence themselves; the arrest and swift conviction of boys claiming to be bystanders was denounced by the left as a 'new Dreyfus Affair'. Photographs taken during the 1979 May Day demonstration show the police attacking the march stewards.[54] Meanwhile, the autonomists, having caused their confusion and destruction, fade away. The result, however, is an embittered atmosphere between the authorities and the political opposition groups, an atmosphere that is exacerbated by the comparison of this sort of violence with terrorism, and the guilt by association that the authorities heap upon the demonstrators themselves.

Second, there is a continuing background of warfare between various groups on the right and left. Attacks on Communist Party headquarters by right-wing groups, the killing of a left-wing picket in Reims in June 1977 by members of the French Confederation of Labour (CFT) — a right-wing 'union' comprising a number of ex-barbouzes — bombings of left-wing bookshops, etc., by quasi-fascist or anti-semitic groups, these and other fairly isolated incidents indicate the tension that exists across the political spectrum. And third, there is in France, as in all Western societies today, a mood of fear about violence and crime in general. Increased police patrols seek out vandals in the Métro.[55] Unemployed youths and secondary school students imitate the autonomists.[56] And a government report, solemnly issued in 1977, waffles on about the social causes of violence; its only concrete proposals call for an increase in the numbers of police and the efficiency of the courts.[57] In both of these types of violence the image of terrorism comes quickly to mind, but to ask whether or not there is a causal connection between the incidence of terrorism and the incidence of these more sporadic forms of low-level violence cannot be proved.

Finally, our last category of contemporary pseudo-terrorism in France is just that — the appearance and disappearance of small groups with revolutionary names that flare up and then die out. In September 1978, three youths claiming to be members of the Armed Revolutionary and Anarchist Terrorist Movement admitted having carried out twenty bomb attacks in Lorraine in the previous year. They denied having political motives; they merely wanted 'to be talked about'.[58] More serious were the Armed Nuclei for Proletarian Autonomy (NAPAP) and the International Revolutionary Action Group (GARI), which carried out a number of attacks in the mid-1970s. They were said to have close contacts with the Red Army Faction, and GARI, which was located mainly in the Southwest, was said to have links with Spanish terrorist groups. NAPAP bombed the front door of the Justice Minister in 1977; killed a former Renault night watchman who had himself killed the Maoist militant Pierre Overney in 1973; bombed the CFT headquarters; was involved in the wounding of the Spanish military attaché in 1975 and the killing of the Bolivian ambassador in 1976; and kidnapped a Renault executive in 1972.[59] GARI kidnapped the director of the French branch of the Banco de Bilbao in 1974 and may have been attempting to bomb the then Interior Minister, Michel Poniatowski, in Toulouse in 1976 when the bomb went off prematurely, killing two militants.[60] But both groups were said to lack the motivation for cold-blooded murder and to be hierarchically weak.[61]

In general, however, the *gauchiste* leaders of 1968 and the organisations that grew out of that period and lasted into the 1970s rejected terrorist methods.[62] But while France has not developed an indigenous terrorist threat, other, less intense forms of political violence have been widespread, mirroring the political conflicts that do not find ready expression in the interplay of the official party system. In this, the pattern of violence reflects the intensity and the plurality of French political culture and the intertwining of the revolutionary and democratic traditions. However, the images of contemporary terrorism have not for all that been kept out by some sort of cultural *cordon sanitaire*. And the state has not lacked instruments to counteract the perceived threat, although it has not had to resort to the extensive measures that have characterised many other countries, especially in Europe.

REPRESSIVE TOLERANCE: THE REACTION OF THE FRENCH STATE

The French political system has not reacted to the terrorist threat in a paranoid fashion. It is not thought that the social order is in danger, and the demand for special measures has in the main been resisted. In the words of the Justice Minister Alain Peyrefitte, 'It is not possible to reply to terrorism by a state terrorism which would draw us into a spiral of terrorism.'[63] However, two facts stand out. First, the French state is in a powerful position in any case, for reasons linked with the nature of French bureaucracy and executive power. And second, the special measures that have been taken by the government, while modifying the relationship between the state and the citizen only incrementally, have nonetheless eroded the latter's rights in certain ways.

A striking feature of the position of the French state is the discretion the government can exercise in matters relevant to terrorism and violence. This is not merely a matter of specific legal dispositions, but derives partly from the strengthening of the executive power under the leadership of a strong President in the Fifth Republic. The President, who holds office for a term of seven years, has certain *de facto* and *de jure* powers, in terms of both administrative decisions and emergency legitimacy, that ensure that coordinated action is the norm rather than the exception. His ability to control the nomination (and resignation) of the Prime Minister and of the members of the government means that politically delicate questions are usually decided in accordance with his preferences. In a more direct way, the ability of the President to decide alone (after only formal consultations) whether or not to apply Article 16 in an emergency gives him the ultimate authority if the security of the state is threatened. The use by de Gaulle of Article 16 in 1961, at the height of the OAS threat, provided a precedent that has not required repeating since that time. And given the centralisation of the French administration generally, particularly control over the police and the defence structure, decisions relevant to terrorism usually escape parliamentary or public scrutiny. These decisions can be placed in two categories: those concerning the maintenance of domestic law and order; and those involving other countries or foreign nationals.

On the domestic plane, control of any sort of violent or potentially violent political activity can involve prevention and administrative action, on the one hand, or *ex post facto* repression and judicial action on the other. In terms of preventive action, the government has, for example, the power to declare a 'state of siege' (Article 36 of the constitution) as well as a state of emergency under Article 16. In a state of siege, the military takes over essential police powers. Furthermore, the Council of Ministers, under the

Law of 3 April 1955, can declare a state of 'urgency', in which case the powers of the police are extended considerably.[64] In a more prosaic sense, the government has the power, exercised through the Prefect, Sub-prefect or Mayor, to ban demonstrations or marches on the public highway (decree-law of 23 October 1935).[65] But a more important provision is the Law of 10 January 1936, which allows the government to dissolve associations or *de facto* groupings 'whose aim is to attack by force the republican form of government or whose activity will prevent the carrying out of measures concerning the re-establishment of republican legality'. In terms of administrative resources, a liaison bureau in the Interior Ministry and in each region links all police forces and coordinates the information available to the police; files of suspects are set up and distributed nationally.[66] 'Special Intervention Units', composed of anti-commando brigades responsible to the Interior Ministry and two gendarmerie units responsible to the Defence Ministry, were established in 1972—4. Also, a parachute regiment and the Foreign Legion are held in reserve.[67]

Judicial action also provides the government with certain powers. First, special procedures or courts can be chosen. For example, there is the special procedure of *flagrant délit* (which literally means 'caught in the act'), which both gives the judicial police exceptional powers if a crime is in the process of being carried out (and limited to the period of time in which the crime is in progress) and provides for a rapid judicial procedure. This process was greeted with protest and scepticism when applied to the alleged autonomists arrested during the demonstration of 23 March 1979, as it prevented a full defence from being presented. But the most dramatic procedure is provided by the existence of the State Security Court, set up in 1963 as the successor to the special military tribunals established to try OAS leaders in the preceding two years. All offences involving state security in times of peace can be tried by this court, on which military and civilian judges sit together (if the crime is related to national defence, the military judges are in a majority). Its jurisdiction covers the entire country (no territorial limits to the examining magistrate's powers of investigation), but it sits in a military precinct in Paris to which access is difficult, even for lawyers. The public prosecutor cannot decide whether or not the prosecution may go ahead; that decision must be made on the written order of the Justice Minister. The period of time a prisoner can be held without going before a magistrate is extended from forty-eight hours to six days, and twelve days in cases of urgency. Certain restrictions on searches and seizures are lifted, and there is no limit to the period of remand. Appeals are limited more strictly than in ordinary courts, and the instruction procedure is controlled only by written documents. Reasons for decisions are not given unless damages are awarded. And defence lawyers are subject to more stringent controls.[68]

Second, the government can apply the *loi anticasseurs* of 1970, which can make individual organisers and participants responsible for the results of violent acts or assaults carried out as the consequence of 'a concerted action by a group using direct force'. Aimed directly at violent demonstrations, the law has always been something of a political hot potato; according to *Le Figaro*, it has been applied with prudence, taking into account the common defence that the defendants were mere pawns. Magistrates are said to be hesitant to make defendants pay for damages (other means exist of providing for these), although this would seem to have been one of the main aims of the law.[69] Attempts to pass other special laws have not been so successful, however. In 1976, a bill attempting to make the registration of associations subject to the approval of the Prefect was withdrawn from parliament, and another bill permitting the generalised searching of cars was struck down by the Constitutional Council. However, a stretching of the *flagrant délit* procedure was used to justify the systematic searching of cars at the time of the kidnapping of the Belgian industrialist Baron Empain in January 1978.[70] Indeed, the police were regularly accused of abusing their files of suspects and their limited powers of search, especially at times like the Schleyer kidnapping, when they felt that they had to prove to the Germans that they could mount efficient operations too.[71] The various intelligence services — the DST charged with preventing subversion from abroad, and the Renseignements Généraux in the Interior Ministry — also played an important clandestine role in government attempts to deal with potential terrorism. But the only special law dealing with a specific terrorist offence is a law of 1971 that sets out specific penalties for hostage-taking: life imprisonment if the hostage is kept for more than a month; 10—20 years if less than a month; and 2—5 years if the victim has been 'voluntarily' freed in less than five days.[72] It must also be remembered that the death penalty still exists in France.

The government's discretion in the matter of foreign nationals is great indeed. In the first place, whatever the other rules in force, the Ordinance of 2 November 1945 gives the government power to decide where a foreign national is allowed to reside — and even to expel him summarily — if the Interior Minister judges his presence to be a menace to 'public order or public credit'.[73] The preamble to the 1946 Constitution — still in effect, as it was adopted unchanged in the 1958 Constitution — states: 'Any person persecuted because of his action in favour of liberty has the right of asylum on the territories of the Republic.' The Geneva Convention of 1951, extended to cover all countries by the Bellagio Protocol of 1967, applies in France, and asylum is usually granted automatically when a refugee has set foot on French soil. Sometimes the clause in the Convention that states that a refugee must have justifiable cause to believe that he would be persecuted in his own country is interpreted widely — as when members of Salazar's secret police were admitted in 1975. But the combination of this clause and the constitutional requirement that the refugee must be persecuted for his action in favour of liberty are occasionally strictly interpreted. As we have already seen, seven Basque activists were returned to Spain in 1979 although they had previously enjoyed political asylum; and the extradition of Klaus Croissant, one of the lawyers of the Red Army Faction, to Germany in 1977 was justified by the Justice Minister, Peyrefitte, on exactly these grounds.[74] Furthermore, asylum is not unconditional. A circular of 2 July 1974 requires the refugee: (1) not to interfere with the domestic politics of the host country; (2) not to bring the political quarrels of his own country onto the national territory in a violent manner; and (3) not to endanger the internal or external security of the host country nor to endanger its diplomatic relations.[75] During the first ten months of 1976, France expelled 3595 foreigners,[76] but during the entire year only 161 were actually extradited.[77] This latter figure, indeed, represents a normal year.

The European Convention on the Suppression of Terrorism was adopted in Strasbourg in November 1976 and signed in January 1977. It greatly restricts the notion of political crimes, although it includes a safeguard clause that either is meaningless or vitiates the text of its usefulness. A great deal of opposition to this text developed in France, as it was seen as a serious threat to the cherished concept of France as a land of asylum. A young law lecturer wrote in *Le Monde:*

> It suffices to think that if such a treaty had existed in another epoch, France would have been obliged to extradite Santiago Carrillo to Franco's Spain and Mario Soares to Salazar's Portugal, not to mention General de Gaulle, a terrorist *par excellence* in the terms of the text, whom the British government would have had to send back to Vichy in 1940![78]

Of course, that was in another era, and the signatories were all liberal democracies now. But the case of Klaus Croissant came to be a symbol of the deficiencies of the new approach.[79] The opposition stretched across the left and left—centre of the political spectrum, and strongly present was the League of the Rights of Man.[80] Although it was intended to present the Convention to parliament for ratification in the spring session of 1978, it has still not yet been presented. Giscard d'Estaing's further proposal of a 'common judicial area' would seem, in these circumstances, to have been stillborn.

In more limited areas, France did sign and ratify the Hague Convention of 1970 on air piracy, but did not even sign the subsequent Montreal Convention of 1971.[81]

Essentially, however, the French government retains a great deal of discretion over political refugees on its territory. The tradition of granting political asylum on a large scale has been maintained. In the domestic arena, ordinary criminal law is still the basis for dealing with violence and terrorism, although the existing structure of that law and of the administrative weapons in the hands of the executive means in effect that further special legislation would not be necessary. In any case, the vigilance of radical intellectuals, left-wing groups and even old-fashioned liberals has made a paranoid over-reaction less credible in the French context.

CONCLUSIONS

The terrorist threat thrives on evoking the existential dread of the social order, which it hopes to force to undermine its own legitimacy. France, however, has been fairly immune from this pressure. In fact, the concept of terrorism itself is a complex one to apply in the context of contemporary French society and politics. The analyst is caught between the narrow definition of terrorism — in which case France is characterised by non-terrorism rather than terrorism — and the very broad definition — in which case all anti-system groups, whether revolutionary or merely dissenting, violent or non-violent, ideological or sectional, active or merely sympathising, come to be seen as potentially subversive and thus become vulnerable to greater repression. This is no mere technical dilemma in the age of modern communications, where media shorthand and the aims of 'terrorist' groups combine symbiotically in a ritual threat of social breakdown, symbolically leading mass publics to internalise the fear felt by the participants in the in fact highly circumscribed 'incidents' that are the raw material of effective news coverage.

That the image of terrorism is diffuse in France is the consequence of two major factors. The first is the lack, fortuitous or otherwise, of an active, visible, coherent indigenous terrorist organisation. Thus terrorism appears as a foreign phenomenon, and linkages with the domestic social order must be by way of analogy rather than through self-evident factual demonstration. An anti-terrorist consensus remains a somewhat abstract formula and is unlikely to lead to policy decisions, pressures for immediate action or the suspension of disbelief in the benefits of bureaucratic repression that is necessary for the acceptance of special legislation and emergency measures. The second, which is inextricably intertwined with the first, is France's political culture, with its unique mixture of revolutionary, liberal—democratic and paternalist—administrative elements, where the label 'left' is often adopted by right-wing groups, where the Declaration of the Rights of Man and Citizen is re-proclaimed in the preamble to every constitution, and where the effervescence of intellectual radicalism is regarded as a political and cultural resource underlying France's humane and civilising mission in the world. Despite the low-level political violence that does exist, and despite the erosion of the social, economic and political pluralism that nurtured the French political tradition, its cultural power is still paramount.

In a world in which terrorism seems to be in decline, France has done better than many others in maintaining its commitment to those values that must underlie a genuine democratic pluralism.

Notes and References

1. See S. Cobler, *Law, Order and Politics in West Germany* (Harmondsworth: Penguin, 1978); L'Europe de la répression, ou l'insécurité d'état. *Actes,* special edition, supplement to no. 17 (Spring 1978).
2. L. Dispot, *La machine à terreur* (Paris: Grasset, 1975).
3. G. Almond and S. Verba, *The Civic Culture: Political Attitudes and Democracy in Five Nations* (Boston: Little, Brown, 1965), pp. 312—13.
4. Consider W.L. Shirer, *The Collapse of the Third Republic* (London: Heinemann, 1969) among others.
5. D. Thomson, *Democracy in France since 1870* (London: Oxford University Press, 5th edn, 1969) and S. Hoffmann, 'Paradoxes of the French political community', in Hoffmann, *et al. In Search of France* (Cambridge, Mass.: Harvard University Press, 1963), pp. 1—117.
6. S. Hoffmann, 'Heroic leadership: the case of modern France', in L.J. Edinger (ed.), *Political Leadership in Industrialised Societies* (New York: Wiley, 1967), pp. 108—54.
7. R. Rémond, *The Right Wing in France from 1815 to de Gaulle* (Philadelphia: University of Pennsylvania Press, 1966) and J. Touchard, *La gauche en France depuis 1900* (Paris: Editions du Seuil, 1977).
8. See P.G. Cerny, 'The new rules of the game in France: coalition-building and institutional learning, 1974—79', in P.G. Cerny and M.A. Schain (eds), *French Politics and Public Policy* (London: Frances Pinter; New York: St. Martin's Press, 1980).
9. M. Crozier, *The Bureaucratic Phenomenon* (London: Tavistock, 1964), Part IV.
10. G. Michelat and M. Simon, *Classe, religion et comportement politique* (Paris: Presses de la Fondation Nationale des Sciences Politiques and Editions Sociales, 1977).
11. J. Marceau, *Class and Status in France: Economic Change and Social Immobility 1945—1975* (Oxford: Oxford University Press, 1977).
12. V. Wright, *The Government and Politics of France* (London: Hutchinson, 1978).
13. E.R. Curtius, *The Civilisation of France: An Introduction* (New York: Vintage, 1962; originally published 1929).
14. S. Hoffmann, 'The Vichy circle of French conservatives', in Hoffmann, *Decline or Renewal? France since the 1930s* (New York: Viking, 1974), pp. 3—25.
15. M. Duverger, *La Ve République* (Paris: Presses Universitaires de France, 1963).
16. For a discussion of de Gaulle's views on leadership, see P.G. Cerny, *The Politics of Grandeur: Ideological Aspects of de Gaulle's Foreign Policy* (Cambridge: Cambridge University Press, 1980), chs 1—3.
17. J. Hayward, Dissentient France: the counter political culture. *West European*

Politics, 1, no. 3 (October 1978), pp. 53—67; for a classical Lipsettian view, see H. Waterman, *Political Change in Contemporary France: The Politics of an Industrial Democracy* (Columbus, Ohio: Merrill, 1969).
18. Hayward, *op. cit.*
19. M.A. Schain, *The French Communists in Power* (London: Frances Pinter, forthcoming 1981).
20. J.-R. Tournoux, *L'histoire secrète* (Paris: Plon, 1962). Also P. Chairoff, *Dossier B . . . comme barbouzes* (Paris: Alain Moreau, 1975).
21. For an understanding of the army's position, see J. Planchais, *Une histoire politique de l'Armée: de de Gaulle à de Gaulle, 1940—1967* (Paris: Editions du Seuil, 1967); cf. O.D. Menard *The Army and the Fifth Republic* (Lincoln, Neb.: University of Nebraska Press, 1967).
22. For a sympathetic treatment of the FLNA, see F. Fanon, *Sociologie d'une révolution: l'an V de la Révolution algérienne* (Paris: François Maspéro, 1978; originally published 1959).
23. Details of the political context of the Algerian War and independence can be found in P.M. Williams, *French Politicians and Elections 1951—1969* (Cambridge: Cambridge University Press, 1970).
24. Cerny, *The Politics of Grandeur,* pp. 60—1.
25. On the OAS, cf. Tournoux, *op. cit.,* and R. Gaucher, *Les terroristes, de la Russie tsariste à l'O.A.S.* (Paris: Albin Michel, 1965), pp. 279—343.
26. C. Plume and P. Démaret, *Target: De Gaulle* (London: Secker and Warburg, 1974).
27. A. Grosser, *La IVe République et sa politique extérieure* (Paris: Armand Colin, 1961), p. 9.
28. For an example of this paranoia, see R. Moss, *The Collapse of Democracy* (London: Abacus, 1977).
29. For a more detailed comparative treatment, see J. Bowyer Bell, *A Time of Terror: How Democratic Societies Respond to Revolutionary Violence* (New York: Basic Books, 1978).
30. See the three-part series La France, terre d'asile. *Le Monde,* 26, 27 and 28/9 November 1976.
31. C. Dobson and R. Payne, *The Carlos Complex: A Study in Terror* (London: Coronet, 1978), pp. 81—2.
32. 9 August 1978. The debate on preventive capability and the legal situation will be referred to again in part II of this chapter.
33. *Le Monde,* 2 August 1978.
34. *Ibid.: Le Figaro,* 3 August 1978.
35. *L'Aurore* and *Le Figaro,* 22 May 1978.
36. Dobson and Payne, *op. cit.,* pp. 55—6; *Le Figaro,* 22 May 1978.
37. *Le Monde,* 29 March 1979.
38. *The Observer,* 4 August 1979.
39. *Le Monde,* 2 February 1979.
40. *Le Monde,* 9 February and 3 March 1979.
41. *Le Matin,* 18 October and 24 October 1978.
42. See *Le Point,* 8 May 1978, and Dobson and Payne, *op. cit.,* pp. 84—91.
43. *Le Point,* 31 October 1977.
44. See *Le Monde,* 6 March 1979.
45. *Libération,* 16 January 1979.
46. *Le Monde,* 27 June 1978 and *Le Figaro,* 1 July 1978.
47. *Le Monde,* 5 July 1978.
48. *Le Figaro,* 27 June 1978.

49. See *Le Monde,* 8 February and 1/2 April 1979. *Le Point,* 2 January 1978, mentions the Corsican who bombed the houses of eight of his wife's lovers. Nonetheless, more bomb attacks were set by Corsicans than by any other group.
50. *Le Monde,* 11 January 1979.
51. *Le Monde,* 16 September 1978.
52. *Le Matin,* 25 July 1978.
53. *Le Monde,* 5 July 1978.
54. *Le Matin,* 2 May 1979.
55. *Le Nouvel Observateur,* 14 April 1979.
56. *Le Monde,* 16 January 1979.
57. *Réponses à la violence,* Rapport du comité présidé par Alain Peyrefitte (Paris: Presses-Pocket, 1977), 2 vols.
58. *Le Monde,* 20 September 1978.
59. *Le Quotidien de Paris,* 28 May 1977; *Le Matin,* 22 October 1977; and *Le Figaro,* 24 October 1977.
60. *Le Monde,* 11, 15 and 24 May 1974; and *Le Figaro,* 11 March 1976.
61. *Le Figaro,* 24 October 1977.
62. *L'Express,* 31 October 1977.
63. *Le Monde,* 28 October 1977.
64. 'L'Europe de la répression', *op. cit.,* p. 3.
65. *L'Aurore,* 31 March/1 April 1979.
66. R. Marcellin, *L'Ordre public et les groupes révolutionnaires* (Paris: Plon, 1969), pp. 53—64.
67. *Le Monde,* 20 October 1977.
68. M. Laval, La Cour de Sûreté de l'etat. *Actes,* no. 10 (Spring 1976), pp. 2—6. Also, La Cour de Sûreté de l'Etat dans le système judiciaire français. *Actualités-Documents,* Paris, Délégation Générale à l'Information, no. 111 (n.d).
69. *Le Figaro,* 15 January 1979.
70. *France Nouvelle,* 6 March 1978.
71. *Libération,* 23 February 1978.
72. *Le Monde,* 20 March and 25 June 1971; *Le Figaro,* 4 October 1977.
73. *Le Monde,* 14 December 1978 and 9 January 1979.
74. *Le Nouvel Observateur,* 28 November 1977.
75. 'La France, terre d'asile', *op. cit.*
76. *Le Monde,* 30 October 1976.
77. *Le Figaro,* 21/2 August 1977.
78. *Le Monde,* 20 July 1977.
79. *Le Matin,* 22 September 1977.
80. F. Julien-Laferrière, La Convention européenne pour la répression du terrorisme. *Après-demain,* no. 211 (February 1979), pp. 43—5.
81. La Lutte internationale contre le terrorisme. *Problèmes Politiques et Sociaux* no. 259 (30 May 1975) La Documentation Française, pp. 48—52.

CHAPTER 5

Nationalists without a Nation: South Moluccan Terrorism in the Netherlands

Valentine Herman and Rob van der Laan Bouma

INTRODUCTION

Like many other West European countries, the Netherlands has not been immune from terrorist attacks in recent years. Since the late 1960s there have been a number of occasions on which the Dutch government, its agents, policies and property — as well as those of foreign governments and multinational companies in the Netherlands — have come under violent political attack. The terrorist groups that have mounted incidents in the Netherlands over the last ten years or so can be divided into two broad categories: on the one hand are 'indigenous' groups such as the Red Youth movement, which claimed responsibility for a number of bomb attacks in the late 1960s and early 1970s; on the other hand are 'imported' groups such as the Japanese Red Army, which seized the French embassy in The Hague in September 1974, and the Provisional IRA, which claimed responsibility for the murder of the British ambassador in The Hague in March 1979. The Netherlands is far from being unique in having experienced either indigenous or imported terrorism. Many — perhaps most — European countries (both East and West) have spawned their own varieties of indigenous terrorist in recent times: terrorism 'pays', and its profitability has led to its widespread imitation. And, as the tentacles of transnational and international terrorist organisations have extended their reach, many West European countries have also experienced imported terrorism.

The distinctive characteristic — and most widely known aspect — of contemporary Dutch terrorism is attributable to its South Moluccan perpetrators and their desire to realise the Republic of the South Moluccas; it is they who provide the focus for this chapter. We shall begin with an

119

historical examination of the relationship between the Netherlands and Indonesia. Second, we shall focus on the social, economic and political conditions of the South Moluccan community in the Netherlands. Next we shall undertake a detailed examination of the main incidents of South Moluccan terrorism in the Netherlands. Finally, we shall consider the responses of Dutch governments to both South Moluccan and international terrorism.

Definitions of terrorism abound. However, for the purpose of this chapter, we define non-governmental terrorism as:

> The considered and systematic use — or threatened use — of widespread, offensive violence, murder and destruction aimed at governmental employees and the general population, as well as public and private property, in order to force individuals, groups, communities, economic entities and governments to modify or change their actual or proposed behaviour and policies so as to concede to the terrorists' political demands.[1]

With this definition of terrorism in mind, we undertake our examination of South Moluccan terrorism in the Netherlands.

THE SOUTH MOLUCCANS AND THE DUTCH: HISTORICAL PERSPECTIVES[2]

The origins of South Moluccan terrorism can be found in the colonial history of a group of islands some 7500 miles away from the Netherlands that now form part of the Indonesian archipelago. Searching for spices, the Dutch first arrived in the Moluccas in 1599 landing on Ambon, the island from which most of the South Moluccans now living in the Netherlands originated. The Portuguese had arrived there sixty-five years earlier, but they were hated by the native population because of the strong pressure put on them to become Roman Catholic. Expecting the Dutch to be more tolerant towards them, the Moluccans requested the Dutch to drive out the Portuguese, which they eventually did.

As an expression of their gratitude, Muhammadan monarchs signed the 'Eèuwig verbond' (eternal alliance) contract with the Dutch: this guaranteed the Moluccans freedom of religion, pledged their loyalty to the Dutch authorities, and contributed to the establishment of the Dutch East Indies Company's monopoly of trade in the islands. The Dutch were not benevolent colonisers, and their repressive measures led to increased poverty and the decimation of the Moluccan population.

Although the military might of the Dutch enabled them to expand their hegemony over the whole archipelago, resistance to their rule was frequent, and the response of the Dutch often bloody. Twice, in the late eighteenth and early nineteenth centuries, the Moluccas were transferred to the British, but on both occasions were returned to the Dutch despite the protests of the Moluccans. Conditions in the islands became so bad that in 1864 the Dutch government had to terminate its monopoly of the spice trade and the use of forced labour. From then on the Dutch government adopted a more liberal policy towards the colonies, which started being exploited by private companies.

During the rule of the Netherlands in the then Dutch East Indies, many South Moluccans became Christians and thus had a common religion with the Dutch. Many South Moluccans were recruited into the Royal Netherlands Indies Army (KNIL), which acquired fame and notoriety through the effectiveness of the fierce Moluccan soldiers. In the early part of the twentieth century South Moluccans joined the KNIL in large numbers; in 1939, 10–20 per cent of the adult male population of Ambon served in the army. This had two main consequences. First, the Moluccan soldiers were sympathetic to the Dutch, whom — from 1864 onwards — they came to see as benign partners: an attitude markedly different from that shown towards the rapacious and exploiting colonists of earlier centuries. Second, it led to resentment amongst other natives of the East Indies (since the KNIL had helped the Dutch to conquer these other islands), who identified the South Moluccans with the Dutch 'imperialists'.

On the surrender of the Japanese (who had acquired the archipelago in 1942) to the British, Sukarno and Hatta[3] were forced by young nationalists to proclaim an independent 'Republic of Indonesia' in Djakarta on 17 August 1945. This brought to an end almost 350 years of foreign rule over the islands, interrupted only by the exigencies of war and competing colonialisms; it was also the harbinger of a series of bloody and bitter battles between the British (who arrived in the islands in September 1945 to disarm the Japanese) and Indonesians in Java. When Dutch troops returned to the islands in October 1945, fighting continued as the Dutch sought to re-establish their prewar colonial authority over an Indonesian population that during the Japanese interregnum had developed an army of over 100,000, mass organisations, and — most importantly — a strong nationalist sentiment, which had been encouraged by the Japanese.

The Dutch government did not want to accept an independent Indonesia; their preference was for a federal United States of Indonesia, which would consist of a number of states and form with the Netherlands a Dutch–Indonesian Union.[4] By contrast, Indonesia wanted the continuation of the unitary Republic. On 24 December 1946, the state of East Indonesia (Negara Indonesia Timor) — which included the South Moluccas — was formed. On 25 March 1947, the Dutch and the Indonesians agreed on a formula for the establishment of the United States of Indonesia as part of a new Dutch Commonwealth. This provided that the Indonesian Republic would govern Java and Sumatra, while the Outer Islands were to be administered separately.

The agreement lasted but a few months. Differences in interpretation led to the so-called 'police action' — an all-out attack on Java and Sumatra by Dutch land-forces, commandos and the KNIL — which was the subject of world criticism. Under strong pressure from the United Nations' Security Council, the Netherlands and the Republic of Indonesia signed a new agreement aboard the American carrier Renville. This too proved to be shortlived, as the Dutch were not prepared to allow Indonesia either to conduct its own international relations or to control its own armed forces. Repudiating the Renville agreement, the Dutch undertook a second 'police action', overrunning territory beyond the lines drawn at the cease-fire, and blockading the port of Java. Again they were censored by world opinion, especially by the United States of America who, after an attempted *coup d'état* by the Indonesian Communist Party, saw Sukarno as a possible partner against Moscow's influence.

Continuing political instability in the archipelago and international pressure led to the convening of the Round Table Conference to decide Indonesia's future in The Hague between 23 August and 2 November 1949. The conference decided that Indonesia would be a federation, and that any state unwilling to join it could negotiate a special relationship with Indonesia and the Netherlands. The conference resolutions were approved by the Netherlands, the Republic of Indonesia, representatives of already existing states (such as East Indonesia) and the United Nations' Commission for Indonesia (which played a supervisory role in the conference). Representatives of separatist movements in Minahassa and Ambon were not invited to participate in the conference on the same terms as the other parties, and refused to participate in it at all. The Round Table Agreements of The Hague transferred the sovereignty of the archipelago from the Netherlands to the Republic of the United States of Indonesia on 27 December 1949, and marked the formal end of the Dutch Empire in the East Indies.

When the United States of Indonesia achieved their independence, the Negara Indonesia Timor, including the South Moluccas, became one of the sixteen states of the new federation. Under the agreements of the Round Table Conference, every state had the right to negotiate special relations with the federation and with the Netherlands; it soon became obvious that these were empty words. 'Indonesia: one and indivisible from Sabank to Merauka' became the rallying cry, and President Sukarno used the Indonesian army — manned almost exclusively by Javanese soldiers unquestionably loyal to him — to conquer those islands that resisted unification. In April 1950, only two of the sixteen states maintained a separate existence, the others being placed under the central government of Djakarta. In East Indonesia, resistance continued, but when on 21 April 1950 a revolt on Celebes was suppressed, it became clear that the existence of the Negara Indonesia Timor was nearly ended.

The South Moluccas, fearing Javanese domination, had no desire to be part of a unitary Republic of Indonesia and, claiming that they had the right of self-determination under the Round Table Agreements, seceded from Indonesia. On 25 April 1950, the Republic of the South Moluccas (RMS) — separate from both East Indonesia and the Republic of the United States of Indonesia — was proclaimed in Ambon, with the following 'Declaration of Independence':

> To grant the real will, wishes and demand of the people of the South Moluccas, we hereby proclaim the independence of the South Moluccas, de facto and de jure, with the political structure of a republic, free from any connection with the Negara Indonesia Timor and the Republic of the United States of Indonesia, on account of the fact that the Negara Indonesia Timor is unable to maintain her position as a part of the United States of Indonesia in accordance with the 'Den-Pasar-regeling' which is still valid now and concerning the resolution of the Council of South Moluccas of March eleventh, 1947, while the Republic of the United States of Indonesia has acted incompatible with the resolutions taken at the Round Table Conference and its own Constitution.
>
> Ambon, April 25th, 1950[5]

One month later, Negara Indonesia Timor — minus the RMS — was incorporated by decree into the unitary Republic of Indonesia.

Indonesia regarded the Moluccan Declaration of Independence as an act of rebellion, and initially tried to end the RMS' existence by peaceful means between April and August 1950. These failed, and in September of that year Indonesian troops landed in Ambon. Fighting took place between Indonesian and South Moluccan forces until November when organised resistance was overcome and the Indonesian national flag was flown in the town of Ambon. The short, but unhappy, life of the independent RMS had lasted but seven months. Notwithstanding this military defeat, the fight against the Indonesian Republic continued in the islands until the 'president' of the RMS — Dr Christiaan Soumokil — was arrested by an Indonesian patrol on the island of Ceram in 1963 and taken to Djakarta where he was executed in 1966.

The Round Table Agreements provided for the dissolution of the 65,000 member KNIL before 26 July 1950. The soldiers were offered the choice of either transferring to the Indonesian Army or being demobilised and having their transport paid to a place in the former Dutch East Indies where they wanted to settle. Few of the 8000 Moluccan soldiers in the KNIL wanted to join the Indonesian Army, as they feared reprisals from the Indonesian troops against whom they had previously fought. The Moluccans wanted to be demobilised in the Moluccas, but this was unacceptable to the Indonesian government as the islands were not yet unified and it feared resistance from the former KNIL troops. This contributed to the delay in disbanding the KNIL, which, by July 1950, still contained 17,000 men. To fulfil the terms of the Round Table Agreements, the remaining troops were 'transferred' to the Royal Dutch Army on 24 July 1950, and two days later the KNIL was dissolved.

When Indonesia gained control over the Moluccas in November 1950, 4000 Moluccan former KNIL soldiers, then members of the Royal Dutch Army, remained in Java. Permission was given for this group to be demobilised in the Moluccas, and the Dutch arranged dates for them to be transported there. However, the Moluccans refused to go as they did not want to be demobilised in the territory of the unified Republic; some of them wanted to go to the Netherlands: they argued before the courts that their lives would be endangered if they were demobilised in territory controlled by Indonesia. The government opposed this view, but lost the case even on appeal to the Supreme Court, which forbade the government to demobilise the soldiers on the territory of the Republic of Indonesia against their will. Neither of the alternatives that the soldiers wanted — demobilisation in Ceram (where resistance to the Republic was still continuing) or in the Dutch territory of New Guinea — was acceptable to either one, or both, of the Indonesian or Dutch governments.

Eventually the Dutch government arranged for the Moluccans to be transported to the Netherlands where a total of 21,300 soldiers and their dependants arrived between March and May 1951. On arrival, they were immediately discharged from the Dutch army. In the words of Wittermans and Gist this

> ... was a traumatic experience for them because it completely altered their cherished status, shattered their self-image, blighted their hopes, and spread confusion as to their identity. They were humiliated; they felt betrayed, morally shocked. Was this attack on their status to be the reward for their service and loyalty to the Dutch? ... Their attitudes of friendliness toward, and confidence in, the Dutch turned to hostility and distrust.[6]

At first the Moluccans staged a series of mass demonstrations to draw attention to their cause and to persuade the Dutch government to do what they considered to be its duty: to put pressure on Indonesia and to bring the South Moluccans' case before the United Nations (in 1954, 50 per cent of the Dutch population supported the latter demand[7]). However, the Netherlands had never recognised the RMS nor supported its goals.

The South Moluccans thought that their stay in the Netherlands would be brief, and that soon they would return to a free Moluccan republic. For their part, the Dutch government also imagined that the South Moluccans' stay would be short, as it was thought that the inclement Dutch climate and feelings of homesickness would lead to a majority of the South Moluccans swiftly returning to their homelands. Public policies towards the South Moluccans were based on this assumption. As we shall see in the next section, the government's initial attitudes towards the South Moluccans were responsible for turning what had begun as a political problem on the other side of the world into one that would lead to unforeseen political and socio-cultural manifestations on its own doorstep.

THE SOUTH MOLUCCANS IN THE NETHERLANDS: SOCIO-CULTURAL PERSPECTIVES

Anticipating their early return to the South Moluccas, the Dutch authorities initially housed the new arrivals in some fifty special 'settlement areas' ('woonoorden': former army and concentration camps and camps that had in the past been used to accommodate temporary government workers); by Dutch standards these were primitive, but to the Moluccans they were satisfactory. In 1960, following the recommendations of the Verwey-Jonker Committee,[8] the government began to move the South Moluccans to purpose-built 'open' residential areas. Frequently these moves were accompanied by violent protest from the South Moluccans who feared that their cultural identity, solidarity and social control over their own people would be undermined. By 1968, 20 per cent of the South Moluccans remained in the 'woonoorden', 20 per cent were dispersed throughout the country, and 60 per cent lived in residential areas. Although the latter are overcrowded, the government is reluctant either to expand existing areas or to build new ones.

When the South Moluccans arrived in the Netherlands, the government assumed responsibility not only for their housing but for all other aspects of their lives. The Moluccans were not expected to find jobs in the Netherlands and, indeed, the trade unions — fearing the competition of low-price labour — were opposed to them doing so. Because the Moluccans envisaged that their stay in the Netherlands would be temporary, there was little incentive for them to integrate into Dutch society.

In 1956, when economic conditions in the Netherlands had improved and when it was apparent that the South Moluccans' stay would not be shortlived, the *zelfzorgregeling* (self-help rule) was introduced. This stated that, wherever possible, the South Moluccans would support themselves and not rely on government assistance. However, the Moluccans could only find jobs of low occupational status. Over the years they have experienced little or no upward social mobility. In 1976, it was estimated that the percentage of unemployed South Moluccans was twice as high as that of the native Dutch.[9] Young Moluccans have found it especially difficult to find employment, and this, plus other factors, has given rise to several problems. It is widely recognised that the incidence of petty theft, crimes of violence and the use of drugs is much higher amongst South Moluccan youth — especially males — than amongst Dutch youth. The South Moluccans have not found it easy to adapt to, or benefit from, the Dutch educational system. About 70 per cent of South Moluccan families speak Maleis at home, and this has caused difficulties in the education of their children. The Moluccans have frequently urged the government to provide bi-cultural educational programmes, but these requests have been rejected on the grounds that such programmes would only increase the problems that young South Moluccans have in adapting to Dutch society. Additionally, the Moluccans have claimed that the government has used the educational system to 'Hollandise' them so that they will give up their allegiance to the RMS.

In the fields of housing, occupation and education successive Dutch governments and administrative agencies have adopted different policies towards the Moluccans than they have towards other ethnic immigrant groups such as the Indonesians. Public policy towards the 100,000 Indonesians on their arrival in the Netherlands in 1950 (as a result of the ending of Dutch hegemony over the archipelago) was based on their full and rapid integration into Dutch society (by ensuring their rapid dispersion throughout the country, arranging special job training programmes, etc.). There was no equivalent policy towards the South Moluccans; as a consequence, the degree of the Moluccans' integration or otherwise into Dutch society was dependent upon the Moluccans themselves. In many instances, the treatment received by the South Moluccans since their arrival in the Netherlands has reinforced their isolated position, marginal status and ethnic solidarity.

The South Moluccan community's support for the RMS has not lessened since their arrival in the Netherlands. It was expected that, as time passed, the ideal of an independent RMS would fade away in the second and third generations of South Moluccans (who had never seen 'their country') and as the older and original generations of South Moluccans died out; this has not happened. Indeed, the ideal of the RMS is supported by a vast majority of the South Moluccans[10] — this notwithstanding the fact that even Dr Manusama has told his followers that they might not live to return to the Moluccas, but that it would fall to their granchildren or perhaps their great grandchildren to do so. While most of the original generation of the South Moluccans have reluctantly resigned themselves to this long-term realisation of their dreams, it has come to be increasingly rejected by the younger South Moluccan community.

Until recently the first generation of the South Moluccans has sought to return to the Moluccas through exerting moral pressure on the Dutch government, hoping that it would both honour the promises it made to them in the 1950s and take the political and diplomatic initiatives necessary to bring about the RMS: to them the RMS was a memory of the past and a vision of the future. In contrast, the second and third generations of the South Moluccans have called for more direct and more radical activity on behalf of the RMS than was conducted in the past. Younger South Moluccans have increasingly come to repudiate the current leadership of the Moluccan community and the South Moluccan 'government-in-exile'[11] and have bitterly condemned them for their political myopia. (Until 1979, there were two

South Moluccan governments-in-exile. Throughout this chapter we refer to the government-in-exile in the Netherlands led by J.A. Manusama. The other government-in-exile was based in New York and had close relations with the African state of Benin. In December 1978 its president, I. Tamaela, died of a heart attack in Benin. This government was founded in 1969 at the time of a split in the South Moluccan community. Since then its influence has been less than that of Manusama's government.)

Whereas the South Moluccans have been united in challenging the legitimacy of the Indonesian government to rule over 'their' islands, the younger generations of the Moluccan community have transferred this challenge to the Dutch government. This is reflected in the targets against which South Moluccan political violence has been directed since the mid-1960s. The execution of Dr Soumokil by the Suharto government in Djakarta in 1966 sparked off a series of militant actions in the Netherlands undertaken by South Moluccan groups to draw attention to their demand for an independent RMS. On 26-27 July 1966, the Indonesian embassy in The Hague was set on fire shortly after the arrival of Dr Soumokil's widow in the Netherlands. On 31 August 1970, the residence of the Indonesian ambassador in Wassenaar was occupied for eleven hours by thirty South Moluccans who killed a policeman and seized several hostages. The purpose of this occupation was to bring about a meeting between President Suharto (who was due to arrive in the Netherlands the next day) and Dr Manusama, the president of the South Moluccan government-in-exile; this event can, in retrospect, be seen as the forerunner of later South Moluccan terrorist activities. During April 1974, an Indonesian Airways office was set on fire and an attempt was made to kidnap the Indonesian consul-general in Amsterdam. In December 1974, the police prevented a clash between pro-Indonesian and RMS supporters in The Hague, but the latter marched upon the Vredespaleis (the seat of the International Court of Justice) where they caused extensive damage. Whereas this violence was initially directed against Indonesian property and personnel in the Netherlands, subsequently it was aimed at Dutch targets. This became evident when it was officially announced on 1 April 1975 that the police had discovered a South Moluccan plot to occupy the Royal Palace at Soestdijk and kidnap Queen Juliana: eventually fifteen South Moluccans were imprisoned for their part in this.

The transfer of political violence by the South Moluccans to the Dutch 'host' government is of considerable importance in understanding the factors contributing to South Moluccan terrorism. According to Macfarlane, 'The most distinctive feature of the state is its claim to the allegiance of its members, an allegiance which is exclusive, all-embracing and unconditional.'[12] While this may be valid in certain contexts, it accurately describes neither the Dutch state's original claim to the allegiance of the South Moluccans on their arrival in the Netherlands, nor the allegiance the South Moluccans have subsequently been willing to give to the Dutch state.

Indeed the South Moluccans' allegiance is to not one but two states — the actual Dutch one within which they live, and the ideal RMS state, and to neither is their allegiance 'exclusive, all-embracing and unconditional'. In the past, as long as their identification with — but not allegiance to — the Dutch state was greater than to the RMS, protest against Dutch authorities was infrequent and non-violent. When, however, the South Moluccan's identification with, and allegiance to, the RMS became greater than to the Netherlands, and when this became politicised and radicalised, the potential for violent political protest against the Dutch state, its agents, property and authority increased; but not to the stage where allegiance was to be completely withdrawn from the Dutch state (as it could not be displaced by the RMS one), or to the stage where that state was to be overthrown.

In a pamphlet published on the twenty-fifth anniversary of the establishment of the RMS, Dr Manusama expressed the political predicament of the South Moluccan community: should they continue to follow the 'respectable road' to the RMS, or adopt a 'hard approach', which some had been pursuing since the Wassenaar incident of 1970?

> For many years our political leaders have, for the purposes of the recognition and respect of our people's rights, as a rule gone the 'respectable road' of presenting petitions, sending telegrams of protest, etc., to focus the attention of the world on the injustice that has been done to our people for such a long time: but they have done so in vain. It is easy to understand that many people have of late come to doubt that by proceeding on this road we shall ever attain the proposed object. Indeed, there are those who think that only a hard approach, in the course of which violence should not be avoided, can lead to the desired success . . . The concrete issue is whether the road we have as a rule gone along so far should make way for a clearly hard approach: a hard approach in the sense that practising violence where and when considered necessary is accepted as a weapon.[13]

Shortly afterwards, some South Moluccans chose the 'hard approach'; our task now is to see where this led.

SOUTH MOLUCCAN TERRORISM IN THE NETHERLANDS[14]

When Surinam attained its independence from the Netherlands on 25 November 1975, Queen Juliana read a speech that proclaimed that '. . . all people have a right to their own country'. One week later, an unexpected twist was given to this sentence when two coordinated acts of South Moluccan terrorism took place.

On 2 December, seven armed South Moluccans stopped the inter-city train from Groningen to Amsterdam near the village of Beilen, killing the driver and a soldier who attempted to escape. Over seventy passengers on the train — many of them pensioners travelling on concessionary tickets —

were held hostage. On the first day, three women and a child were released from the train, carrying with them a list of the terrorists' demands. These included: that they should be provided with a plane to fly to an undisclosed destination; that the Dutch government should publish a lengthy statement in every newspaper publicising the South Moluccans' grievances; that the government should present a television broadcast telling of the injustices done to the South Moluccan people; that the leaders of the South Moluccan community should be allowed a television broadcast and a press conference; that a meeting should be held between the Indonesian government and the South Moluccan government-in-exile; and that the Dutch government should raise the South Moluccan issue at the United Nations. Later that day six passengers escaped from the train, and the next day another hostage was released carrying further demands from the kidnappers.

The train was surrounded by police, troops and armoured cars. Two crisis centres were established: a local policy centre in the immediate area of the train manned by civilian, police and military authorities and advisers, and a national crisis centre in the Justice Ministry in The Hague. Mr Andries van Agt, the Minister of Justice, announced the government's position towards the terrorists:

> They have demanded that they should be allowed to leave with hostages. We have never given in to such demands, even when Japanese terrorists were holding the French Ambassador last year, and we shall not give in now. Furthermore, now that these men have killed, we cannot allow them to leave Holland at all.[15]

Dr Manusama negotiated with the terrorists on 3 December; later that day, seventeen passengers and the guard escaped from the train. The next day, the kidnappers made new demands, which included: the release of all South Moluccan 'political prisoners' from jail in the Netherlands (among them being the South Moluccans imprisoned following the discovery of the plot to capture the Royal Palace); that the Netherlands should arrange independence talks for their homelands under the auspices of the United Nations; and an ultimatum, which if not met would result in the killing of the hostages. On the expiry of the ultimatum later that day, one hostage was shot dead and his body thrown from the train; Prime Minister Den Uyl referred to this as 'cold-blooded murder'. The kidnappers handed to another South Moluccan mediator — Protestant clergyman, Reverend Samual Methiari — a declaration in which they claimed that their action was the result of 'Indonesian imperialism' and the Dutch government's 'deliberate blocking of all roads to a peaceful solution' of the question of South Moluccan independence.

An explosion on the train on 5 December injured one of the South Moluccans and three hostages, all of whom were taken to hospital. Later that day, a government spokesman said, 'Holland will not make any political concessions to end the hostage affair.' The next day, the gunmen dropped their demand for safe passage out of the country, but by then a position of stalemate had been reached: the government was not prepared to meet the terrorists' demands; the terrorists were unable — or unwilling — to exert further pressure on the government. Four mediators — including Dr Manusama and Mrs Soumokil, the widow of his predecessor — met with the remaining terrorists and secured the release of two elderly hostages. After the meeting, Dr Manusama sent a telegram to the Secretary-General of the United Nations asking that the world should consider the South Moluccan case; he also appealed to the International Red Cross for assistance in resolving the crisis. The siege continued, its monotony alleviated only by regular deliveries of food to the train, the comings-and-goings of mediators, and occasional military manoeuvres in the train's proximity. On 14 December — twelve days after the start of the ordeal — the remaining twenty-eight hostages were set free as the terrorists surrendered to Dr Manusama.

The second incident in 1975 began on 4 December (two days after the hijacking of the train) when six armed South Moluccans stormed and occupied the Indonesian consulate-general in Amsterdam: neither the consul nor the vice-consul were in the building at the time as they were both at a meeting to discuss the Beilen hijack. However, thirty-two people, including seventeen schoolchildren, were inside the consulate; several consular officials escaped through windows, but one man fell and died from his injuries five days later. One of the gunmen made a telephone broadcast live on Dutch radio from the consulate in which he maintained, 'We are not murderers: the Dutch have made murderers of us.' As if to prove his point, five of the youngest children were freed on the night of 4—5 December. Later, and after the intervention of Rev. Methiari, more children were set free.

The terrorists' initial demands were similar to those of the gang on the train; in addition, they demanded that a debate should be held between the Indonesian ambassador, Lieut.-General Sutapo Yuwono Projohandoko, and Dr Manusama. Earlier the ambassador had informed the Dutch government that he would not agree to a meeting with the South Moluccans: Foreign Minister Max van der Stoel was told that it was up to the Dutch to solve the problem caused by the terrorists. The remaining children were released from the consulate after an assurance was given that a meeting would be held between the Indonesian political counsellor and Rev. Methiari. The South Moluccans wanted the Indonesians to listen to their demands for an independent republic: this is precisely what the political counsellor was reported to have done, as he did not speak at the eighteen-minute meeting held on 8 December.

The same day the terrorists announced further demands. These included the freeing of Moluccan 'political prisoners' in Indonesia under the auspices of Amnesty International; a meeting between President Suharto and Dr Manusama in Geneva; and the freedom of all South Moluccans in their homeland to discuss a free republic. The terrorists claimed that the Dutch were responsible for the Moluccan problem, and recalled that thousands of Moluccans had died fighting for the Netherlands against the Japanese. The Indonesian response was unequivocal. President Suharto dismissed the terrorists' demands as 'ridiculous', and Dutch radio broadcast a report that the Indonesian Foreign Minister wanted to remind the South Moluccans in the Netherlands that they had family and friends in Indonesia, stating that it would be 'a shame' if 'reprisals' were carried out against Moluccans in Indonesia.

After the surrender of the Beilen gunmen, Rev. Methiari urged the occupiers of the consulate to surrender. Late on 19 December they agreed to do so, providing the Dutch government agreed to hold discussions with South Moluccan leaders. This the government agreed to do, on condition that the South Moluccan delegation was representative of the Moluccan community; fifteen days after the siege began, the terrorists surrendered to Dr Manusama and Rev. Methiari.

Sixteen months later, the precarious truce that had come to exist between the South Moluccan and Dutch communities was shattered when two further terrorist incidents took place. On the morning of 23 May 1977, two groups of South Moluccans staged coordinated assaults on a train and a school in North Holland.

Two South Moluccans stopped the Rotterdam to Groningen express near Assen where they were joined by seven other terrorists armed with machine-guns and other weapons. Several passengers quickly escaped from the train, and a number of elderly people and children were released; over fifty hostages remained. A few minutes after the hijacking of the train, four South Moluccans entered a primary school in Bovensmilde (about twelve miles from Assen); fifteen South Moluccan children in the school were immediately released, and 105 children — aged between six and twelve — and five teachers were taken prisoner. This second incident in particular aroused local passions: taxi-drivers from Groningen offered to take the children's places, and children at two primary schools with a large concentration of South Moluccan pupils were swiftly evacuated after threats were received that the children would be taken hostage as a reprisal. On hearing of the incidents, Premier Den Uyl's initial reaction was, 'Our first priority is to get the children out.' The areas around the train and the school were immediately sealed off by several thousand troops and police, who also kept the Dutch and South Moluccan communities in Bovensmilde from attacking one another. Telephone communication was established with both the train and the school and, after initial hesitation, the two terrorist groups accepted the supply of food, blankets, medicine and other items.

The leaders of the South Moluccan community quickly condemned the attacks. Dr Manusama criticised the 'low mentality' of the terrorists, stating that their actions 'in no way serve our ideal to create an independent South

Moluccan republic'. Indonesia's attitude was equally uncompromising: the Minister of Defence and Security said that the problem was essentially an internal affair for the Netherlands. After an emergency cabinet meeting, Mr Den Uyl declared, 'Democracy cannot bow to terrorism.' When asked how the government would deal with the terrorists, he replied, 'Patience is the watchword, but we are prepared to use controlled violence if necessary.' The government also announced that the general election due to take place in three days' time would not be postponed because of the incidents.

On 24 May, the terrorists made their demands known. First, the government should release the fourteen South Moluccans imprisoned after the 1975 sieges of the train and the consulate, as well as the seven South Moluccans convicted for their part in the plot to kidnap Queen Juliana. Second, the government should provide transport to Amsterdam's Schiphol airport where a Boeing 747 jumbo-jet, fully crewed and fuelled, should be waiting to take the two groups of terrorists, the twenty-one released prisoners and an unspecified number of hostages to an undisclosed destination. The South Moluccans also stipulated that if these demands were not met by 2.00 p.m. on 25 May, hostages would be killed. To emphasise their seriousness, hostages with nooses around their necks were paraded outside the train.

The government's response was unflinching. Justice Minister Van Agt insisted that there could be no negotiations with the terrorists until the children held at the Bovensmilde school were released. Mr Den Uyl stated that the government would not allow any hostages to leave the country. As it was known that both groups of terrorists had radios, the government was reluctant to make further statements that might have compromised its position or endangered the safety of the hostages.

The deadline passed without incident. On 26 May, three seriously ill children were released from the school. The next day the remaining children — about half of them suffering from gastro-enteritis — and one teacher were also released. The four other teachers remained as hostages. On 31 May the terrorists requested the government to provide a mediator to conduct negotiations to end the sieges. (Earlier they had said that they would shoot any negotiators sent by the government.) Disagreements arose between the terrorists and the government as to whom should be appointed. Both sides rejected each other's initial choice of mediators, and it was not until 3 June that agreement was reached on two mediators — Mrs Soumokil and Dr Hassan Tan, a chest specialist. The mediators spent six hours talking to the South Moluccans on the train on 4 June. The following day, two pregnant women were released from the train, and on 8 June, a sick man was also allowed to leave. A further four hours of talks took place on 9 June, but made no progress to end the impasse: 'we leave the country or we die', proclaimed the terrorists. In a statement, the mediators spoke of '. . . the serious situation which has now developed because of the obstinate attitude of both sides. The Dutch and South Moluccan peoples must know how fatal the consequences must be.' Dr Tan also gave a warning that the Netherlands might be on the brink of a race war. Via the mediators, the government warned the gunmen that unless the hostages were released unharmed, violence against the South Moluccan community could break out.

As the sieges neared the end of their third week, the authorities' patience was exhausted. On 11 June both the train and the school were taken by force. At daybreak, a detachment of marines, supported by ground troops, stormed the train while six jets flew overhead. A short fight took place in which six South Moluccans and two hostages were killed, while seven hostages, two marines and a South Moluccan were injured. The remaining two South Moluccans were captured unhurt, and forty-nine hostages released unharmed. At the same time as this assault, another detachment of marines broke into the school at Bovensmilde capturing the four South Moluccans and rescuing the four teachers.

Premier Den Uyl reported to the Dutch parliament on 14 June that 'In the end there was no other way than force. We were and are convinced that if we had not taken action, the outcome would have been far more serious.'[16] He revealed that the government had initially offered the South Moluccans safe conduct out of the country if they released the children, but after doing so the terrorists had insisted on taking hostages with them. This was unacceptable to the government, which then withdrew its free exit offer.

The most recent South Moluccan terrorist incident began on 13 March 1978, when three gunmen occupied the Drenthe provincial government offices near Assen seizing seventy-one hostages, including two provincial councillors. Mrs Tineke Schilthuis, the Queen's Commissioner for the province of Drenthe — who it was thought was the gunmen's prime target — escaped along with about 600 of the office's employees. The South Moluccans rounded up the hostages, shot dead a provincial planning official and threw his body out of a window. They also started firing at passers-by, wounding five people.

Soon after the terrorists occupied the building the Justice Ministry received a letter signed by the hitherto unknown South Moluccan Suicide Command, which demanded the release of twenty-one Moluccans imprisoned for earlier terrorist actions; $13 million ransom; and an aircraft to take them, the twenty-one released prisoners and fifty hostages to an unspecified destination. Justice Minister Job de Ruyter stressed that the government's main concern was the safe return of the hostages, and that it would follow the policy of previous governments and not accede to the terrorists' main demands. Soldiers and police surrounded the building, and a specially trained anti-terrorist marine squad was flown in. The security forces planted eavesdropping devices in the building to detect the movements and plans of the gunmen and the location of the hostages. The next day, two representatives of the South Moluccan community met with the gunmen to discuss their demands. They secured the release of a female hostage, but the terrorists refused to negotiate on their terms to free the others, and warned that if a getaway bus were not provided by 2.00 p.m. they would begin to shoot their hostages in pairs at thirty-minute intervals.

Forty-five minutes after the expiry of the deadline, the anti-terrorist squad stormed the building: in the ensuing battle, six hostages were injured and one of the provincial councillors received serious stomach wounds from which he died in hospital one month later. Mr De Ruyter disclosed that the decision to use the anti-terrorist squad had been taken after a shot had been heard during a telephone conversation with the South Moluccans, which, they claimed (falsely, as it turned out), had killed the first of the hostages. Premier Van Agt asserted that '. . . it was clear that a non-violent solution was in the realms of the impossible and by failing to go ahead with what we did, we would have put the lives of the hostages seriously at risk.'[17] He also appealed to the Dutch nation not to hold the entire South Moluccan community in the Netherlands responsible for the action of the terrorists.

The effects of terrorism on public opinion

It is instructive to consider the effects of South Moluccan terrorism on both the South Moluccan community and Dutch public opinion. The terrorist incidents have badly divided the South Moluccan community and revealed tensions between moderate and militant elements. In the midst of the 1975 sieges, the South Moluccan Council in Holland — of which both Dr Manusama and Rev. Methiari were members — issued a statement that, while regretting the murder of the civilians on the train, supported the gunmen's actions and agreed with their motives. Dr Manusama, who had already begun negotiating with the gunmen, dissociated himself from the statement, and in radio and television broadcasts called on the gunmen to free their captives and surrender. Two days later, Dr Manusama's approach became more militant. After a meeting of the Badan Persatuan — the political body representing a majority of the South Moluccans in the Netherlands — he announced the conditions for the calling off of the sieges: first, the Dutch had to guarantee a meeting between President Suharto and himself; second, the Dutch should proclaim their belief in the justice of an independent RMS. However, it was questionable whether the moderate leadership of the Badan Persatuan could exert any control over the gunmen, or the militant South Moluccan Youth Movement from which they came; indeed, the leader of the Youth Movement rejected a government appeal to act as a mediator with the gunmen in the consulate. Later the Rev. Methiari was to warn the gunmen that he would cease to mediate if they did not consider his orders on behalf of the leaders of the South Moluccan community. The moderate South Moluccan leaders expressed much less sympathy for the terrorists who carried out the 1977 sieges than they did for their predecessors in 1975, and Dr Manusama publicly condemned their irresponsibility. In the midst of the 1977 sieges, the South Moluccan Youth Movement and the Liberation Front of the Republic of the South Moluccas — both militant organisations — called for the government to make a political gesture to end the sieges and offered to act as mediators. They criticised the government for concentrating on the fate of the hostages and ignoring what they considered were the wider issues. While the government wanted mediators to be drawn from the moderate South Moluccan community, the gunmen wanted them to come from their militant organs.

While the trial of the survivors of the 1977 incidents was being held, the police decided to 'clean up' the South Moluccan housing-estates in Bovensmilde and Assen. The areas were sealed off and armed police, backed up by armoured cars and personnel carriers, went through the estates seeking weapons and plans for other attacks, as the whole South Moluccan community was under suspicion of plotting further incidents. In a massive display of force, the police fired shots into Moluccan homes, harassed women and children, and police vehicles flattened the Moluccans' gardens. The Moluccans met this force with hostility but not violence. The operation's main outcome was a hardening of Moluccan attitudes against the Dutch authorities, although the police later announced that they were studying the details of a South Moluccan plan, discovered during the search, to stage a further action involving the seizure of hostages.

Emotional crowds gathered in Assen and Bovensmilde in June 1977 when the Dutch authorities handed back the bodies of the terrorists killed in the rescue operation on the train. 5,500 South Moluccans attended their funeral, and as the *cortège* drove through the Moluccan quarter, almost all houses flew the flag of the RMS at half-mast.

While the leaders of the South Moluccan community were sympathetic to the 1975 attacks and embarrassed by the 1977 ones, they evinced no support whatsoever for the gunmen who seized the provincial government offices in Drenthe in 1978: South Moluccan leaders in Assen denounced the 'suicide commando'. The South Moluccan community is badly divided on operational lines over the question of how to reach an independent RMS. Younger South Moluccans have lost faith in their elders, whom they criticise for spreading the ideals of the RMS while doing little to realise them. However, notwithstanding these intergenerational differences — or 'respectable approach' versus 'hard road' to achieving the RMS — at the 1977 funeral, and during 'clearing-up' actions in Assen and elsewhere, the South Moluccan community has united in its opposition to the Dutch government.

Public opinion in the Netherlands has not been sympathetic to the South Moluccan terrorists, and relations between the Dutch and Moluccan communities has deteriorated as a result of it. During the 1975 sieges, a South Moluccan was beaten up outside Amsterdam's central station, two others were thrown off a stationary train by irate passengers at Rotterdam, and there were reports that railwaymen refused to carry South Moluccans on their trains. Hundreds of people queued in Rotterdam to sign a petition calling for harsher penalties against terrorism, and expressed their anger against the gunmen and their support for the government. The government's handling of the train and consulate hijackings was supported by 63 per cent of the population, while only 22 per cent were critical of it; 69 per cent thought the hijackings ended well under the circumstances, 23 per cent that they ended badly. Public opinion was more divided in its attitudes towards the perpetrators of the hijackings: 41 per cent believed that they deserved understanding, 44 per cent that they did not.[18]

The public's feelings were outraged by the capturing of the schoolchildren at Bovensmilde; the terrorists' release of fifteen South Moluccan children from the school only exacerbated racial elements of a dangerously tense situation. Public opinion was firmly behind the government's handling of the train and school hijacking (90 per cent supportive versus 7 per cent critical); 74 per cent thought the incidents ended well, 7 per cent that they ended badly. Only 27 per cent of the population believed that the terrorists deserved understanding; 67 per cent believed that they did not.[19]

Immediately after the ending of the 1977 hijackings, public opinion was divided on government policy towards the South Moluccans. While 38 per cent of the public thought that the government had done too little for the South Moluccan community after the 1975 hijackings, 42 per cent thought that it had done enough, and 7 per cent that it had done too much. Two out of three members of the public agreed with the statement that the South Moluccans 'should be placed under intensive control, even if this gives our country the appearance of a police-state'. In addition, 68 per cent thought that there was a certainty that further South Moluccan terrorist action would occur, and 28 per cent thought that there was a good chance that it would happen again; only 4 per cent believed that there was no likelihood of further outbreaks of South Moluccan terrorism.[20]

In the past, the Dutch held a widespread belief that all South Moluccans were loyal to the Netherlands: now there is an equally widely held belief that all South Moluccans are potential terrorists.[21] While neither view is correct, the switch from one to the other reflects the negative effect that South Moluccan terrorism has had on Dutch public opinion.

Terrorism and the courts

Changing Dutch and South Moluccan attitudes towards the terrorists have been mirrored by their treatment in the courts. The trial of the seven South Moluccans who hijacked the train in December 1975 took place in March 1976. With reluctance, the judges agreed to the defence argument that the political background of the South Moluccans formed an essential element of their trial and, within limits, they were allowed to explain their political motivations. The public prosecutor called for twelve- to eighteen-year sentences on the gunmen; the court imposed fourteen-year sentences on them. Judge Frans Fliek stated:

> The Dutch authorities will have to do everything in their power to understand the position of the South Moluccans living in Holland. On the other hand, the South Moluccans will have to recognise the limitations and obstacles lying in the way of their independence ideals.[22]

At the trial of the seven South Moluccans responsible for the siege of the Indonesian consulate, the public prosecutor called for seven-and-a-half-year sentences. In court he expressed admiration for the accuseds' courage and willingness to sacrifice themselves for an ideal. The prosecutor also suggested that the Dutch authorities and the leaders of the South Moluccan community should reach an agreement guaranteeing that there would be no more hijackings or taking of prisoners. If this could be achieved, convicted gunmen could be regarded as 'prisoners of war . . . whose pardon would be automatically considered once hostilities had ceased'. The court eventually sentenced the seven to six years in jail.

In September 1977, eight South Moluccans stood trial in Assen for their part in the sieges of that year. On this occasion, neither the judge nor the public prosecutor expressed sympathy for their cause. The prosecutor sought ten-year sentences for the seven surviving gunmen, and a four-year sentence for the eight accused of planning the raids; they received sentences of six to nine years and twelve months respectively.

After the occupation of the Drenthe provincial government building, three South Moluccans were brought to trial in June 1978. The public prosecutor sought eighteen-year jail sentences for two of them, and fifteen years for the third. The court denied that the three had been 'driven by political motives' and sentenced each of them to fifteen years imprisonment.

An important outcome of the 1975 events was the establishment of a joint Dutch—South Moluccan commission. On the ending of the sieges, Prime Minister Den Uyl announced that the government would begin talks with the South Moluccan community. The Moluccan delegation was to be representative of their community, and Mr Den Uyl did not rule out the possibility that members of the militant South Moluccan Youth Movement could be included in it. While the South Moluccans could express their views on an independent RMS, Mr Den Uyl made it clear that they must not create 'illusions that the Netherlands cannot satisfy', and that the Netherlands must continue to live with the South Moluccan community. The first meeting took place on 17 January 1976, and a decision was taken to appoint a commission — half Dutch and half South Moluccan — to provide a permanent forum for the raising of grievances and the discussion of their possible solutions. The commission was to deal with problems arising from the fact that 'in the South Moluccan community in the Netherlands, political ideals are being pursued which the Netherlands' Government cannot support but whose existence and gravity it recognises.'[23] Four months were needed to form the commission, which met throughout 1976. Whatever it achieved as a forum for discussion, it did not prevent the terrorist actions of 1977; after these, it was decided to enlarge the ten-member body by bringing in representatives of the younger South Moluccan community. The government also decided that it would ban South Moluccan paramilitary organisations, uniformed private armies and vigilante units. Furthermore, while advocating closer police surveillance of South Moluccan areas, more searches for illegal arms and tighter conspiracy laws, it recognised that it was impossible completely to eliminate future terrorist acts.

In mid-1978, the government announced a new socio-cultural package worth about 8 million guilders (approximately £2 million) aimed at meeting some of the South Moluccans' grievances. The package guaranteed the pensions of the original KNIL soldiers who came to the Netherlands; promised to build up to 6000 apartments dispersed throughout the country (rather than in existing residential areas) to ease the growing South Moluccan housing problem; made extra money available for special educational programmes; and guaranteed employers additional premiums for taking on young unemployed Moluccans.

FIGHTING TERRORISM

Successive Dutch governments have responded to the various outbreaks of South Moluccan terrorism we have chronicled above in two distinct ways. On the one hand, they have introduced a series of social, cultural and economic measures designed to improve the position of the South Moluccans in Dutch society and, in so doing, to undermine some of the possible causes of terrorism. This is, necessarily, part of a long-term process. On the other hand, governments have been concerned with the short-term problem of fighting terrorism, that is dealing with particular terrorist operations, as well as taking measures to prevent their occurrence. These include protecting military, governmental and selected civil installations; restricting the availability of arms to civilians; protecting public figures; collecting and processing information about dissident groups; etc. In this final section we shall consider how certain organisational and judicial aspects of the fight against both South Moluccan and other forms of terrorism have been organised in the Netherlands.

It is impossible to provide a full inventory of government measures designed to combat terrorism, as many of them are cloaked in confidentiality: this applies, for example, to many of the activities of the Dutch secret service. Questions were asked by members of parliament in 1973 about the government's anti-terrorist measures.[24] Prime Minister Biesheuvel announced that a series of measures had been taken to fight terrorism: two groups of sharpshooters — one recruited from the state police, the other from the army — had been formed; in addition, a group of marines was to receive special training in close-combat fighting.[25] It was also announced that army units would be made available during terrorist incidents to provide some assistance to the police.[26]

These measures introduced two innovations in the state's interior violence apparatus: the involvement of the army in domestic affairs, and the introduction of 'shoot-to-kill' teams. Parliament established a committee to examine the measures, and the government gave its assurance that the sharpshooters would only be used after the Minister of Justice had given permission initially to send the sharpshooters to the scene of a terrorist incident and, subsequently, for them to be sent into action.[27] These precautions were followed when the sharpshooters played a part in ending the 1977 sieges of the train near Assen and the school at Bovensmilde: for the first time the sharpshooters were used in an offensive capacity.

Further anti-terrorist units have also been established, of which the Landelijke Bijstandsteam Terreurbestrijding and the Brigade voor speciale beveiligingsopdrachten are the most important. The former is a police team that specialises in the collection and coordination of information concerning the taking of hostages; the latter, an anti-terrorist squad recruited from the military police. (The Dutch anti-terrorist units and police have received advice from anti-terrorist specialists from the FRG, as well as from British Special Air Services officers.) In addition to these nationally organised units, local police forces of several large cities have formed specialised teams responsible for dealing with suspected terrorists and armed criminals.

The organisation of the state's response to specific terrorist incidents — especially in situations where hostages have been taken — also warrants attention. The authorities were totally unprepared when South Moluccans seized the Wassenaar residence of the Indonesian ambassador in 1970: they had neither a specific policy for bringing an occupation to a speedy and satisfactory conclusion, nor a general policy for dealing with terrorists and their threats. As the division of responsibilities amongst the forces trying to end the occupation was ill defined, and as the coordination of their activities was badly handled, it became clear that, given the widely anticipated growth of international terrorism at that time, a more organised response to future terrorist attacks was necessary.

In the Netherlands, the police perform two main functions: first, they exercise a judicial function in tracing and arresting perpetrators of crimes and, second, they are responsible for the maintenance of public order. Authority for carrying out the judicial function lies with the regional public prosecutor who is responsible for the police when they trace and arrest criminals. The mayor of a town in which there is an infringement of public order is charged with commanding the police when they try to restore order. When hostages are taken during terrorist incidents, the police are called on to perform both their functions. The question arises as to what is the chain of command in these instances. Is the public prosecutor or the mayor to exercise command? Responsibility for conducting anti-terrorist activities has been given to the public prosecutor, with ultimate responsibility for their deployment resting with the Minister of Justice. This judicial solution has been criticised by those who have argued that in terrorist situations the maintenance of public order — specifically the safeguarding of hostages — should receive priority.[28]

In each instance since 1970 in which hostages have been taken, two decision-making centres have been immediately established. At the local level, a policy centre has been established manned by, amongst others, the provincial governor, the mayor(s) of the townships or territories in which the terrorist action took place, the chief commissioner of the local police or the district commissioner of the state police, the Attorney General of The Hague, and the regional public prosecutor concerned. Also attached to each policy centre have been consultants (including medical officers and psychiatrists) and commanders of the military police and marine corps. At the national level, a crisis centre has been established in The Hague, which has supervised the policy centre. Among the members of the crisis centre have been ministers of Interior and Justice; in the past, prime ministers have also been closely involved with the activities of the crisis centre.[29]

Attention must also be given to legal aspects of the fight against terrorism. The Dutch legal system has two special laws that can be used in exceptional circumstances: the *oorlogswet* (war law), which provides for the transfer of powers from civilian to military authorities, and the *Wet Buitengewone Bevoegdheden Burgerlijk Gezag* (law concerning the special competences of civil authorities). The latter can be used in situations where the constitutional order and existence of the nation are menaced by rebellion, or where serious threats to public order exist or are threatened. It grants the civil authorities exceptional powers, such as restricting the freedom of the press, searching houses and individuals and imprisoning people where there is a suspicion that they are a threat to the public order. To date, neither of these laws has been used in the fight against terrorism, although the provincial governor of North Holland — who has participated in several local policy centres — has stated that the government has exercised the powers provided under them in previous terrorist situations.[30] However, the government's legal basis in, for example, searching for weapons in the South Moluccan residential area in Assen in 1977 without formally invoking the special competences law, has been challenged by some legal experts.[31]

In a number of Western European countries (for example, Greece, West Germany, Italy and the United Kingdom), anti-terrorist legislation has been introduced to provide a judicial defence for the liberal—democratic state. While such laws restrict the freedoms and civil rights of terrorists, they have the same effects on innocent civilians: perhaps the best known example of this is West Germany's controversial *Berufsverbot*.[32] Although anti-terrorist legislation has not been introduced in the Netherlands to date, two proposals — the European Convention on the Suppression of Terrorism and an arms and ammunition law are at present under discussion. The European Convention is subject to criticism mainly on the grounds that the Dutch legal system can be overruled by the systems of less democratic states. At the time of writing (June 1979) the convention is being considered by an advisory committee of the government. When the committee has given its opinion on the measure, parliament will decide whether or not to ratify it.

The arms and ammunition law — which has received initial parliamentary consideration — is designed to give the civil authorities special powers to search houses, luggage, boats, etc. in cases where there is a reasonable suspicion that arms and ammunition are illegally possessed. It gives such powers not only to the police, but also to customs officers and to controllers of dangerous materials. Although the proposed law has been introduced to harmonise Dutch legislation with that of its Benelux partners,[33] the government has admitted — in an explanatory memorandum attached to the proposal — that there are no deficiencies in existing laws.[34] The measure has also come under criticism because of the wide range of powers given to the authorities, and also because of the difficulties involved in ascertaining where 'reasonable suspicion' exists. The question must also be posed whether the benefits of legislative harmony are greater than the curtailment of civil liberties that the legislation will entail if it is passed.

CONCLUSIONS

From our analysis of South Moluccan terrorism in the Netherlands a number of conclusions can be drawn. During the period of South Moluccan terrorism, four factors have remained constant. First, the Dutch government has refused to accede to any of the terrorists' main demands. In each of the three outbreaks of terrorism, the government maintained an uncompromising attitude to blackmail while at the same time preserving the well-being of hostages. Over and above agreeing on mediators and supplying food, medicines and a limited amount of material goods necessary to alleviate the plight of the hostages, the sole concession that the government has made was at the end of the Indonesian consulate siege in 1975, when it agreed to hold a meeting subsequently with representatives of the South Moluccan community.

Second, the government has not taken up the South Moluccan cause in the international arena; in fact it has not changed its policies towards Indonesia in any way at all. On 26 January 1978, the government presented a declaration to parliament stating that 'for judicial, historical and political reasons' the Netherlands could not 'recognise or support an autonomous South Moluccan republic'.[35] This unequivocally and unambiguously deprived the South Moluccans of their sole major ally in reclaiming the islands from Indonesia. The Deputy Prime Minister and Interior Minister, Mr Hans Wiegel, stated that the government would continue to respect the South Moluccans' right to their traditions, religion and language, and, if the South Moluccans so wished, would continue to integrate them into Dutch society.[36] Parliament decided that the Dutch and Indonesian governments should play an active part in solving the South Moluccans' political problems. This was not, however, to damage Dutch—Indonesian relations.[37]

Third, the South Moluccans have failed to win support for themselves. Unlike the Palestinians and the Namibians, their struggle for independence has not won them the sympathy of major international powers, or public opinion, or even the support of the 'puppeteers of international terrorism' such as Libya or Algeria. In Laqueur's words, 'They are the proletariat of the terrorist world.'[38]

Finally, the Indonesian government has been resolutely immovable over both the terrorists' general demands for an independent South Moluccan republic and their specific demands (meetings with President Suharto, the release of 'political prisoners', etc.) to achieve this. Similarly, it has steadfastly maintained that the problem of South Moluccan terrorism in the Netherlands is the responsibility of the Netherlands, not Indonesia.

While the above things have not changed as a result of South Moluccan terrorism, others have. First, while in 1975 the original South Moluccan terrorists' demands were explicitly directed to bringing about an independent RMS — a United Nations debate on the issue, a meeting between the Indonesian government and the South Moluccan government-in-exile, etc. — those of their 'successors' in 1977 and 1978 have had a different focus — freeing their 'comrades' (convicted in 1975) from jail and escaping with them from the Netherlands. The nationalist focus of the terrorism has radically changed over this period: terrorism by South Moluccans metamorphosed into terrorism by South Moluccans for other South Moluccans.

Second, the government has changed its social, cultural and economic policies towards the South Moluccan community, establishing a permanent forum for dialogue, and provided extra assistance in the housing, occupation and education fields. Whether the government policies in these areas, and changes in them, have been a cause, effect or mitigating influence on South Moluccan terrorism is not our concern here; suffice it to note that they have not been unconnected with it.

Finally, the way in which the government has dealt with terrorists has also changed. In 1975, the train and consulate gunmen were 'talked out' after a lengthy siege. In 1977, the tactics changed: even longer sieges were ended by a military operation. In 1978, the occupation of the provincial government offices was also ended by a military operation, but after a comparatively short time. Over this period, the 'Dutch approach', involving psychiatrists talking out terrorists in sieges, was replaced by a military solution similar to that employed by anti-terrorist squads in the FRG and Israel.

As we have shown above, unlike terrorist groups in many other countries, the aims of South Moluccan terrorists have not been to overthrow the state; rather they have been to focus public attention on their cause, and to get the Dutch government to exert pressure on their behalf in the international arena and honour its earlier commitment to an independent RMS. In the face of intransigent Indonesian policy towards their people, the Dutch 'betrayal' of their cause and public indifference to their plight and ignorance of their circumstances, South Moluccan terrorists hoped that a combination of concerned public opinion and Dutch political and diplomatic action would lead to the realisation of the RMS. This has not happened. The Indonesian government's attitude towards the South Moluccans is still negative; the Dutch government no longer sympathises with their cause; the public has by now become hostile to them; the international community is deaf to their pleas; and the South Moluccans in the Moluccas are indifferent to the plight of their former countrypeople. The South Moluccans have become nationalists without a nation.

What the consequences of this are must remain unclear. The demise of terrorist activity will not follow from an awareness that an independent RMS is an unrealisable ideal. What is more likely is that their terrorism will continue in pursuit of less South Moluccan-specific ideals. If the focus of South Moluccan activism shifts from pursuit of the RMS to a more radical critique of capitalist society, South Moluccans will come into closer contact with terrorist groups espousing anti-colonialist, anti-imperialist and nationalist ideals than they have to date. This will have the effect of internationalising South Moluccan terrorism, at the same time channelling its original force into different directions.

Notes and References

1. See R. van der Laan Bouma and J. Wiersma, Terrorisme en burgerlijke grondrechten. *Civis Mundi, 17* (1978) pp. 210–15; and also P. Wilkinson, *Terrorism and the Liberal State* (London: Macmillan, 1977), esp. p. 49.
2. For the history of what is now the Republic of Indonesia, see: D. Woodman, *The Republic of Indonesia* (London: The Cresset Press, 1955); L. Fisher, *The Story of Indonesia* (London: Hamish Hamilton, 1959); H. Soebadio and C. A.

du Marchie Sarvaas (eds), *Dynamics of Indonesian History* (Amsterdam: North-Holland, 1978). Works specialised on the history of the Moluccas include: H. J. de Graaf, *De geschiedenis van Ambon en de Zuid-Molukken* (Franeker: Wever, 1977); B. van Kaam, *Ambon door de eeuwen heen* (Baarn: In den Toren, 1977); T. Pollmann and J. Seleky, *Een gouden regen in den vreemde; kleine Molukse geschiedenis* (Amsterdam: Bijvoegsel Vrij Nederland no. 35, 1978); E. Utrecht, *Ambon; kolonisatie, dekolonisatie en neo-kolonisatie* (Amsterdam: Van Gennep, 1972).

3. Sukarno and Hatta had been very active in nationalist movements in Indonesia. In 1927 Sukarno founded the Indonesian Nationalist Party. Both Sukarno and Hatta spent long periods in prison until they were released by the Japanese in 1942. Sukarno became the first president and Hatta the first vice-president of the 'Republic of Indonesia'.

4. For these developments, see: De problematiek van de Molukse minderheid in Nederland. *Handelingen 1977—1978,* 14915 no. 2, appendix 1, pp. 70—126; A. and H. Algra, *Dispereert niet* (Franeker: Wever, n.d.), part 5, pp. 169—242.

5. Department of Information Service of the Republic of the South Moluccas, 'Confrontation with a quarter of a century of discrimination of the South Moluccan right of self-determination' (Eindhoven, 1975), p. 32.

6. T. Wittermans and N.P. Gist, The Ambonese nationalist movement in the Netherlands: A study in status deprivation. *Social Forces, 40* (1962), pp.309—17, at p. 312.

7. Nipo, press release, no. 648 (February 1954).

8. The Verwey-Jonker Committee (named after its chairperson) was set up on 24 September 1957 by the Minister of Social Work to study problems concerning the South Moluccans. Its report ('Ambonezen in Nederland', April 1959) had a great influence on Dutch policy towards South Moluccans.

9. *Social and Cultural Report, 1976* (The Hague: Staatsuitgeverij, 1977) p. 219.

10. J. Persijn, Uit de schaduw van het verleden, legende en realiteit van het Molukse vraagstuk. *Internationale Spectator, 30* (1976) pp. 103—10, J.E. Ellemers, Minderheden en beleid in Nederland: Molukkers en andere catagorieën alloctonen in vergelijkend perspectief. *Transaktie, 7* (1978) pp. 20—40.

11. K. Bais, Het rommelt in de Zuid-Molukse jeugdbewegingen. *Jeugdwerk nu, 9* (24 August 1977) pp. 4—5.

12. L. Macfarlane, *Violence and The State* (London: Nelson, 1974), p. 26.

13. Department of Information service of the RMS, *op. cit.,* pp. 29—30.

14. For a detailed description of the events, see: Gebeurtenissen rond de treinkaping te Beilen en de overval op het Indonesische consulaat-generaal te Amsterdam. *Handelingen 1975—76* 13756, no. 1—4; De Gijzelingen in Bovensmilde en Vries. *Handelingen 1977—1978,* 14610, no. 1—2; Gijzelingen Assen 13—14 maart 1978 (The Hague: Rijksvoorlichtingsdienst afd. interne voorlichting, 1978); Gijzeling Assen 13—14 maart 1978. *Handelingen 1977—1978,* 14968.

15. *The Times* (London), 3 December 1975.

16. *The Times* (London), 15 June 1977.

17. *Ibid.,* 15 March 1978.

18. Nipo, press release, no. 1749 (9 January 1976).

19. Nipo, press release no. 1851 (24 June 1977); press release, no. 1852 (28 June 1977).

20. Nipo, press release, no. 1853 (1 July 1977); Bureau Lagendijk 'Enige meningen over de gijzelingen' (7 July 1977).

21. For a comparative analysis of public opinion towards terrorist groups see:

V. Herman and R. van der Laan Bouma 'Martyrs, murderers or something else? Terrorism in the Netherlands, the United Kingdom and the Federal Republic of Germany' (unpublished manuscript, Erasmus University).
22. *The Times* (London), 27 March 1976.
23. *Keesings Contemporary Archive,* 28 May 1976, p. 27756.
24. Earlier, the Chief of Police of Groningen had pointed to the possibility that in extreme cases in the fight against terrorism a policeman could receive the command shoot to kill (inauguration speech K. Heijink, 19 January 1973). See L. van Haaren, De overheid en het Terrorisme. *Algemeen Politieblad* (16 June 1973), pp. 279—82.
25. The letter in which the Prime Minister announced these measures to parliament is known as the 'Terreurbrief', 22 February 1973 (*Handelingen* 12000, no. 11).
26. See: P. van Reenen, *Overheidsgeweld, een sociologische studie van de dynamiek van het geweldsmonopolie* (Alphen aan den Rijn: Samsom, 1979).
27. See: Inzet lange-afstand-schutters is uiterste maatregel als alle andere middelen gefaald hebben. *De Nederlandse Gemeente* (April 1973) pp. 185—7.
28. See: J.J.H. Pop, Herstel van orde en veiligheid bij terroristische acties primair. *De Nederlandse Gemeente* (20 April 1973) pp. 181—4; L. van Haaren, *op. cit.,* p. 280; and A.R. Haakmat, De bestrijding van terreuracties, juridische en polemologische visies vergeleken. *Intermediar* (25 November 1977).
29. For an impression of the functioning of these centres and the relations between them, see: F.J. Kranenburg, Gijzeling, rechtsorde, openbare orde. *Algemeen Politieblad* (10 April 1976) pp. 195—201.
30. *Ibid.,* p. 196.
31. See: *Sociaal en Cultureel Rapport 1978* (The Hague: Staatsuitgeverij, 1978), p. 165; and G.E. Langemeijer, Terrorisme, uitlevering, asyl. *Socialisme en Democratie* (March 1978) pp. 111—21.
32. In official language the 'Radikalen-Erlass' of 28 January 1972. For information about the West German situation, see M. Blank, *et al., Wohin treibt der Rechtsstaat?* (Berlin: Pahl Rugenstein, 1977).
33. C.P.A. Aler, De politiebevoegdheden in het wetsontwerp wapens en munitie. *Delikt en Delinkwent, 7* (1977), pp. 433—50.
34. *Handelingen 1976—1977,* 14.413, no. 3, p. 20.
35. *Keesings Contemporary Archive* 4 August 1978, p. 29121.
36. *Ibid.*
37. *Trouw,* 30 May 1978. A motion, which parliament did not approve, wanted the Dutch government to bring the South Moluccan case before the United Nations.
38. W. Lacqueur 'Terrorism — a balance sheet', in W. Lacqueur (ed.), *The Terrorism Reader: A Historical Anthology* (New York: Signet, 1978), pp. 251—66, at p. 259.

CHAPTER 6

Terrorism in Northern Ireland: the Case of the Provisional IRA

E. Moxon-Browne

INTRODUCTION

A leading exponent of the concept of 'political terrorism' has argued that it is characterised, above all, by 'amorality and antinomianism'.[1] In other words, the political terrorist regards himself as exempt from existing moral codes because the political goals he seeks to achieve justify the methods he uses. It follows, therefore, that in many cases an act of political terrorism will be arbitrary, indiscriminate and unpredictable to those who are its actual or potential victims.

However careful we are in defining terrorism or terrorists we cannot escape making something of a subjective judgement. It is because someone is 'terrorised' by an act that the act itself becomes a terrorist act and its perpetrator a terrorist. Yet an element of randomness or unpredictability is a vital ingredient in the definition, too, since the timid driver who is 'terrified' when the policeman produces a notebook, does not automatically regard the policeman as a terrorist! Legitimacy is another ingredient, albeit subjective, in our judgement of whether someone is a terrorist. The familiar argument as to whether a certain group are 'terrorists' or 'liberation fighters' revolves around the perceived legitimacy of the group in question. The distinction between terrorism and guerrilla warfare can become blurred in the public mind when efforts are made by the state to discredit the guerrillas by calling them terrorists.

In the light of these preliminary remarks, it is not easy to label the Provisional IRA (PIRA) as a terrorist group and leave it at that. The IRA has waged a campaign of intermittent violence in Ireland for about sixty years. Its resilience and longevity, if nothing else, make it exceptional in European terms. But its view of itself as 'the legitimate Republic' and its belief that the Dublin government (to say nothing of British rule in Northern Ireland) is a gross usurpation, distinguish it sharply from other subversive groups in Europe like ETA, the Brigate Rosse, the Baader—Meinhof and the South Moluccans, none of whom can lay claim to the sort of ancestry that purports to make them the true repository of the nation's honour. And it is easier to describe these European groups as terroristic since their campaigns tend to be spasmodic, irrational and, apparently, devoid of widespread support. The IRA, on the other hand, displays some of the characteristics of a guerrilla movement, and it is instructive to reflect on Wilkinson's distinction between 'guerrillas' and 'terrorists':

> Guerrillas may fight in small numbers and with often inadequate weaponry, but they can and often do fight according to conventions of war, taking and exchanging prisoners and respecting the rights of non-combatants. Terrorists place no limits on means employed and frequently resort to widespread assassination, the waging of 'general terror' upon the indigenous civilian population . . .[2]

The present campaign of the PIRA does not fall wholly into either of these categories. Certainly, even those most hostile to the PIRA find no difficulty in seeing their campaign as essentially a guerrilla campaign;[3] and certainly the PIRA sees itself as an 'army' fighting a war against an alien power in order to achieve national liberation. However, if we return to Wilkinson's conception of 'political terrorism',[4] we find that the PIRA campaign falls quite easily into his third category, which he calls 'revolutionary terrorism' (the other two being 'repressive terrorism' and 'sub-revolutionary terrorism'), whose main characteristics are:

> Always a group phenomenon, however tiny the group, with a leadership and an ideology or programme, however crude. Develops alternative institutional structures. The organisation of violence and terrorism is typically undertaken by specialist conspiratorial and paramilitary organs within the revolutionary movement.[5]

Even if it is accepted that the PIRA indulges in a form of 'revolutionary terrorism' as described here, the tactics are classic guerrilla tactics. The PIRA is unusual in engaging in both rural and urban guerrilla warfare with equal success, although in the current campaign the emphasis is on the urban areas and, even outside those areas, there is a tendency to concentrate on the dislocation of inter-urban communications. The theorists of guerrilla warfare argue the merits of rural and urban campaigns[6] but, for the IRA, the memories of the desolate border campaign of 1956—62 are probably enough to settle the argument.

In sum, then, although the term 'terrorist' is widely used to describe the PIRA, especially in Northern Ireland, it is important to keep in mind the differences between the PIRA and other groups in Europe that are similarly described. The term 'terrorist' has obvious pejorative overtones and is a natural weapon in the armoury of the state as it seeks to discredit its opponents. The 'criminalisation' of a campaign that is, to some extent, politically inspired is a theme I shall return to later because it is part of the battle for legitimacy between the state and those who wish to overturn the state.

DEVELOPMENT OF PIRA

The origins of the PIRA lie in the split of the IRA into two wings in 1969—70 over tactics. This split arose from a growing divergence of views over the appropriate response to the civil rights campaign in the North. The Official IRA (OIRA), as it became known, had been strongly influenced by the aims of the civil rights campaign, and also by the need to tackle problems like unemployment, bad housing, and so on, in the South. The virtual abandonment of the Catholic ghettoes to face Protestant attackers in 1969—70, and the taunting gable-end slogans 'IRA = I Ran Away' that followed, marked the parting of the ways. The OIRA called a cease-fire in 1972, but the PIRA went over to the offensive and, except for some short-lived 'cease-fires', have held the initiative ever since.

To understand the stance of the PIRA since 1972, it is useful to recapitulate, however briefly, the earlier history of the IRA from which the present PIRA considers itself to be a direct descendant.[7] In general terms, the IRA was born out of the struggle to rid Ireland of British rule. In 1916, the first attempt to establish a thirty-two-county republic had failed. The 1920 Government of Ireland Act, which gave the predominantly Protestant six north-eastern counties their own parliament, was regarded by the IRA as a betrayal of the nationalist cause. This sense of betrayal was expressed in a brief, but bitter, campaign of violence. On 7 January 1922, the Dail narrowly accepted, by 64 votes to 57, a Treaty that gave dominion status to the new twenty-six-county Free State. Links with Britain that remained, and stuck in the throats of the anti-Treaty Sinn Fein ('Ourselves Alone') party, included a Governor-General, an oath to the Crown for members of the Dail (TD's), and some concessions to Britain over military bases. Sinn Fein, under de Valera, contested the 1923 elections but refused to take up its seats on the grounds that the institutions of the Free State were illegitimate. However, finding this abstentionism unproductive, de Valera formed the Fianna Fail ('Soldiers of Destiny') party in 1926. The new party consisted of those who, although essentially opposed to the Treaty settlement, had decided to follow de Valera's pragmatic *volte-face* and participate in the Free State institutions. In the 1927 elections, the new party won forty-four seats, entered the Dail, but refused to take the Oath. In the meantime, the IRA continued to wage an intermittent campaign of violence against the fledgling State, and this led to the passing of special legislation: the Public Safety Act in 1923, and the Juries Protection Act in 1929.

Continuing violence from the IRA in the 1930s was a constant reminder that it claimed to represent the 'real Republic', a claim that still found some sympathy among the public at large. After 1932, when de Valera formed his first government, the IRA was further emasculated by a policy of absorption. The Special Branch became staffed by ex-IRA men; and a volunteer militia was set up to give potential IRA members regular pay and a uniform to wear. As Bowyer Bell puts it: 'Old grievances were transformed into new loyalties to the government.'[8] On the constitutional side, de Valera endeavoured to create something resembling the 'real Republic': the Governor-General was replaced by an obscure Fianna Fail politician; land annuities were no longer paid to the British government; and, in 1937, a new constitution omitted any mention of the Crown and defined the national territory as the thirty-two counties. This policy of mollifying the IRA could not be carried much further, and it still failed to satisfy hard-core Republicans who sought an end to partition — something that de Valera himself recognised could not be achieved by force.

Thus, by 1939, the IRA had been partly crushed and partly absorbed into Fianna Fail. The war, however, gave the IRA the chance to harass Britain over the question of partition and a campaign was launched in Britain that culminated in an incident in Coventry where five people died and sixty were injured. At the same time, de Valera cracked down harder on the IRA in Ireland. The Offences Against the State Act was passed in 1939; military tribunals tried IRA suspects, hundreds of whom were interned in the Curragh. By the end of the war, the IRA was seriously weakened by this constant harassment and its principal *raison d'être*, the problem of partition, showed no sign of being resolved.

Fianna Fail showed that it sympathised with the aspirations of the IRA, if not with its methods, when it mounted an international publicity campaign on the partition issue in the postwar period. In 1948, a coalition government took office consisting of Fine Gael ('Tribe of Gaels'), the party that had accepted the Treaty in 1922 and consequently suffered from a conservative and pro-Commonwealth image, and Clann na Poblachta ('Family of the Republic'), an ephemeral party founded in 1948 and advocating a strong blend of Republicanism and social reform. This Inter-Party Government, as it was known, took Ireland out of the Commonwealth with the Republic of Ireland Act (1949) in the hope that the ghost of the 'real Republic' might cease to haunt the political landscape. But, precisely because measures like these did nothing to erode the partition of Ireland, an IRA guerrilla campaign flared in the border areas from 1956 until 1962. This campaign was dealt with by governments North and South according to a pattern that was now well established: internment, some censorship, and special judicial procedures. Once again, by the late 1960s the IRA appeared to be totally shattered. North—South relations had rarely been as amicable and, consequently, partition had ceased to be a burning issue.

In 1968, a totally new chapter in the history of the IRA was ushered in — a chapter that is still far from closed. The concentration of power in the hands of the Unionist Party since 1921 had led to a certain complacency in its own ranks and growing dissatisfaction among the Catholic minority with its virtual exclusion from meaningful political activity. The civil rights protest marches, which started peacefully enough, were quickly perceived by Loyalists as attempts to subvert the state in Northern Ireland. Clashes with the police became so serious that, in August 1969, the British army had to intervene; and its increasing presence thereafter testified to the rapidly deteriorating situation: 3000 troops in 1969, 13,000 in 1970, and 21,000 in 1972. Although the army came initially to protect the Catholic ghettoes, goodwill soon turned to hostility as the burden of the military presence intensified in the minority areas. The low point undoubtedly came when internment without trial was introduced in August 1971. This measure, which was aimed almost exclusively at Catholics, proved to be largely ineffective since many active terrorists succeeded in eluding the 'sweep' and many moderate Catholics became further alienated from the institutions of the state. The IRA had already claimed its first killing of a British soldier on 6 February 1971, and the violence that preceded internment continued unabated thereafter. Bombings became a part of everyday life. Describing the variety of bombs that terrorists can use, Clutterbuck covers almost all the IRA tactics:

> The terrorist bomb may be posted in a letter or a parcel; it may be put in a shopping bag, with a time fuse, in a pub, a bus-station or a tourist centre like the Tower of London, and left to blow up indiscriminately whoever may be there. It may be left in a suitcase or carton in a station baggage room, in the baggage compartment of a public building. It may be locked in the boot of a car; or it may simply be a booby trap to be set off by any simple action, such as opening a door or treading on a floorboard.[9]

On 21 July 1972, twenty-two bombs exploded in Belfast, killing nine people and injuring over a hundred. In August 1976, the British ambassador in Dublin was killed when a landmine blew up his car; and a similar device was used to kill four men from the Royal Ulster Constabulary (RUC) near Bessbrook (Co. Armagh) in early 1979. In August of the same year, Lord Mountbatten died when his yacht was blown up off the coast of Co. Sligo. Besides bombs, snipers have taken a steady toll of soldiers, policemen and civilians. But by no means all the killing has been done by the PIRA. In January 1972, British paratroopers killed thirteen men in Londonderry during a civil rights march (Bloody Sunday) and, in early 1978, a group of men were shot dead while planting bombs at Ballysillan Post Office (in Belfast). Moreover, there have been numerous 'tit-for-tat' assassinations both within and between the two communities in Northern Ireland, not least among the various Protestant paramilitary groups (e.g. Ulster Defence

Association, Ulster Volunteer Force, Ulster Freedom Fighters, etc.).

The worsening security situation after 1969 led inexorably to greater British involvement in the Province. Not only was military assistance stepped up, as has been indicated, but the British government tried to impress on the Stormont government the need for various concessions to minority demands. When these reforms proved to be too little and too late, the British government resumed direct responsibility for the Province under the Northern Ireland (Temporary Provisions) Act, which was passed in March 1972. This Act suspended the Stormont government and its powers became vested in a Secretary of State for Northern Ireland while the twelve MPs continued to represent the Province at Westminster. This system of government, known as 'direct rule' to distinguish it from the devolved government it replaced, has been in operation ever since (except for the brief spell of 'power-sharing' government between January and May 1974).

The position of the Republic's government has been difficult throughout this latest PIRA campaign since the killings have been largely confined to Northern Ireland. Although the Irish government was obviously concerned with the plight of Catholics in the North, there was little direct help that could be given to 'our people'. This feeling of frustration was most intense in the wake of the Bloody Sunday deaths. For many people in the South, the IRA had the same concern as the government for the welfare of the Catholic ghettoes, but whereas the government could only make vain promises ('we will not stand idly by'), the IRA was seen to be doing something on the ground. It was not difficult for government ministers in the South to applaud secretly the defensive role of the IRA in the North while publicly condemning violence. The apparent ambivalence of the Irish government has stemmed largely from a sense of helplessness at not being able to influence events in an area where they have no jurisdiction. Conor Cruise O'Brien captures this mood:

> Mr Lynch condemned violence, indeed he did. He also said that 'violence is a by-product of the division of the country'. This seemed to imply that violence would go on as long as partition did, and that those who were responsible for the violence, which Mr Lynch so unfailingly condemned, were those who maintained that partition. Did this imply that the IRA, though a little hot-headed, perhaps, were by and large right?[10]

A similar ambivalence runs through Irish attitudes towards the IRA. Many more people are prepared to tolerate the IRA than actively support it, although few would say so publicly. (The Northern Ireland Attitude Survey of 1978 found that 46 per cent of Catholics and 35 per cent of Protestants agreed that the IRA are 'patriots and idealists'; and the same survey found that 33 per cent of Catholics and 12 per cent of Protestants concurred with the view that 'But for the IRA the problem [of Northern Ireland] would be further from solution'.) In many rural communities in Ireland it is still true that a certain emotional satisfaction is derived from having a known IRA man living in the neighbourhood; and people will do good turns for him even though they publicly disown his methods, and even his aims. This rather schizophrenic attitude towards the IRA stems largely from the complex concatenation of ideas that constitute Republican 'ideology'.

THE IDEOLOGY

'Ideology' may be rather a grandiose term to ascribe to the network of tactics and goals that underlies the PIRA's campaign at the present time. Not only are short-term aims and long-term goals difficult to distinguish, but Republicanism, like any nationalist ideology, weaves together the divergent threads of argument into a messy tapestry. The leitmotiv running through all Republican thought is hostility to the presence of British influence, in any shape or form, in Ireland. But, beyond that, there has been continual disagreement as to how the British presence should be faced. The internal feuding endemic in the Republican movement revolves around 'collabora-tive' and 'triumphalist' strategies — a dichotomy that has now hardened into the split between the OIRA and the PIRA. But this is merely the latest fission: there is no doubt that the 'Republican' strategy of Irish governments, particularly under de Valera, went a long way towards siphoning off much support for the IRA, with the result that the great mass of the population is content with 'half a loaf'.

The resilience of the IRA as a viable movement has puzzled and fascinated observers. There can be few movements in Europe that have shown such powers of survival for over half a century. This is not easy to explain, but one reason for it must be the variety of ideological currents that have been subsumed under the Republican banner. Like a typical 'nationalist' movement, Republicanism has managed to attract adherents from a wide social spectrum — soldiers, scholars, workers — and to include (although uneasily) fascist and socialist tendencies within its ranks.

The major split between the OIRA and the PIRA is sometimes rather superficially classified as a split between the right and the left, but this is something of an oversimplification. The PIRA advocacy of 'national liberation' before 'national socialism' is diametrically opposed to the OIRA strategy of winning over working-class support in both the Republic and the North before pushing for unification.

But, in the meantime, the initiative belongs to the PIRA; and the British presence in Northern Ireland is the *casus belli*. This presence is nothing new, although 'direct rule' arguably makes it more manifest, and the implications of that presence are now perceived more clearly. The PIRA campaign is based on the supposition that a substantial part of the Catholic working class survives in conditions of chronic 'repression'. These conditions are seen to be a direct result of the existence of a sectarian six-county state underwritten by British force. The PIRA claims to have a mission to free the Catholic working class from various injustices, which British rule has done nothing to rectify. In other words, the aspirations awakened by the civil rights movement offered the IRA a new opportunity after a period in the doldrums. As Bowyer Bell puts it:

> By 1962 many others had long since faded away in despair, in disgrace or in dudgeon. The Army [i.e. the IRA] was a husk — its strength eroded, its purpose lost, its future unclear.[11]

The rejuvenation of the IRA in its Provisional guise after 1969 was related to the experiences and the perceptions of the Catholic population in the North. It became plausible for the PIRA's apologists to argue that it was needed as a defence force for the Catholic ghettoes against the incursions of British army raiding parties and Loyalist gunmen. Support for the PIRA in such areas (e.g. Ballymurphy, Turf Lodge) fluctuates according to how the conduct of the security forces is perceived at any particular time. To 'lift' suspects, the army has to conduct searches and 'screen' civilians over a wide area. Inevitably, such searches may be humiliating, distasteful, even violent, but not necessarily so. To some of the people living in these areas, it may on occasion be difficult to distinguish between the 'lawlessness' of the IRA and the 'lawlessness' of soldiers who, under vague and sweeping legislation, combine the roles of policeman, judge and executioner. Thus a participant-observer in a Belfast ghetto writes:

> Soldiers not only apprehend and detain suspects, they beat them. They interrogate with illegal methods ranging from ill-treatment to torture. They wreak vengeance for their dead comrades.[12]

Alienation from the state in Northern Ireland is bound to be exacerbated if those who purport to serve the state fall below its own proclaimed standards of impartiality. Such alienation is the lifeblood of PIRA recruitment. Widespread cynicism results when allegations of brutality involving the security forces are either ignored by the authorities or 'whitewashed' in an official enquiry. And, as Boyle *et al.* point out, the use of judges to chair such enquiries does not remove them from the arena of political controversy, it simply taints the judicial system with political bias.

Support for the PIRA tends to be more constant when it confines itself to defensive operations. The offensive role is much more controversial since it invites retaliation by the security forces in the very areas the PIRA claims to protect. Indeed, it is sometimes argued that the PIRA itself generates the conditions that justify its continuing campaign. As for their offensive operations in rural areas, the PIRA has argued that these are a way of distracting the British army's attention from the Catholic ghettoes. Such guerrilla operations also inflict casualties on the security forces in a way that is calculated to sap morale among the troops themselves and sow seeds of doubt in the minds of the British public.

The resilience of the PIRA in the face of the forces ranged against it is explained by the reservoir of passive support it enjoys. The image of a small band of ruthless criminals holding a cowering population to ransom is a comforting illusion, but it has little to do with reality. While the PIRA argues that 'repression' can only be ended by expelling Britain and uniting Ireland, this long-term goal is probably less attractive than the resolution of short-term grievances within Northern Ireland. Thus the key to the elimination of violence lies not with a purely military strategy but with the creation of a political atmosphere in which the PIRA would become virtually redundant, and where tacit support would be transformed into outright rejection.

A major focus of allegiance among Catholics is the Church. One indication of the strength of this allegiance is the effort made by the PIRA to reconcile its own activities with the doctrines of the Church. Traditionally, of course, the Roman Catholic hierarchy has given short shrift in public to the IRA. The local priests deprecate the violence of the PIRA but without condemning their long-term goal. The PIRA response to intrusions from the Church is either to argue that political and religious matters should be kept separate (i.e. that priests should mind their own business) or to justify their campaign in quasi-religious terms. Thus:

> The Provisionals argue they can be good Catholics by appealing to the ultimate sanctity of the conscience. They strive to make a distinction between religious and political dogma and they reserve the right to use violence in a just war.[13]

The Catholic Church has generally taken the line that government security forces should be supported provided they behave within the law. Thus, while many priests privately aspire to a thirty-two-county Ireland, they do not condone the use of violence to achieve it. However, the Church has been careful not to alienate its own supporters by turning a blind eye to a more insidious form of violence — that practised by the state. In a joint statement in 1971 the Catholic bishops in Northern Ireland condemned all violence as being 'contrary to the law of Christ' and alluded to 'some particularly cold-blooded murders in recent weeks'. They then went on to condemn:

> . . . another form of violence which is also shameful and contrary to the law of Christ. We refer to the process known as 'interrogation in depth' as it has been practised in Northern Ireland in recent months. Men have been kept hooded and standing, with arms and legs outstretched . . . These were men who had been imprisoned without trial . . . The solution to our present tragic situation will never be found in violence or counter-violence.[14]

One is often asked for what sort of Ireland the PIRA is fighting. The ordinary member of an Active Service Unit is not politically sophisticated. He may believe he is fighting for the end of British rule in Ireland or for a 'thirty-two-county Republic' but, beyond that, the political planning has been left to Provisional Sinn Fein (PSF) which is the political wing of the PIRA, and is not a proscribed organisation either in the Republic or in Northern Ireland. From the point of view of the state, the existence of PSF is important since it allows for some sort of communication with the PIRA without too much political embarrassment. PSF and the PIRA view themselves as the 'civil' and 'military' wings, respectively, of the Republican movement in which they play equal and complementary roles, although, in fact, the major decisions relating to military and political matters tend to be taken by the Army Council within the PIRA.

Eire Nua, or the 'new Ireland' envisaged by PSF, would be based on a federation of the four historic provinces — Ulster, Connacht, Leinster and Munster. The federal capital would be located in Athlone but substantial powers would be reserved to the four provincial parliaments of which one, Dail Uladh (the parliament of Ulster), would have a Protestant majority. Below the provincial level, power would be further delegated to regions and, below them, to the *pobol* (district councils for communities of 10,000—40,000 people). Thus Eire Nua would be *pobol pobol* — a community of communities. The economic aspects of the New Ireland would also be fundamentally different: the nationalisation of key industries; the severing of foreign control; departure from the EEC; and the greater exploitation of Ireland's 'natural resources'. Culturally the Irish language would become predominant. In foreign affairs links would be forged with the Third World.

The whole complexion of this political and economic programme is a studied repudiation of the major influences on the Irish economy and political system in the twentieth century. The economic programme rejects the 'modernising' forces of foreign investment, which have tied Ireland so closely to Britain and to Europe. The political programme rejects the high degree of centralisation that characterised British rule before partition and government in both parts of Ireland thereafter.

In the meantime, however, PSF has two main concerns: to end British rule in Ireland, and to secure an amnesty for all political prisoners. Prisoners have always played an important part in Republican tradition. The escapes, the hunger strikes, the martyrdoms: these have been recurring events that are every bit as important as the achievements on 'active service'. The idea that laws and justice go together has not been readily apparent to IRA men. The law itself has been tarnished in each generation by the actions of 'over-zealous' servants of the state: the Royal Irish Constabulary (the police in Ireland before partition); the Black and Tans (police auxiliaries brought to Ireland in 1920 and dressed incongruously in a mixture of black and khaki uniforms); the B-Specials (an auxiliary, and overwhelmingly Protestant, reserve police force in Ulster from 1922 to 1969); the Paras (British army paratroop regiments). Historical memories are continually revived by modern analogies. Burton cites an example from present-day Belfast:

There are memories like those of old Mrs. Johnson who told me how, as a young girl she had seen a man abducted by the Black and Tans. He was found dead later on in the day. Mrs. Johnson sees the British troops of today in the very same street as latter-day Tans.[15]

Part of the explanation for the long survival of the IRA lies exactly in this repetitiveness — the fact that contemporary events so often evoke vivid and bitter memories that, in themselves, are enough to stiffen resistance and exclude compromise.

This obduracy is very apparent in the current prisoners' protest. Known as the H-blocks protest because of the H-shaped buildings at the Maze prison, the prisoners' action started on 14 September 1976. Just under 400 prisoners, mostly Republican, are refusing to wear prison clothes as part of their campaign to achieve 'political status'. For two reasons, this campaign is of central concern to the PIRA. First, it challenges the state's view that the PIRA campaign is not 'politically motivated'. Second, it is linked in the Republican mind with a string of prison protests stretching back to the 1920s. The release of the first H-blocks' protester, Kieran Nugent, in May 1979 gave the press a chance to hear, at first hand, what the protest involved. Of Kieran Nugent himself, the *Irish Times* wrote:

His background helps to explain the stubborn courage of the H-block prisoners. He comes from a family of 10 in the Lower Falls, Belfast. After a decade of war and generations of neglect this ghetto has become a wasteland. Its people have always known repression and for them a united Ireland represents the prospect of a fair chance in life.[16]

and of the protest in general:

How do they endure these conditions? 'Mind over body' was the clichéd expression. Shared privation has created a sense of solidarity among these tough working class men; they are strengthened by the ministry of their church and by the devotion of relatives and friends . . .[17]

The H-blocks' protest is probably the most burning issue of contention between the state and the PIRA at the present time. Its symbolic value outweighs its material implications both to the protesters and to the government. The government is just as unwilling to reverse its view that 'convicted criminals must be treated as criminals' as the PIRA is to accept the view that they are criminals.

THE RESPONSE OF THE STATE

The division of the island of Ireland into two political units is not only a major grievance for the PIRA, it is also one of the main obstacles to a successful pursuit of the PIRA by the two states concerned. During the sixty years of partition, the activities of the IRA have rarely had a uniform impact in both North and South; perceptions of the IRA have not been similar, nor have the strategies used to tackle IRA violence.

In the period since 1969, it has been Northern Ireland that has borne the brunt of the PIRA's campaign. The existence of two jurisdictions in Ireland has meant that the PIRA has been able to elude security forces in the North by disappearing south of the border. This has led opinion in the North to regard towns like Dundalk and Castleblayney as 'bases' from which the PIRA has been able to launch incursions into the North. No amount of cross-border cooperation can replace the 'right of hot pursuit'; and it is undoubtedly a considerable frustration to the British army in the North that, whereas the great mass of the population (including terrorists) can cross the border quite freely, the army must observe the territorial limits of the Republic most scrupulously.

In the legal sphere, there has been anti-terrorist legislation on the books in both the Republic and Northern Ireland virtually without a break since 1920. Despite the fact that British governments (and Northern Ireland politicians) accuse the South of being a 'haven for terrorists', 'soft on the IRA' and so on, the anti-terrorist legislation in the Republic is probably a greater infringement of civil liberties than is tolerated in any other Western liberal democracy at the present time. In one respect, at least, the PIRA was much worse off in the Republic up to 1974 than it was in the United Kingdom in that it was a proscribed organisation there and, since 1976, the IRA has been denied all publicity through the media — something that is not yet the case in the United Kingdom.

The Republic's main judicial response to subversive organisations like the IRA has been the Offences Against the State Act (1939), which has been amended on more than one occasion since to take account of the current PIRA campaign. In 1972, Part V of the Act was invoked to establish the Special Criminal Court. This consists of an uneven number of judges (usually three) and no jury. The Court is intended to deal with cases where a threat to the state is involved and where there is reason to believe that normal jury trial would not suffice. Except for the lack of a jury, the Court's procedure is supposed to follow that of a normal court. Even so, the Court did not succeed in securing many convictions against the PIRA until the end of 1972 when the Dail passed another amendment, which made it easier to secure such convictions. This amendment placed the onus on an individual to repudiate any published allegation that he was a member of the IRA; failure to do so would be taken as evidence of such membership.[18] Moreover, henceforward, a statement by a senior garda officer that a person is a member of the IRA would be taken as evidence of such membership.[19] The burden of proof, once again, fell on the individual to disprove membership of an illegal organisation. In this respect, the Republic's legislation is more stringent than similar legislation in Northern Ireland. In yet another amendment to the Act in 1976, in the wake of the killing of the British ambassador in Dublin, spokesmen for illegal organisations were not allowed to appear on radio or television, or be quoted in the press. Again, the contrast with British legislation can be noted, since the interview with a spokesman for the Irish National Liberation Army (INLA) on BBC television in mid-1979 would have been illegal in the Republic, although many viewers in the Republic can, in fact, pick up BBC television programmes. (The INLA claimed responsibility for the assassination of Airey Neave, a prominent Conservative MP who was widely expected to be Secretary of State for Northern Ireland in the event of the Conservative party coming to power.)

Needless to say, the rather draconian provisions of the Offences Against the State Act, and its several amendments, have given rise to some concern in the Republic that the normal judicial process, with its protection for the accused, has been seriously jeopardised. This feeling has been exacerbated by the fact that the Special Criminal Court has been used for cases that were not obviously 'political' in nature,[20] although the distinction between 'political' and 'non-political' offences is not one that this Act recognises.[21]

The other piece of legislation worthy of mention is the Criminal Law Jurisdiction Act (1975), which is designed to extend the criminal law to cover crimes committed in Northern Ireland and Britain. A procedure is established whereby a court can obtain evidence from witnesses too frightened to travel for the purpose. A reciprocal Act has been passed in Britain (The Criminal Jurisdiction Act), which makes complementary provisions. This pair of Acts constitutes a rudimentary foundation for the kind of comprehensive legal cooperation that will be needed throughout the British Isles if the full weight of the law is to be felt by any illegal organisations like the PIRA. Even this modest beginning had a difficult passage through the Dail, although its enactment was greatly accelerated by bomb explosions in Dublin streets. The major stumbling block still remaining is the refusal of the Republic to extradite suspects to the United Kingdom for offences that can be regarded as 'political'. The Irish constitution is cited as the reason for this refusal — article 29.3 declares: 'Ireland accepts the generally recognised principles of international law as its rule of conduct in its relations with other States'.

In Northern Ireland, the principal anti-terrorist legislation was the Special Powers Act (1922), which was replaced by the Emergency Provisions Act in 1973. This Act has been amended from time to time since 1973 and the latest consolidated Act dates from 1978. By far the most controversial aspect of emergency legislation has been the power to imprison without trial. In 1975, detention without trial was considerably modified. The power became vested in the Secretary of State to make 'interim custody orders', which were subject to review. The numbers of people detained under the new procedure gradually fell. It is widely agreed that mass detention without trial proved to be counter-productive since so many innocent people became enmeshed in the process and consequently disaffected from the judicial system. The fact that detention operated so much more against Catholics than Protestants did nothing to win 'hearts and minds' in the minority community to support the forces of law and order.

Another aspect of the emergency legislation has been the suspension of trial by jury. The argument here is that in a society where juries were being constantly challenged and intimidated, the normal process of law cannot operate. The 'Diplock courts' (so called after the judge who recommended their establishment in the 'Report of the Commission to consider legal procedures to deal with terrorist activities in Northern Ireland') have undoubtedly streamlined the judicial process; and there have been no serious allegations of bias in their operation. The Gardiner Committee, reporting in 1975, concluded that, although a return to jury trials should be achieved as soon as conditions permitted, the Diplock system was not, in itself, a major source of grievance.[22] Nevertheless, public opinion in Northern Ireland remains in favour of a return to trial by jury.

Other aspects of emergency legislation include arrest without a warrant; prolonged periods for holding suspects without charges being brought; and special powers for the police to search. The Prevention of Terrorism Act (1974), which was passed in the aftermath of the Birmingham bombs (November 1974) when twenty civilians died, proscribed the IRA and increased police powers against terrorist suspects. The most controversial aspects of this Act, however, have been the powers to exclude any person from Britain who is suspected of being a terrorist.[23] Even people resident in Britain for less than twenty years can be expelled across the Irish Sea to either Northern Ireland or the Republic. The Act also empowers police at ports to detain people for questioning if they think they may have some useful information. The maximum period for such interrogation is seven days (with the Home Secretary's approval). From 1974 to June 1979, 4146 persons were thus detained for questioning — mainly at Liverpool and Heathrow Airport. Under 'exclusion orders', in the same period, 140 people were removed from Britain to Northern Ireland, and 29 to the Republic. About 90 per cent of the people detained at ports have no charges brought against them. A recent report from the National Council for Civil Liberties says the Act 'nullifies the remedy of a writ of habeas corpus, by making it lawful for the police to arrest on extremely wide grounds'; and it claims that fingerprint records and photos of all those questioned are kept in police files.[24]

CONCLUSIONS

The foregoing discussion on the judicial response to the PIRA brings us to the central problem for any liberal—democratic government that faces violent subversives operating on its territory: how far the due process of law can be set aside to take account of the special circumstances prevailing. In Northern Ireland, this dilemma continues to be acute. On the one hand, the situation clearly demands special emergency measures and these have been applied with varying degrees of stringency during the past ten years. On the other hand, the further the judicial system in Northern Ireland becomes removed from norms operating elsewhere in the United Kingdom, the more difficult it is to win support for the state's attempts to maintain law and order. Successive governments have wanted to avoid playing into the hands of the PIRA by creating anything resembling a 'police state' in that part of the United Kingdom but, at the same time, they have had to avoid giving the impression that a certain level of violence is acceptable provided it does not 'spill over' into Britain. Since 1975 the general thrust of security policy has been to treat PIRA acts of violence as ordinary crime and deal with them in the courts. This policy has entailed ignoring any claims that PIRA activities are politically motivated; and it has also entailed giving the police in Northern Ireland the most sophisticated equipment and training for their fight against this sort of 'crime'. The army, as a corollary, has found itself being used increasingly as an armed police force in 'support of the civil power' rather than an army proper that could go over to an offensive role. Opinion differs sharply over whether the army should be allowed a 'free hand' to 'root out the terrorist' or whether the present restrained profile should be allowed to continue in the interests of avoiding political controversy. From the army's point of view, the present policy is far from satisfactory as evidenced by the fact that the PIRA is still alive and well. First, the 'yellow card', which restricts the circumstances in which a soldier can open fire, means that he must wait for the terrorist to take the initiative.[25] Second, the fact that the army is used as a police force in areas where the RUC is regarded as unacceptable, suggests that soldiers ought, in some cases, to have police powers.[26] For example, soldiers are not normally expected to enforce the law in such matters as motor tax evasion, speeding, or drunken driving. Third, although the army is supposed to be 'aiding the civil power' (i.e. assisting the police), this role can be vague and ambiguous since soldiers are, by definition, called upon to perform tasks that would not normally be dealt with by a police force (e.g. an ambush, a major riot, a political strike, a sniper, the defusing of bombs), and so may be less inhibited in the methods used. Finally, and most crucially, despite public statements to the contrary, the army feels it cannot succeed in the task it has been assigned. As one army officer has remarked, the soldiers sometimes feel that they and the IRA are face to face in the ring while the government acts as referee blowing the whistle when either side oversteps the mark! Since 1972, when the army was at its most active in Northern Ireland, public opinion has, on balance, been favourable to its presence. For example, a poll in 1979 found that 47 per cent of Catholics and 91 per cent of Protestants think that the 'interests of N. Ireland would be better served by the army remaining'.[27] But it is also true, as was said earlier, that the excesses of the security forces have been a source of grievance in some of the Catholic ghettoes and a boost for recruitment to PIRA.

The durability of the PIRA depends, however, on much more than the conduct of the security forces. The guerrilla fish do have the water they need to survive. The 'water' consists of a proportion of the Catholic population that feels that it does not receive a 'fair deal' in the Northern Ireland of today. Such a 'fair deal' would consist of both tangibles and intangibles ranging from a notion of 'justice' at one extreme to jobs, houses and leisure amenities, at the other. The role of the PIRA has been to capitalise on these perceptions of injustice and link them to a broader struggle. As Burton puts it:

> The IRA has managed to activate from the favourable social struggle of the Catholic communities, a politics of civil rights through national liberation.[28]

As long as this sense of grievance remains, the PIRA will be able to find 'safe houses'. As long as economic and social deprivation persist, as long as the law is enforced in a half-hearted and capricious manner, as long as it seems that some people are above the law, then the battle for legitimacy cannot be won by the state. The attempt to 'criminalise' the PIRA has not succeeded because, in the battle for legitimacy, it is not enough to hurl insults at one's opponents. Legitimacy has to be demonstrated by example.

Support for the PIRA is stronger than many observers will care to admit. In an editorial, the *Guardian* used the turnout of 7000 for an IRA demonstration on 12 August 1979 to calculate the real measure of support for the PIRA:

> If 3 per cent support the IRA and another 5 per cent give it acquiescence, there are 250,000 people ready to turn a blind eye . . . Add to those the mass of people in any society who shrug away from involvement in things they do not like and the sea is large enough for many a guerrilla to swim in.[29]

This support could, however, be decimated if the sense of injustice that pervades the ghettoes could be eradicated. This is not to argue that the gun would be put on the shelf overnight or, indeed, ever, but that the 'sea' in which the 'fish' swim would become dangerously shallow.

In sum, I have argued that the PIRA is not simply a terrorist movement in the accepted sense of the term. Its longevity, its history and its goals suggest that it is deeply rooted in the society in which it operates. Although it indulges in acts of terror from time to time, it also fights a military campaign against what it perceives to be an alien army. Unlike the Baader—Meinhof

Group, the Brigate Rosse and other terrorist groups, the PIRA's aims are feasible, internally consistent and find some measure of support among the wider population. In essence, the PIRA represents the 'cutting edge' of a movement that finds roots in the frustration of relative deprivation experienced by a section of the Catholic community in Northern Ireland.

Notes and References

1. P. Wilkinson, *Political Terrorism* (London: Macmillan, 1974), p. 16.
2. *Ibid.,* p. 80.
3. C.C. O'Brien in his *States of Ireland* (London: Panther, 1974), for example, draws on the Maoist analogy of guerrilla 'fish' needing the 'water' of popular support in order to survive.
4. P. Wilkinson, *Terrorism and the Liberal State* (London: Macmillan, 1977), p. 55.
5. *Ibid.,* p. 56.
6. See, for example, C. Guevara, *Guerrilla Warfare* (Harmondsworth: Penguin, 1969); and R. Debray, *Revolution in the Revolution?* (Harmondsworth: Penguin, 1968).
7. For this section, I rely heavily on J. Bowyer Bell, *The Secret Army* (Cambridge, Mass.: MIT Press, 1970) and *A Time of Terror* (New York: Basic Books, 1978), pp. 204—33.
8. Bowyer Bell, *A Time of Terror,* p. 209.
9. R. Clutterbuck, *Living with Terrorism* (London: Faber, 1975), pp. 75—6.
10. O'Brien, *op. cit.,* p. 261.
11. Bowyer Bell, *The Secret Army,* p. 337.
12. F. Burton, *The Politics of Legitimacy* (London: Routledge and Kegan Paul, 1978), p. 107.
13. *Ibid.,* p. 104.
14. *Violence in Ireland* (Dublin: Veritas Publications, 1977), pp. 125—6.
15. Burton, *op. cit.,* p. 69.
16. *Irish Times,* 18 June 1979.
17. *Ibid.*
18. Offences Against the State (Amendment) Act 1972, 3(1)b.
19. *Ibid.,* 3(2).
20. M. Robinson, Special Court abuses. *Hibernia,* 6 December 1974.
21. P. Waterworth, 'Northern Ireland — the administration of justice in the light of civil disorder, and sectarian violence' (BA (Hons) dissertation, University of Durham, 1978), p. 66.
22. 'Report of a Committee to consider, in the context of civil liberties and human rights, measures to deal with terrorism in Northern Ireland', cmnd. 5847 (1975) para. 29. See also, for a critique of the Diplock courts and other special judicial measures, K. Boyle *et al., Law and State: The Case of Northern Ireland* (London: Martin Robertson, 1975).
23. The Prevention of Terrorism Act (1976) Part II.
24. *Belfast Telegraph,* 24 August 1979.

25. Wilkinson, *Terrorism and the Liberal State*, p. 157.
26. R. Evelegh, *Peacekeeping in a Democratic Society* (London: Hurst, 1978), *passim.*
27. Reported in *New Society*, 6 September 1979.
28. Burton, *op. cit.*, p. 128.
29. *The Guardian*, 29 August 1979.

CHAPTER 7

The European Community and Terrorism: Establishing the Principle of 'Extradite or Try'

Juliet Lodge

Nothing in the Treaty of Rome establishing the European Economic Community (EEC) obliges its signatories to pursue or adhere to a common policy regarding the suppression of terrorism. Indeed, terrorism is outside the jurisdiction of the EEC's institutions. Nevertheless, the events of the late 1960s and 1970s impressed upon many states, and notably those in the Community with contiguous borders, the need to act in concert and to make common arrangements if terrorist offences were to be countered effectively. The two principal European organisations within which steps have been taken to realise these aims are the Council of Europe and the EEC. More than seventeen mainly West European countries belong to the Council of Europe. Its membership base is, therefore, broader than that of the EEC, and includes the EEC's member states: Belgium, Denmark, France, the Federal Republic of Germany (FRG), Ireland, Italy, Luxembourg, the Netherlands and the United Kingdom.

The Council of Europe took the lead in 1973 in working towards the adoption of anti-terrorist measures by its members; but the EEC did not seriously begin concerted appraisal of anti-terrorist measures until 1976. The impetus for Community action has emanated largely from the European Parliament and draws inspiration from the Council of Europe's Convention on the Suppression of Terrorism. This is not surprising in view of the overlapping membership between the EEC and the Council of Europe, but is problematic in that, as we shall show, for various reasons some Community members have been unwilling to see a comparable Community agreement drafted and enforced. This may seem paradoxical in view of the fact that EEC member governments must in part have been motivated to explore the adoption of common principles in this area by the inadequacy of existing international provisions and by a desire to intensify cooperation among themselves on the matter.

However, the delays in achieving agreement on Community action against terrorism relate to a number of considerations. Apart from political factors and difficulties arising from the differences between civil law states like France and common law states like the United Kingdom, it must be realised that the adoption of a common Community 'policy' on terrorism has important implications not simply for the jurisdiction of the member states and the nature of their mutual and reciprocal obligations, but that it would be tantamount to an extension of the EEC's competence to a sphere hitherto the prerogative of the member states, and hence imply that Community judgments and law in this area would be binding and assume precedence over national law, as in other areas covered by EEC regulations. As has been amply demonstrated in other policy areas in the EEC, the compartment-alisation of policy is replete with difficulties since the integration of one or more sectors has ramifications for others. This was one of the considerations underlying the French proposal to deal with terrorism in the EEC not by Community regulations *per se* but through the creation of a common judicial area (*un espace judiciare européen*). Differences of opinion over the advantages of either approach complicated attempts within the EEC to concert action against terrorism.

It will be useful to consider the EEC's progress in this area after a brief scrutiny of the development and content of the European Convention on the Suppression of Terrorism, which has earned the EEC's broad but qualified approval. Since it would be erroneous to believe that action during the 1970s to combat terrorism proceeded only at the national level and within the Council of Europe, it should be remembered that the United Nations (UN) has attempted to promote international cooperation on the suppression of terrorism with limited success. Consideration of its efforts being outside the scope of this chapter, I shall turn to the Council of Europe's activities in respect of measures to suppress terrorism by regulating extradition principles.

THE COUNCIL OF EUROPE

The hijacking of aircraft and the need to combat terrorism both by preventive devices like stringent screening and security measures at airports and by agreements on the extradition of terrorists prompted action by the Council of Europe. One of its primary objectives was to establish a common definition of the notion of a 'political offence' so that terrorists should not be able to evade prosecution by claiming that their deed was politically justifiable. Terrorist deeds endangering the lives of innocent people were, therefore, to be regarded as criminal offences, and signatories to the Council of Europe Convention on Terrorism were to undertake either to prosecute or to extradite terrorists. As will become apparent, this was to be no easy task.

In considering the Council of Europe's endeavours, it will be useful to recall that it was felt that national legislation regarding terrorism, and more especially the extradition or prosecution of terrorists claiming to have been in pursuit of a political aim, was too divergent to be effective; that a more harmonised practice other than existing measures based on reciprocal, bilateral arrangements was desirable; and that the Geneva Convention on the High Seas, the Tokyo Convention of 1963, the Hague Convention of 1970 and the Montreal Convention of 1971 needed to be supplemented by additional measures if terrorism was to be combated successfully.

Each of the conventions was deficient in some respect. The Geneva Convention, relating to piracy, governs

> any illegal acts of violence, detention or any act of depradation, committed for private ends by the crew or passengers of a private ship or aircraft and directed against another ship or aircraft on the high seas, or persons or property thereon, or against a ship, aircraft, persons or property in a place outside the jurisdiction of any state, any voluntary participation in the operation of a ship or aircraft with knowledge of facts making it a pirate ship or aircraft, and inviting or assisting such acts.[1]

According to Charles Fletcher-Cooke, this means that unless a hijacked aircraft attacks another, the hijacker(s) fall outside the laws of piracy.[2] Moreover, whereas acts of piracy seem to be directed at a ship or aircraft and at persons or property on it, in the case of hijacking, the persons on board the aircraft are often the indirect objects of hijackers and are used in an instrumental manner to elicit certain undertakings from the main objects — governments — regarding some cause or goal that the hijacker wishes to further or attain.

The Tokyo Convention is designed to meet the deficiencies of the Geneva Convention on the High Seas by providing for the state in which an aircraft is registered to exercise jurisdiction over offences (except political offences, but including hijacking and acts affecting the aircraft's safety) committed on board — the aim being to allow a state to seek the extradition of those who commit offences on board an aircraft registered with it. However, while the state of registration may commence extradition proceedings, the extradition of the offender(s) extends only between contracting states, and acts that the offender(s) claim(s) to be politically justified are normally excluded unless the aircraft's safety is infringed.

Both the Hague and Montreal conventions seek to overcome the deficiency of the Tokyo Convention. They govern hijacking, interference with the safety of aircraft, aircraft destruction and offences regarding not just the state of registration but the state of landing, the state where the offence took place and any state 'leasing' the aircraft. Signatories to these conventions are required to prosecute or extradite offenders. However, the weakness of the conventions lies in their not being universally applicable: if offenders escape to a non-contracting state that either lacks extradition arrangements with the contracting state, or has measures not covering the offence in question, or accepts a plea of an offence being politically justifiable, they might escape prosecution. The Council of Europe's members were anxious above all to clarify and eliminate the 'political offence' caveat. In 1972, in response to the recommendation of the Consultative Assembly of the Council of Europe,[3] the Committee of Ministers set up an *ad hoc* Committee of Senior Officials to study the legal aspects of international terrorism. However, the Consultative Assembly felt that this in itself would not contribute in the immediate future to a reduction of terrorist acts. Accordingly, during its 25th session in May 1973, the Consultative Assembly adopted *Recommendation 703* on international terrorism. Condemning international terrorist acts, this stated that 'regardless of their cause [these] should be punished as serious criminal offences involving the killing or endangering of the lives of innocent people'. The Consultative Assembly, noting 'the disappointing response of the international community' to combating terrorism, believing that this made 'joint action' by the Council of Europe's members 'all the more necessary and urgent', and deploring 'the fact that the political and material support of a certain number of governments and organisations permits acts of international terrorism',[4] called upon the Council's Committee of Ministers to invite the governments of the Council's member states, *inter alia*, 'to establish a common definition for the notion of "political offence" in order to be able to refute any "political" justification whenever an act of terrorism endangers the life of innocent persons'.[5]

In addition, the Consultative Assembly called upon the Committee of Ministers to invite the Council of Europe's members:

to ratify, as a matter of urgency, the Tokyo, Hague and Montreal conventions against hijacking and unlawful interference with civil aviation;

'to use all their political and economic influence to dissuade the States concerned from pursuing a policy which allows terrorists to prepare their acts or to reside or find asylum on their territory';[6]

to coordinate their proposals for action at United Nations level;

urgently to convene a special conference of the Council of Europe's members' Ministers of the Interior or other Ministers responsible for the police and internal security to elaborate proposals and coordinate measures aimed at preventing acts of terrorism on the regional basis of the Council of Europe's member states;[7] and

to 'take seriously into account the fact that, failing effective and urgent European governmental action, parliamentary and public opinion will openly support retaliatory action by the airline pilots and international transport workers against services to and from offending states'.[8]

The Committee of Ministers examined this recommendation and on

24 January 1974 adopted resolution (74)3 on international terrorism. The Committee of Ministers was convinced that extradition is a particularly effective measure for ensuring that perpetrators of terrorism who allege political motivation should not escape either extradition or punishment. The resolution emphasised the importance attached to extradition and set out principles to guide member states when faced with a request for extradition. Member states should be guided by the following principles:

> 1.   When they receive a request for extradition concerning offences covered by the Conventions of The Hague for the suppression of unlawful seizure of aircraft and of Montreal for the suppression of unlawful acts against the safety of civil aviation, offences against diplomatic agents and other internationally protected persons, the taking of hostages or any terrorist act, they should, when applying international agreements or conventions on the subject, and especially the European Convention on Extradition (of 13 December 1957), or when applying their domestic law, take into consideration the particularly serious nature of these acts, *inter alia:*
> — when they create a collective danger to human life, liberty or safety;
> — when they affect innocent persons foreign to the motives behind them;
> — when cruel or vicious means are used in the commission of those acts.
> 2.   If it refuses extradition in a case of the kind mentioned above and if its jurisdiction rules permit, the government of the requested state should submit the case to its competent authorities for the purpose of prosecution. Those authorities should take their decision in the same manner as in the case of any ordinary offence of a serious nature under the law of that state.
> 3.   The governments of member states in which such jurisdiction is lacking should envisage the possibility of establishing it.[9]

Underlying the above principles is the notion that Council of Europe members share a set of common values, beliefs and understanding as to the tenets of legal practice in liberal democracies, along with common understanding as to what is meant by 'cruel and vicious means' under the third principle. Clearly, the aim of the resolution is to persuade governments to ensure the prosecution of terrorists.

The problem with the Committee's resolution lay not in its objective but in the weakness of the Committee's jurisdiction. While the Committee could not issue a recommendation to member governments unless it was unanimous, the recommendation is not binding on the Council of Europe's members. Moreover, even conventions established under the Council of Europe are binding only on those states that ratify them.[10] Nevertheless, the resolution was intended to lead to the conclusion of a convention to combat terrorism that the member governments would ratify. The matter was, therefore, discussed by the Council of Europe's Conference of European Ministers of Justice. This was formed in 1961 and grew out of the deliberations of the Council's European Committee on Crime Problems, which had been established by a decision of the Committee of Ministers in June 1958, and whose members consist of senior officials from Ministries of Justice. They have promoted the exchange of information and research relating to the prevention of crime and the treatment of offenders. The involvement of the Ministers of Justice themselves in the Council of Europe's work was deemed desirable in view of their specialised competence and knowledge. Generally, they meet biennially and assist in directing the Council's legal programme.[11]

Following the issue of the Committee of Ministers' resolution on international terrorism, the Conference of European Ministers of Justice met in Obernai, France, on 22 May 1975. Predictably enough, in view of the terrorism experienced in Western Europe during the 1970s, they stressed the need for coordinated action to combat terrorism, and alluded to the possibility that terrorist acts committed specifically for 'political' ends might jeopardise and paralyse the liberal—democratic institutions of the Council of Europe's member states. The ministerial initiative for European-based action in this field having been taken by the Conference of European Ministers, at its 24th plenary session the same month the European Committee on Crime Problems suggested to the Committee of Ministers the establishment of a committee of governmental experts to scrutinise problems raised by new forms of concerted acts of violence. This was authorised in June 1975. The Council of Europe's Directorate of Legal Affairs provided the secretariat for the committee, which prepared a European Convention on the Suppression of Terrorism at its first two meetings on 6—8 October 1975 and 2—6 February 1976 respectively. The Committee of Governmental Experts' work on the problems associated with measures for the improvement of international cooperation during and after the commission of an act of terrorism continued and no report was expected before March 1980.[12]

The draft convention was submitted to the European Committee on Crime Problems in May 1976, and thence to the Committee of Ministers for approval — as well as to the European Ministers of Justice who, at their tenth conference on 3—4 June 1976 in Brussels, expressed the hope that the Committee of Ministers would consider the draft convention expeditiously. In November 1976, the Committee of Ministers approved the convention's text and opened it to signature by the Council of Europe's member states on 27 January 1977, all of whom except Ireland and Malta signed it that day; Spain (which acceded to the Council of Europe in November 1977) signed it on 27 April 1978. The convention entered into force on 4 August 1978 after ratification by Austria, Sweden and the FRG, and subsequently by Denmark on 27 June 1978 and the United Kingdom on 24 July 1978. The difficulty with the convention lies both in the reluctance of several of the Council of Europe's member states to ratify and be bound by it, and in the provision of exceptions to the extradition clauses. Realisation of the convention's limitations encouraged members of the EEC to examine what steps could be taken, at least within the Community, to concert measures against terrorism. Prior to scrutinising these, it will be useful to consider the anti-terrorist measures and principles contained in the Convention on the Suppression of

Terrorism.

Perhaps most significant is the attempt to fill the lacuna in the Council's European Convention on Extradition and in the Convention on Mutual Assistance in Criminal Matters (of 20 April 1959). Under the former, article 3, paragraph 1, provides that extradition shall not be granted in respect of a political offence. While one of the intentions of this article was to protect those seeking to elude prosecution for alleged political crimes by governments not respecting basic human rights, it was felt that the principle could be abused by terrorists themselves infringing innocent people's liberties and lives. The Council of Europe's members felt that given the climate of mutual confidence among them, their democratic nature and their respect for human rights safeguarded by the institutions set up under the Convention for the Protection of Human Rights and Fundamental Freedoms (of 4 November 1950), their governments would not blatantly disregard the obligations imposed on them in respect of human rights. At the same time, they argued that the human rights of both those accused or convicted of terrorism and their victims or potential victims had to be safeguarded.

The internationalisation of terrorism was seen as the main reason why resort to measures complementing or modifying, where necessary, existing extradition and mutual assistance arrangements among the Council of Europe's member states would be an appropriate and effective way of combating terrorism in Western Europe. For extradition purposes, therefore, the Convention on the Suppression of Terrorism provides, under article 1, that certain specified offences shall never be regarded as 'political':

an offence within the scope of the Hague Convention for the Suppression of Unlawful Seizure of Aircraft of 16 December 1970;

an offence within the scope of the Montreal Convention for the Suppression of Unlawful Acts against the Safety of Civil Aviation of 23 September 1971;

a serious offence involving an attack against the life, physical integrity or liberty of internationally protected persons, including diplomatic agents;

an offence involving kidnapping, the taking of a hostage or serious unlawful detention;

an offence involving the use of a bomb, grenade, rocket, automatic firearm or letter or parcel bomb if this use endangers persons;

an attempt to commit any of the foregoing offences or participation as an accomplice of a person who commits or attempts to commit such an offence.

Under article 2, other specified offences may not be regarded as 'political' notwithstanding their political content or motivation, which provides member states anxious to avoid obligations to extradite with an escape clause. While article 1 eliminates the possibility of a state that has received an extradition request invoking the political nature of the offence to justify non-compliance with the request, it does not create an obligation to extradite. At most, it qualifies article 3.1 of the European Convention on Extradition by stipulating offences that contracting parties to the Convention on the Suppression of Terrorism may no longer regard as 'political'. The traditional rights of political refugees and others enjoying political asylum under other international arrangements to which the convention's signatories are party are not affected by the convention. The convention also recognises that for legal or constitutional reasons a contracting state may not be able to comply fully with article 1 and, therefore, allows for reservations under article 13. If extradition is refused in accordance with article 13, the state, if it has jurisdiction over some offences committed abroad by its nationals, can prosecute the offender in place of extraditing him/her after receiving a request for extradition from a contracting state whose jurisdiction is based on a rule of jurisdiction existing equally in the law of the requested state. Article 7 establishes an obligation for a state refusing extradition to submit the case to its competent authorities for the purpose of prosecution without undue delay, and no exception may be invoked. Prosecution then follows the law and procedure in force for offences of comparable seriousness. Articles 6 and 7 are designed to meet the differences in the principles of jurisdiction between states whose domestic courts have, under their criminal law, jurisdiction over offences committed by nationals wherever committed and those where the domestic courts' competence is based generally on the principle of territoriality.[13] Although the convention does not make extradition mandatory, article 8 establishes an obligation to grant assistance in cases involving offences under both articles 1 and 2, and provides that assistance may not be refused on the sole ground that the offence is of a political character. This, therefore, modifies article 2(a) of the European Convention on Mutual Assistance in Criminal Matters, which allows states to refuse assistance in cases of political offences.[14]

The overall intended effect of the Convention on the Suppression of Terrorism is obvious: the plea that a terrorist act is politically inspired, justifiable and defensible is no longer to be regarded as justifying non-prosecution of a terrorist. The problems with the convention remain not simply in its limited regional applicability and caveats, but in the fact that terrorists may still escape prosecution or extradition if they land or seek refuge either in a country not party to the convention or to the various UN provisions, or in one that does not have reciprocal arrangements with members of the Council of Europe regarding the prosecution and extradition of terrorists committing offences within the regions of the Council of Europe's member states. Recognition of this led the Consultative Assembly to advocate political and economic measures in such instances, and the European Parliament has adopted a similar line in its deliberations on combating terrorism. Let us consider now the EEC's endeavours to concert action against terrorism.

The European Community

Not until 1976 did EEC Ministers start consultations on anti-terrorist measures. However, the European Parliament, which has exercised its rights to issue opinions on all matters of topical interest during the 1970s, had been active before this, and remains committed to promoting the conclusion of anti-terrorist measures that will close loopholes in existing conventions to which some or all EEC member states are party. EEC consideration of measures to combat international terrorism embraces six main elements, which concern attempts to secure agreement among the member states:

to approve and accept measures, to apply to the EEC as a whole, similar to and adapted from the Council of Europe's Convention on the Suppression of Terrorism;

to adopt, in the EEC, a common system for the extradition of terrorists;

to consider creating a common EEC judicial area to assist the EEC's members in combating criminal offences;

to encourage the study of problems associated with terrorism, including the abuse of diplomatic bags;

to impress upon countries, notably in the Arab or Third World, that have given havens to terrorists perpetrating offences on EEC members' 'territory', that trade and political relations with the EEC are, thereby, likely to be endangered;

to act to promote more adequate firearms' control in furtherance of the European Convention on the Acquisition of and Possession of Firearms.

All these issues have given rise to numerous difficulties in the EEC and raised a number of legal niceties as to the legal basis for any Community action in these areas since — with the arguable exception of the last two elements listed above — they fall outside the scope of the EEC's competence as delineated by the Rome Treaty. However, the spate of terrorist activities throughout the 1970s, either indigenous to a Community member state or commenced or committed in an EEC country and/or involving their aircraft, embassies, diplomatic personnel or nationals, led the European Parliament's members (MEPs) to press for the adoption of measures to combat terrorism. Although they have also considered national anti-terrorist and anti-subversive measures in force (such as the FRG's *Radikalenerlass* — the Radicals' Decree), space limitations preclude their examination here. Suffice it to note, therefore, that MEPs have been vigilant of the potential abuse, by governments, of measures designed to combat terrorism. Furthermore, concern with respect for human rights has also featured in deliberations over trading relations with the Lomé (African, Caribbean and Pacific countries) and Arab countries, and has an external dimension relevant to the discussion of terrorism at the supranational level.

EEC member governments themselves have adopted a cautious attitude towards this question. This is owing both to fears concerning the impact of any common EEC legislation on existing national measures, and to concern that the sovereignty of individual member governments in this sensitive area should not be compromised. When, in April 1976, EEC Council president Gaston Thorn was asked by Mr Yeats (European Progressive Democrat: Ireland) when the EEC Ministers of the Interior would meet to discuss matters pertaining to terrorism as provided for by the Rome summit, Thorn brushed aside the question, but significantly conceded that 'it would be preferable if the terrorists themselves knew the effects of our common action before your Parliament'.[15] The fact that MEPs are at liberty to pass motions and resolutions on terrorist matters does not imply a commensurate freedom for EEC ministers to act in furtherance of MEPs' wishes. Rather, to the extent that EEC ministers have shown themselves willing to consider and concert action in this sphere, they have done so necessarily mostly within the context of Foreign Ministers' meetings and of 'European Political Cooperation' — strictly speaking this is not an EEC institution although participation in it is restricted to EEC members. In many respects, the European Parliament does, however, stimulate their action. Consequently, the focus of the present enquiry will be on MEPs' activities, especially since 1975.

The liberation of the Entebbe hostages in 1976 led to all the party groups in the European Parliament on 6 July 1976 adopting and approving a resolution to combat international terrorism. The resolution not only called on the EEC's institutions to act, but advocated action in respect of Third World countries. In addition, it referred to the need for greater Community cohesion in international organisations considering terrorism. Specifically, the European Parliament called upon

> the Conference of Foreign Ministers, the Council and Commission . . . in the context of European political cooperation and of Community activities, to coordinate energetically and without delay measures to combat international terrorism, and to intensify their efforts to reach suitable mutual judicial assistance agreements with Third Countries; [and called] on the organs of European political cooperation and the European Communities to coordinate their efforts to this end, in particular in the plenary assembly of the United Nations, in the UN Security Council and in the subsidiary organisations of the UN.[16]

The European Parliament's president forwarded the resolution to the Conference of Foreign Ministers, Council of Ministers and Commission. Similarly, eleven days before the Council of Europe's Committee of Ministers signed the European Convention on the Suppression of Terrorism, MEPs pressurised EEC member governments to ratify the convention immediately.[17] The all-party resolution to this effect was designed to underline their conviction that the EEC's credibility in this area would be enhanced by common coordinated ratification of an international agreement by the EEC member governments.[18] This time the resolution was transmitted to the EEC's member governments and parliaments. Even so, it had no discernible effect: member governments felt neither legal nor moral obligations to respond positively to MEPs' resolutions.

During 1977, while continuing to press for stronger national and supranational action to suppress terrorism and to ensure that the perpetrators of terrorist offences in the EEC be duly tried, the European Parliament began considering the wider aspects of terrorism. Its Political Affairs Committee studied terrorism and reported to Parliament on 14 November 1977.[19] On 11 October 1977, both the Socialist and the Christian Democratic groups tabled motions for resolution on terrorism in the EEC.[20] The two motions are interesting in that both go beyond restatement of concern that terrorists should be brought to account. Both embody the sixth element of Community action on terrorism by calling for EEC arms control. Of the two motions for resolution, that tabled on behalf of the Socialist group is the mildest in tone. It also reflects a greater concern with the issue of the constitutionality of anti-terrorist measures than does its Christian Democratic counterpart. This was not surprising in view of the contentiousness in SPD circles of German government anti-terrorist legislation, which some felt was open to abuse by any unscrupulous authorities, and in view of the common desire to protect liberal democracy from terrorist threats.

The Socialist motion, therefore, noted that freedom of expression and freedom of political activity were guaranteed by the EEC's member states (which, the motion pointed out, 'are all democratic'). While condemning unconditionally all acts of terrorism in the EEC, demanding that 'all terrorists in the Community, whatever their motives, be apprehended, charged and punished by due process of the law', and welcoming 'the vigour, stringency and determination with which the governments of Member States beset with terrorism have applied the law', the Socialist motion contained no less than five clauses (out of eleven — the eleventh clause being by way of an instruction to forward the resolution to the EEC Commission, Council of Ministers, and, for information, to the Member States' parliaments) preoccupied with the implications for the maintenance of liberal-democratic norms of anti-terrorist measures. Under clause 4, member governments are encouraged in their resolve that restrictions on freedom should be kept to a minimum; clause 5 insists that parliaments should 'examine the need for full emergency powers at short intervals and suspend special measures as soon as possible'; clause 6 indicates the importance of avoiding 'special measures which cause hostility between sections of the population within the

Community'; clause 9 notes that it remains 'essential that governments should demonstrate to their people their determination to conquer terrorism by means of measures approved in Parliament'; and clause 10 stresses that 'every effort should be made to eliminate the causes of terrorism and, despite the present extent of this problem, to maintain a climate of peace, openness, stability and justice'.[21]

These five clauses amply demonstrate the Socialists' concern that anti-terrorist measures should be subject to proper parliamentary scrutiny and control; that they should be kept to a minimum; that traditional liberal—democratic rights, values and practices should not be infringed by member governments and that governments should not be encouraged to introduce measures antithetical to them by the extent of the terrorist problem. Underlying this, of course, is anxiety that any terrorist claims, notably in the FRG, that the government itself was anti-democratic and a source of state violence against the individual, should not appear to be bolstered by the nature, scope, duration, provisions and application of anti-terrorist measures especially if these could be shown to violate basic constitutionally guarded civil liberties, freedoms and rights.

By contrast, the Christian Democratic, Liberal and European Progressive Democratic motion emphasised the need for joint efforts in the EEC 'to provide effective protection for all citizens and to safeguard democracy in the European Community'.[22] It stressed the need for further preventive measures to combat terrorism, expected the Council of Ministers to adopt measures to strengthen supranational cooperation in combating crimes of violence and terrorism in the EEC,[23] and called upon it to encourage the conclusion of international agreements on anti-terrorist measures.[24] This was an allusion to the failure of all member states to ratify the European Convention on the Suppression of Terrorism, and to the slow progress in the UN towards the conclusion of a convention against the taking of hostages; it clearly expressed the conviction that the EEC's members should be pressurised at the EEC level to take more positive, harmonised and concerted action in international bodies seeking to combat terrorism.

The Christian Democratic, Liberal and European Progressive Democratic motion for resolution shared the Socialists' concern to condemn terrorism, but went further in outlining measures to supplement those already in force or under consideration. While the Socialists had also noted the need for Community action to control the sale of arms, the Christian Democratic, Liberal and European Progressive Democratic motion recommended that the Council of Ministers should consider the following:

(a) the setting up of a permanent conference of ministers responsible for the internal security of the individual Member States;
(b) the harmonisation of legal and administrative provisions on internal security;
(c) the harmonisation of identity card and registration measures;
(d) the harmonisation of arms legislation;

(e) the establishment of an integrated system of investigation within the Community;
(f) the extension of mutual legal assistance between the Member States in the Community.[25]

At the European Parliament's sitting of 12 October 1977 both motions for resolution were referred to the Political Affairs Committee, which was instructed to report to the House at its November part-session. On 20 October 1977, Mr Fletcher-Cooke (European Conservative: United Kingdom) was appointed rapporteur. The Committee considered a motion for a resolution the same day, and adopted it unanimously on 2 November 1977. This motion embraced aspects of both the Christian Democratic, Liberal and European Progressive Democratic and Socialist motions, but was less specific than either in advocating new measures. No mention of arms control was made. Instead, once again, the member states' governments were called upon

> to make full and continuous use of the Community and European Political Cooperation machinery, with the full participation of the Commission . . . and with special conferences as appropriate, in order to improve the already existing cooperation between national authorities within the Community and international bodies outside the Community.

In addition, they were requested to accelerate action in the UN, and reminded of the European Parliament's resolution of 14 January 1977 in favour of the European Convention on the Suppression of Terrorism.[26]

Given that the European Parliament's scrutiny of the terrorism issue in the autumn of 1977 had been motivated by the spate of terrorist acts during the year, the rather unimpressive nature of the Political Affairs Committee's motion for resolution presented to the House on the subject has to be explained. Why was a more dynamic role for the EEC not advocated? Why was there no willingness to encourage the EEC to take the lead in international efforts to combat terrorism? Had the Committee simply assumed that the political climate made such efforts impossible?

When Mr Fletcher-Cooke presented the Committee's report to the European Parliament on 15 November 1977, he attempted to justify the Committee's position. Noting that terrorist activity in Europe aimed at undermining liberal—democratic values, the rule of law and fundamental human rights, and at driving 'the democratic state into the position of an authoritarian and totalitarian tyranny . . .',[27] he admitted that the Political Affairs Committee had chosen deliberately to draft a short report devoid of novelty in the hope that this would guarantee that the report would 'gain the maximum degree of assent'.[28] It had been agreed that 'it would be wrong to ask for any new mechanisms, for any novel departures from the existing weapons at hand'.[29] Moreover, what appeared to deter the promotion of any novel proposals was recognition of the fact that existing conventions on terrorism had yet to be used. It appeared more appropriate that they should be enforced than that another convention should be drawn up.

More importantly, the Political Affairs Committee was unwilling to overlook the European Convention on the Suppression of Terrorism, which it regarded as more significant than any other similar convention. This convention does, of course, have particular relevance to the Community in that it is Euro-centric, having been initiated by the Council of Europe. Mr Fletcher-Cooke argued that its important legal effect lay in the provisions that terrorists should not be able to evade extradition by pleading that their crimes were political offences; that contracting states should not refuse the extradition of terrorists; and that, therefore, a country unwilling or unable — because of domestic law — to extradite terrorists, should, nevertheless, be obliged to try the terrorists itself. In other words, the primary importance attaching to the Council of Europe's convention was the intention to ensure that terrorists should not be above the law, especially in view of the internationalisation of terrorism. For the Political Affairs Committee, terrorism was to be regarded as a crime 'similar to, if not worse than, the old international crime of piracy',[30] and one that, like piracy, should be dealt with differently from other crimes.

Although EEC Ministers of the Interior had discussed ratifying and using existing anti-terrorist instruments, they had not been successful in realising their objectives. The Political Affairs Committee, therefore, urged them to intensify their collaboration in concert with the Commission, and to enforce existing international anti-terrorist measures. This meant that the European Parliament was being advised to do no more than pressurise member governments in respect of existing conventions; this was, to some degree, an admission of defeat. Nevertheless, the resolution was welcomed at least as an expression of the EEC's resolve to resist terrorism by constitutional means. Each of the three speakers — Mr Holst (Socialist: Denmark), Mr Vernaschi (Christian Democrat: Italy) and Mr Berkhouwer (Liberal Democrat: Netherlands) — emphasised the importance their party groups attached to this. In addition, Mr Berkhouwer drew attention to the fact that terrorist offences could originate or be continued inside or outside the EEC, and that terrorists should not escape prosecution, and called for effective measures to counteract international crime.[31] He saw a paradox in the EEC attempting to eliminate barriers between countries while the need for security made them necessary. Going on from accepting the limitations of Interpol, he asked whether a European police information service could not be devised, and greater coordination of effort among the EEC's police forces achieved. He suggested the establishment of an EEC police radio network to provide direct links between the national police forces, and the placement of police liaison officers in the embassies and consulate-generals.[32] This idea represents part of the third element of the EEC's attention to anti-terrorist measures and clearly embraces the concept of international crime.

Mr Berkhouwer also suggested that if terrorists were successfully apprehended and prosecuted, further terrorist acts aimed at achieving the release of terrorists held in national prisons might be avoided by the device of placing terrorists, regardless of their origin, in an international prison under international supervision.[33]

Mr Vernaschi's proposals for combating terrorism dealt with the fifth element to Community action: namely, that regarding the tendency of countries linked to the EEC by association agreements to shelter terrorists. He argued that consideration should be given to suspending trade agreements with such countries, especially those that had ignored the European Parliament's condemnation of their actions in this respect in the past, wherever the actions of their governments conflicted with the European Parliament's policy on terrorism.[34]

In spite of the party groups' support for the resolution and despite their spokesmen's efforts to encourage EEC solidarity against terrorism and a more novel approach to it, both the Council of Ministers' president-in-office, Henri Simonet, and the Commission's spokesman, Viscount Davignon, adopted a cautious attitude. Simonet argued that the issue was far too serious and far-reaching to allow a quick reply to the points raised, and simply assured the House that the points had been noted and would be brought to his colleagues' attention. Viscount Davignon, while generally endorsing the sentiments expressed in the resolution, noted that it was up to the member states to ratify the relevant existing conventions so that their legal positions on the matter be in accord.[35] The Commission, lacking the right to initiate proposals in this sphere, could do little more than support the Parliament and affirm the responsibilities of, and possibilities for, concerted member governments' actions.

When the discussion was resumed on 15 November, Mr Nyborg (for the European Progressive Democrats) also advocated greater harmonisation of efforts along the lines of the German, Spanish and British examples of strengthening airport security,[36] and welcomed the UN General Assembly resolution of 3 November, condemning hijacking and other acts of violence involving civil aviation, which staved off a protest strike by the International Pilots Association. Taking a tough line, however, he advocated the reintroduction of the death penalty for terrorist crimes,[37] which his fellow Dane, Mr Holst (Socialist), rejected as erroneous. Mr Sandri (for the Communist group) supported resistance against terrorism but argued that ultimately the fight against terrorism would be won 'by refusing to resort to emergency laws, and by rejecting the hysteria which cynical elements or unwitting proponents of chaos who exploit events seek to foster among the public in order to turn one nation against another at a European level'.[38] Calling for anti-fascist measures to combat terrorism — a 'combination of security and tolerance, a national respect for truth, and a constant appeal for the unity of our citizens, enabling them to renew their faith in democracy and eradicate this evil which today threatens democracy itself in some of our countries and at a European level' — he appealed, above all, for political cooperation to locate terrorist power centres and to establish the links between their financial backers and instigators.[39] Taking up this theme, Mr Blumenfeld (Christian Democrat: FRG) deplored the member governments' lack of political will to tackle terrorism cooperatively at the Community level.[40]

Endorsing political action, the Commission had, in fact, through its president, assured the German government of its support for its recent antiterrorist action. For the Commission, Viscount Davignon indicated that the Commission urgently wanted the creation of a legal instrument to cover all the EEC's member states, and advocated the ratification of all existing conventions to ensure that there were no differences between the member states. He recalled that the Commission could not deal with terrorism, this being the member states' prerogative, but assured the European Parliament that the Commission would lend its full support to all measures touching its competence or concerning the establishment of appropriate legal instruments.[41] As before, the president-in-office of the Council of Ministers, Mr Simonet, refused to make any commitment to do more than inform his colleagues because, first, the issue concerned mainly Ministers of the Interior and not just Foreign Ministers, and, second, 'when human lives are at stake, I never speak off the cuff'.[42]

On 16 November, MEPs adopted two amendments to the Fletcher-Cooke motion for resolution. The first, tabled by Mr Lagorce on behalf of the Socialists, clarified the preamble by confining the resolution to the EEC on the grounds that other bodies should act outside it. It therefore read:

noting with deep concern the increase in acts of terrorism committed in several Member States of the [EEC] which may begin or be continued outside the Community.

The second amendment, tabled by Mr Durieux (Liberal Democrat: France), referred to problems associated with countries giving havens to terrorists. It stressed the Parliament's unconditional condemnation of all acts of terrorism 'and the authorities of countries which aid and abet them, . . . by making it easier for them to be committed by directly participating in them, in particular by receiving hostages on their territory in defiance of all the precepts of international law and of respect for human rights'.[43]

The resolution was then adopted by the Parliament. However, its adoption did not appreciably advance Community-wide intergovernmental cooperation on combating terrorism. Bilateral cooperation continued, but supranational concertation and harmonisation seemed to depend on the commission of terrorist acts in the EEC. Tragically, a stimulus for greater government cooperation on terrorism was given by the kidnapping in March 1978 of Aldo Moro, president of the Italian Christian Democratic Party.

On 17 March 1978, the European Parliament unanimously agreed to an all-party motion condemning the kidnapping of Aldo Moro and 'all methods of pursuing political ends which pose the gravest threat not only to human life but to freely elected democratic institutions', and noting the House's 'fullest solidarity with the Italian democratic movement in the face of a particularly difficult situation', concern for Moro's safety and condolences to the families of those who lost their lives in the exercise of their duties.[44] This was followed by the EEC heads of government meeting in Copenhagen as the European Council on 7—8 April, which similarly condemned Mr Moro's kidnapping and declared solidarity with the Italian government and people.[45] The European Council adopted a declaration on combating terrorism and expressed concern lest increased terrorism undermine the functioning and principles of society in the EEC. It agreed to give high priority to intensified cooperation to defend the EEC against terrorism and to conduct studies of the problems of terrorism, including the abuse of diplomatic bags;[46] and decided that the relevant ministers should increase their mutual cooperation and submit their conclusions as soon as possible on the proposed creation of a European judicial area.[47] Mr Fellermaïer (Socialist: FRG) deplored the nebulousness of this term.[48] However, discussion of its implications was postponed until the ensuing debate on legal questions, although it was noted that aspects of a Community policy on terrorism might conflict with national laws regarding, for example, the search of houses and might, therefore, not be acceptable to some states.[49]

During the debate on terrorism, Mr Sieglerschmidt (Socialist: FRG) advocated greater police liaison and a simplification of procedures to facilitate police cooperation.[50] Shortly thereafter, during question time, he raised the question of EEC coordination of the sale and supply of arms by EEC member states to countries that, others pointed out, trained and financed terrorists. The Danish president-in-office of the Council of Ministers, Mr Andersen, argued that a common arms procurement policy was not possible, and evaded the question.[51] Over and above stating that the EEC's Ministers of Justice had not met since 1974, Mr Andersen argued against the EEC duplicating efforts of the Council of Europe and in favour of good contact and a sensible division of labour with it.[52] He did not, therefore, meet objections that a European judicial area was intended simply to cover terrorism rather than criminal and civil law. Instead, he simply underlined the differences between the member states, implying not only that harmonisation was impossible, but that it was not worth pursuing.

Moreover, similar arguments were advanced during the debate when the issue of special EEC citizens' rights was discussed — again, to little effect.[53] However, what is clear is that by the spring of 1978, and following Moro's murder,[54] thinking — notably in the European Parliament — about Community action to combat terrorism had gone well beyond concern with the enforcement of a common undertaking to extradite terrorists, and encompassed the related issues concerning the search for and arrest of terrorist suspects, police liaison, arms supply, procurement and sales, the maintenance of EEC citizens' democratic rights, and a common judicial area. Indeed, in May, during question time, Commission President Jenkins agreed with the need for concerted action to combat terrorism in general and arms smuggling in particular. He assured the Parliament that if the Commission lacked the necessary power to take action, it would use its influence to persuade national governments to cooperate closely.[55]

The problem of arms control was to become a preoccupation of the European Parliament during the second half of 1978. This can be attributed both to the realisation that combating abuses in arms procurement, supply and sales was an essential facet of the attempt to curb terrorism, and to parallel developments in the Council of Europe where, on 28 June 1978, the Committee of Ministers presented the European Convention on the Control of the Acquisition and Possession of Firearms by Individuals for signature. This was endorsed by the United Kingdom, Ireland, Denmark and the FRG.

At the September 1978 sitting of the European Parliament, an oral question with debate was tabled on the Socialist group's behalf to the Commission on the standardisation of weapons legislation.[56] It was noted that firearms used to commit acts of violence in EEC member states had often been illegally imported from other member states or from outside the EEC, and that foreigners could acquire firearms almost without formality provided they exported them immediately. Arguing that discrepancies should be eliminated and that harmonisation was vital, Mr Fellermaïer asked whether the Commission favoured the early signature and ratification of the convention as a means of eliminating discrepancies in national legislation; whether the diversity of legislation had 'a direct and unfavourable effect on the functioning of the common market in firearms'; and what additional measures the Commission considered necessary and feasible. Commissioner Davignon replied that while the Commission welcomed what was being done, it was uncertain about the legal basis for any action over and above the cooperation, outside the EEC's framework, of EEC Ministers of the Interior that had begun in 1976.[57] Davignon hinted that Commission action might be possible if the EEC's members agreed that article 235[58] of the Rome Treaty should be the basis for such action. If they did not, the Commission might have recourse to article 100, although action would be difficult to justify since this article concerned the approximation of laws insofar as it was necessary to the functioning of the common market.[59] Article 36,[60] which provides for member states to take measures restricting free trade on a number of grounds, including public policy ('ordre public'), public safety or security, could possibly be invoked. However, action in this area was difficult. Rejecting Viscount Davignon's arguments, Mr Sieglerschmidt argued that action under article 235 was possible and legal.

While it is true that the legal basis for Commission action in this sphere was open to dispute, the problem lay elsewhere: namely, with the unwillingness of EEC member governments to compromise their national provisions on this and matters relating to terrorism in the name of Community harmony. Their failure even to ensure that all of them endorsed the European Convention on the Suppression of Terrorism led to further pressure in 1979 from the European Parliament and notably from its directly elected MEPs. However, some progress towards a common Community attitude on combating and prosecuting terrorists was achieved, after a great deal of haggling, by the EEC's Ministers of Justice. Using the Council of Europe's Convention on the Suppression of Terrorism as a basis for achieving uniformity, in October 1978 they agreed to observe a common stance on extraditing or prosecuting 'without undue delay' EEC nationals accused of terrorist acts. They provided for greater leeway than the Council of Europe in the interpretation of what acts constituted political offences justifying a refusal to extradite, providing the case was referred to the appropriate national authorities for prosecution. In addition, to overcome French objections, the member states supported a Belgian compromise to follow up French proposals for a common European judicial area where, *inter alia*, anti-terrorist measures would be tightly enforced.[61] Discussions about arms control, anti-terrorist measures based on EEC accord regarding the extradition of terrorists, and the creation of a common judicial area proceeded *in tandem* with the broader and equally controversial debate concerning defence and a common arms procurement policy for the EEC. This issue was complicated by the fact that not only was defence explicitly excluded from the Rome Treaty but Ireland was not a member of NATO, France had a special relationship with NATO, and the FRG's access to nuclear weaponry know-how remained contentious.

In 1979, EEC initiatives against terrorism reflected external stimuli and, as before, largely translated themselves into pressure from the European Parliament on the EEC's member governments.[62] These initiatives related to the statement issued at the Bonn summit of 16—17 July 1978 by the heads of state and government of Canada, the FRG, France, Italy, Japan, the United Kingdom and the USA. The latter, determined to intensify their joint efforts to combat terrorism, agreed that:

> . . . in cases where a country refuses the extradition or prosecution of those who have hijacked an aircraft and/or do not return such aircraft, the heads of state or government will take immediate action to cease all flights to that country.
> At the same time, their governments will initiate action to halt all incoming flights from that country, or from any country by the airlines of the country concerned.[63]

They urged other countries to join them in this commitment.

The Political Affairs Committee responded to this in November 1978 when, by letter of 6 November, it requested authorisation to draw up an own initiative report on hijacking. On 16 November 1978, the enlarged Bureau of the European Parliament authorised the Committee to proceed, and its meeting of 22—23 January again appointed Mr Fletcher-Cooke as its rapporteur. At its meeting of 27 February 1979, the Committee considered and unanimously adopted the motion for resolution on hijacking. This was then debated by the European Parliament on 16 March 1979.

The motion began by recalling previous efforts to combat terrorism, and noted that the weaknesses of the International Civil Aviation Organization conventions of Tokyo, The Hague and Montreal in combating hijacking lay both in the insufficient instruments at their disposal and in the failure of some signatories to ratify the conventions. Significantly, it appealed again to the EEC's member parliaments and governments to ratify the European Convention on the Suppression of Terrorism, and listed its resolutions of 14 January 1977 relating to this,[64] that of 16 November 1977 on terrorist acts in the EEC,[65] and that of 12 April 1978 on terrorism.[66] The motion repeated the Parliament's earlier condemnation of all forms of terrorism and of hijacking in particular. However, it went further than earlier resolutions by recommending that penalties should be invoked against states associated with the EEC prone to providing safe harbours for terrorists and hijackers, and so embraced another aspect of Community affairs in an attempt to improve anti-terrorist measures. Under the motion, the European Parliament requested:

> the Member Governments, in the framework of Political Cooperation, to agree on the most suitable methods of combating hijacking, making it their first aim that all the Member States should subscribe to the commitments entered into by the 'Seven' in Bonn, and [urged] the governments of the Member States to persuade governments of other states to adhere to the same agreement.[67]

The Parliament indicated that it expected member states to introduce 'harmonised provisions in their legislation to implement the commitments of that declaration as soon as possible';[68] and expressed the belief that:

> in order to combat hijacking more effectively provision should be made immediately for the introduction of Conventions for the extradition or punishment of those responsible for such acts in agreements drawn up by the Community, such as association, cooperation and trade agreements and in the Lomé Convention with the African, Caribbean and Pacific countries.[69]

This was the most controversial and significant paragraph in the motion. However, anxious to impress upon member governments the desirability of keeping it informed of developments in the field of measures to combat terrorism, the European Parliament requested the Foreign Ministers meeting in Political Cooperation to inform it regularly about progress, and instructed its own president to forward the resolution on hijacking to the Foreign Ministers, the Council of Ministers, the Commission and member states' parliaments.

Explaining the purpose and content of the Political Affairs Committee's motion to the European Parliament on 16 March, Mr Fletcher-Cooke stressed the vulnerability 'by reason of their technically advanced nature' of European countries to terrorism.[70] Bemoaning the difficulties arising from varying interpretations of terrorism and the failure of the UN to achieve more than minimal agreement on its definition, he pointed out that the European Convention on the Suppression of Terrorism showed that progress could be made on a more limited regional basis. He felt that the provision relating to countries linked to the EEC was especially important.

The debate on the resolution revealed that MEPs were keen to ensure that member states should not be obliged to extradite terrorists to countries that might not observe human rights and should, therefore, reserve the right to choose to prosecute themselves if necessary. Speaking on behalf of the Christian Democratic group, Mr Jahn advocated that EEC member states include the Bonn Convention in their anti-terrorist legislation, and welcomed the measures proposed in respect of associated countries. For the Commission, Mr Brunner welcomed the main features of the resolution without reservation.[71] For the Socialists, Mr Sieglerschmidt tabled an amendment to the paragraph relating to associated countries, which, along with the rest of the resolution, was approved and adopted by the European Parliament. The amended paragraph indicated the Parliament's belief that

> in order to combat hijacking more effectively, immediate provision . . . be made, when concluding Community association, cooperation and trade agreements and renegotiating the Lomé Convention, for the extradition or punishment of those responsible for such acts.[72]

Mr Fletcher-Cooke subscribed to the reformulated paragraph whose immediate relevance lay with the reference to the renegotiation of the Lomé Convention that the EEC was conducting with African, Caribbean and Pacific countries.[73]

In spite of a good deal of attention to the whole question of human rights, this hope did not translate itself into a formal undertaking in the second Lomé Convention. The European Parliament's views had not been completely ignored, neither had they had the desired effect. The same was to be the case when the directly elected MEPs considered terrorism and related issues in September 1979. Once again, the issue of arms supply and control arose with deep divisions apparent between those who favoured Community cooperation on the grounds that it would save money and secure the EEC's independence, and those who felt that even discussion of the issue — the Klepsch Report notwithstanding — was outside the European Parliament's competence.[74] MEPs voted 208 to 87 in favour of debating the issue following objections from French Gaullists, Communists and some Socialists that defence and security matters were the exclusive preserve of the member states.

Tending to accept the majority view of the MEPs with caution, the emphasis of the Commission's view was on technical matters: it was argued the aim should be to ensure the cost-effectiveness of defence-related industrial spending — the implication being that the matter could be discussed at a technical level within the context of a common EEC industrial policy. While space limitations preclude detailed scrutiny of this issue here, a link between this and terrorism was made by the Reverend Ian Paisley. Deploring recent Provisional IRA murders, he told MEPs that while the Provisional IRA would be able to continue acquiring arms from the USA in an election year, the Royal Ulster Constabulary would not, and so advocated EEC independence from the USA in this sector.[75]

Following the murder of Lord Mountbatten in August 1979, the whole issue of terrorism and Community action to combat it was debated, often acrimoniously, at the September session of the European Parliament following the tabling of a question by Lady Elles on behalf of the European Democratic group addressed to the Foreign Ministers concerning the nature of progress towards a common system of extradition.[76] Lady Elles noted that terrorist crimes invariably involved a cross-national element and, therefore, made Community harmonisation crucial. She advocated greater police cooperation, a common policy on extradition or prosecution and common extradition procedures; she noted that states seeking accession to the EEC must be kept informed of the contents of any EEC agreement on extradition (such as that then under consideration) and apprised of their obligation to ratify it upon accession.[77]

Before debate on extradition and Lady Elles' remarks could proceed, Mr Skovmand (Danish People's Movement against the EEC) tried to prevent the issue being debated on the grounds that it fell outside the EEC's competence, and that any Community agreement would infringe national sovereignty and extend terrorist activity to those countries such as Denmark that he asserted did not suffer terrorism by virtue of their greater tolerance relative to their neighbours.[78] Mr Skovmand failed in his attempt. Mr Gendebien ('non-attached': Belgium), alluding to the Council of Ministers' opinion of 30 July 1979 supporting the view that the issue fell outside Parliament's competence, argued that since the Council had agreed to reply to Lady Elles' question, it recognised the Parliament's competence; that, moreover, Parliament was 'automatically competent in any matter discussed by the Council of Ministers'.[79]

Although MEPs agreed on condemning terrorism, they differed over the question of extradition for political offences. Lady Elles dismissed fears articulated about the treatment afforded suspects of political/terrorist offences in different member states on the grounds that the Nine were signatories to the European Convention on Human Rights, which, she maintained, represented a sufficient guarantee of offenders' rights.

Clearly, at the root of this issue was the question of respecting human rights guaranteed by either the European Convention or national constitutions or provisions and whether comparable guarantees existed in each member state. Since the EEC had failed, in spite of pressure from the European Parliament, to promote a citizens' charter, the member states shared only commitment, in this respect, to the Convention. However, Lady Elles reminded MEPs that the whole legal basis of the EEC as expressed in the EEC Court of Justice was founded on the rule of law and recognition of the human rights and fundamental freedoms of EEC citizens. Posing a rhetorical question, she asked how the living and working conditions of all the peoples in the EEC could be constantly improved as stated in the Rome Treaty's preamble if people lived in a state of terrorism and in a state of instability caused by those acts of terrorism.[80] This point was reiterated by Mr Almirante ('non-attached': Italy) who stressed that external security could not be guaranteed in the absence of internal security. He continued:

> For this reason let those who speak in defence of the sovereignty of Member States take note of the fact that there is no sovereignty without the certainty of the rule of law and that [this] is undermined and traduced by those who, on the pretext of exercising the old and mediaeval institution of the right of asylum, detain in their own countries, and therefore protect and defend, terrorists or presumed terrorists, who are enemies of our civilisation and the enemies of Europe.[81]

The main body of the debate focussed on the question of establishing and securing Community acceptance of the principle of 'extradite or try'. Replying to Lady Elles' question, Mr Andrews, the Irish president-in-office explained that the EEC member states were considering measures to intensify cooperation among themselves in a number of areas of criminal law, including extradition. In accordance with understandings reached at the fifth, sixth and seventh European Councils, a group of senior officials had contemplated two measures to this end. The first was an agreement between the member states to apply the European Convention on the Suppression of Terrorism; the second, a draft convention on cooperation in criminal matters between the EEC member states and studied in the context of proposals for the creation of a common European judicial area. He explained that the aim of the former was to apply the European Convention on the Suppression of Terrorism within the EEC by regulating each member state's position while taking into account whether or not a member state had signed or ratified the convention, and whether or not a state had made or intended making a reservation to the convention. This was to be accomplished in such a way as to avoid infringing any member state's constitutional requirements.

The draft convention on cooperation in criminal matters is, similarly, mainly concerned with extradition and applies to 'terrorist-type offences' and 'a broad range of offences of a certain gravity'.[82] Its objectives are to require member states to submit cases to their competent authorities for prosecution in certain circumstances where extradition has been refused; to ensure that they have the jurisdictional competence for this; and to establish simplified procedures. The draft is considered as but a first step in the creation of a European judicial area.[83]

When MEPs debated the issues raised by Lady Elles' question and Mr Andrews' reply, not only were exchanges between the Irish and Northern Irish MEPs particularly acrimonious, but many MEPs clearly doubted whether either the European Convention on the Suppression of Terrorism or the draft EEC agreement on its application in the EEC could be effective instruments against terrorism given the number of reservations expressed by individual member states.

Speaking on behalf of the Socialist group, Mr Sieglerschmidt argued that while there may be some validity in the reservation against the European Convention on the Suppression of Terrorism that its geographical scope, from Iceland to Cyprus, was too large, reservations expressed against ratification by any of the EEC member states rested on shaky foundations. He also pointedly warned against any European judicial area being simply conceived as a 'penal area', and advocated it being supported by a European Charter of Human Rights and the introduction of political, economic, social and cultural rights for EEC citizens.[84] Together with speakers from other Groups, he generally endorsed the motion for a resolution even though there was widespread disquiet as to the effectiveness of any agreement on extradition. Mr d'Angelosante (for the Communist and Allies group) noted that international law could limit the possibility of extradition in the case of political offences, and that this was a rule of Italian constitutional law. Moreover, he felt that the 'extradite or try' provision by itself was inadequate and needed supplementing by the harmonisation of national laws, or by the creation of a European judicial area or by an agreement between the EEC member states to solve the problem in a manner appropriate to the requirements of the present day.[85]

Taking up the problem of national reservations against extradition, Mr Lalor (for the European Progressive Democrats) pointed out that Belgium, Denmark, France, the FRG and the Netherlands reserved the right not to extradite their own nationals for political or non-political offences. Yet, the European Council of July 1976 accepted the principle of 'extradite or try'. Where the European Convention on the Suppression of Terrorism was concerned, several states, including Sweden, Italy, Norway and Portugal, entered reservations as to their right to refuse extradition for particular offences. Ireland had not signed the convention, he explained, because of article 29 of its constitution, which states that Ireland accepts the generally recognised principles of international law as its rule of conduct in its relations with other states. However, as an agreement between EEC members was to be based on the principle of 'extradite or try' and met Ireland's constitutional requirements, he assured MEPs that Ireland would sign an EEC agreement.[86]

Arguing that extradition was one, but not the best, way of combating terrorism, Mr McCartin (European People's Party: Ireland) argued that the European Convention on the Suppression of Terrorism had been rendered 'meaningless' by the numerous qualifications entered against it by several signatories.[87] For his part, Mr Ryan (European People's Party: Ireland) suggested that terrorism could be combated as effectively through a system of common law jurisdiction as through extradition requirements.[88] Repudiating the alleged usefulness of extradition arrangements, Mr Taylor (European Democrat: Northern Ireland) argued that the Irish courts had refused many applications for extradition to Northern Ireland on the grounds that political offences were at stake, and Ireland had become 'a haven of safety for wanted IRA suspects'.[89] Mr Almirante ('non-attached': Italy) and Mr van Minnen (Socialist: Netherlands) underlined the difficulty of defining 'political offences',[90] and Mr Gendebien ('non-attached: Belgium) and Mr Chambeiron (Communist: France) referred to the necessity of protecting the right of political asylum.[91] Mr Gendebien also questioned the effectiveness of extradition and suggested that in order to circumvent the problems of defining political offences and trying them at a national level, 'a European Court independent of States and based on the jury system, should be set up to try all political offences and crimes perpetrated on European Community territory'. He noted that such a system would mean that 'extradition between European states for political offences and crimes would be totally abolished, each State undertaking to have its citizens, like those of other EEC States or non-EEC states, tried by the said European Court'. He saw the advantage of this system lying in Europe's reputation being enhanced 'not by the creation of a police "Internationale" but ... by the establishment of legal machinery guaranteeing absolute respect for democratic principles and true defence of rights and liberties in all circumstances'.[92]

Most MEPs were primarily concerned with measures to combat terrorism, although some raised the question of dealing with the causes of terrorism. In spite of their well-founded reservations that extradition was but a partial step towards accomplishing this, and that any EEC agreement concerning the principle of 'extradite or try' might be tantamount simply to a modification of the basic notions behind the European Convention on the Suppression of Terrorism making them compatible with the most restrictive provisions of individual constitutional requirements, they endorsed current efforts to deal with the problem notably by political as opposed to repressive means.[93]

On 27 September, the European Parliament adopted a motion for resolution tabled by Mr Scott-Hopkins and Mr Bangemann on behalf of the European Democratic group and the Liberal and Democratic group respectively concerning a common system of extradition. During the debate on the resolution, Messrs Sieglerschmidt, Ferri and Zagari endeavoured to secure the amendment of paragraph 2, which urged EEC member governments 'to move towards a common system of extradition in the fight against international crime and terrorism'.[94] They sought its replacement by two paragraphs, one requesting the EEC's national parliaments 'to discuss the agreement by the EEC Member States to apply the European Convention on the fight against terrorism, as soon as the agreement by the Nine is submitted for signature and ratification'; the other expressing the hope that they should ratify the agreement having ensured its compliance with constitutional guarantees that any extradited persons should receive fair legal treatment within the meaning of the European Convention on Human Rights.[95] Sieglerschmidt contended that the original paragraph was redundant given that the EEC member states were preparing to sign an agreement on applying the European Convention on the Suppression of Terrorism, and that the conditions governing its ratification needed defining. He argued that paragraph 2(a) of the amendment outlined in general terms the conditions whereby ratification of an EEC agreement on a common system of extradition would be considered desirable.[96] Mr Scott-Hopkins (European Democrat: United Kingdom) spoke against the amendment because many countries had not signed the European Convention on the Suppression of Terrorism. Not being persuaded by Sieglerschmidt's argument, MEPs voted to adopt the original resolution.

A second resolution on a European judicial area was tabled by MEPs fearful lest one come into being by means of a common system of extradition likely both to infringe and reduce the discretion of the judiciary in the member states and, instead of protecting democracy against terrorism, constitute 'a setback for democracy and hence a victory for terrorism'.[97]

Such objections notwithstanding, the EEC member governments — having established a group of legal experts to draft a criminal convention as a first step in establishing a European judicial area[98] — finalised their efforts to agree on the application of a common system of extradition in the EEC. Following the Dublin European Council in November 1979, the EEC Ministers of Justice endorsed an agreement to apply the broad terms of the European Convention on the Suppression of Terrorism to the EEC. It was agreed that a suspect who was not extradited should stand trial where arrested and regardless of where the crime had been committed. The agreement will enter into force upon its ratification by the member states' national parliaments.

Meanwhile, however, an unsuccessful attempt was made in the European Parliament to secure an urgent debate on the motion for resolution regarding the extradition of Franco Piperno[99] (an Italian suspected of being involved in Moro's assassination). Mr Capanna (a member of the Group for the Technical Coordination and Defence of Independent Groups and Members), rejecting Mr Klepsch's (European People's Party: FRG) argument that the motion was unfit to be received by the House, suggested that Piperno was 'the victim of a serious political frame-up',[100] and that the matter fell under the European Parliament's terms of reference since Piperno's extradition had been requested by France. While some MEPs felt that the real question was a Franco-Italian conflict, others felt that the right to political asylum was being eroded. The request for an urgent debate was rejected and the motion for a resolution referred to the appropriate parliamentary committee.[101] What this exchange revealed, however, was the extent of continuing uncertainty over the implications and effects of any common system of extradition in the EEC. Nevertheless, applying the principle of 'extradite or try' in the EEC has been the main weapon, over and above increased inter-state police cooperation, in the EEC's arsenal against terrorism.

During the course of the elaboration of an agreement between EEC member governments to apply the principle, it became apparent that many of the reservations expressed by EEC member states in respect of signing and/or ratifying the European Convention on the Suppression of Terrorism still appeared valid to some of those member states. Consequently, the agreement was watered down to make it palatable to them. However, it would be erroneous to assume that the problems confronting the EEC's member states in this area were especially acute. Rather, the attempts made both to prevent and to advance the conclusion of the agreement illustrated how national interests could be eventually subordinated to the common interest. While it could be argued that the agreement could have been secured on an intergovernmental basis devoid of EEC intervention given the political will, there can be little doubt that membership of the EEC provided a reason for action, no matter how limited and rudimentary, among the member states. The agreement itself showed that the member states could and needed to harmonise certain matters relating to extradition on the basis of a Council of Europe convention without attempts being undertaken to secure the EEC's accession *per se* to the convention (something that had been mooted in respect of the European Convention on Human Rights).[102] At the same time, a sometimes faltering resolve was reinforced by the member states' common interest in securing comparability among themselves on extradition and prosecution matters, coupled with discussion of the establishment of a European judicial area and failure of the UN and Council of Europe to secure speedy ratification of their anti-terrorist instruments on a uniform basis by the EEC member states, as well as the wave of terrorist offences in Europe during the 1970s.

The member governments agreed that terrorist offences were crimes rather than political offences and should, therefore, be subject to prosecution. To this end, they concentrated on securing acceptance of the principle of 'extradite or try'. This did not imply disregard for the need either to determine and eliminate the causes of terrorism (something often stressed in the European Parliament), or to combat terrorism by means of the addition of penal clauses to association agreements with third countries. Rather, the emphasis on apprehending and punishing terrorists, coupled with the example of how even members of a supranational community could weaken the European Convention on the Suppression of Terrorism when they failed to endorse it, led to the attempt to deal with extradition and prosecution of offences before attempting anything more ambitious. Even so, some member states were only prepared to accept this if accompanied by attempts to create broader agreements. Moreover, while it is true that the European Parliament was successful in urging EEC governments to apply provisions of the European Convention on the Suppression of Terrorism, MEPs failed to see a number of the other provisions of their resolutions translated into concrete measures. Yet MEPs' affirmation of the need to respect human rights and to encourage others to do so had filtered through to the appropriate authorities and provides a moral if not legal pressure on them to heed them. Even so, the effectiveness of such moral suasion has yet to be proved.

In conclusion, it is clear that progress towards a common EEC policy against terrorism has proved highly problematic and the adoption of further measures is likely to become even more difficult with the accession of Greece, Spain and Portugal to the Community. In the meantime, although EEC member governments have at least agreed on the desirability of their all applying key provisions of the European Convention on the Suppression of Terrorism, some — Italy, Denmark and France — have already stated their intention to make use of their right to maintain reservations in respect of 'political offences'. How effective the agreement among the EEC member states will be in combating terrorism remains to be seen.

Notes and References

1. C. Fletcher-Cooke, *Terrorism and the European Community* (London: European Conservative Group, 1979), p. 8.
2. *Ibid.*
3. Consultative Assembly of the Council of Europe, *Recommendation 684* (1972).
4. Consultative Assembly of the Council of Europe, 25th Ordinary Session, *Recommendation 703 (1973) on International Terrorism.*
5. *Explanatory Report on the European Convention on the Suppression of Terrorism* (Strasbourg: Council of Europe, 1977), p. 5.
6. *Recommendation 703, op. cit.*, 6(i)(b).
7. *Ibid.*, 6(ii)(a and b).
8. *Ibid.*, 6(iii).
9. *Ibid.*, Appendix, pp. 29—30.
10. For a discussion of the Council of Europe's powers, see A.H. Robertson, *The Council of Europe* (London: Stevens & Sons, 2nd edn, 1961); and the summary

in his *European Institutions* (London: Stevens & Sons, 3rd edn, 1973), pp. 36—71.

11. *Ibid.,* pp. 59—60.
12. I am obliged to H.-J. Bartsch of the Council's Legal Affairs Directorate for clarifying this point.
13. This is explained especially well in the Council of Europe's *Explanatory Report,* pp. 16—17.
14. *Ibid.,* p. 18.
15. *The Sittings* (European Parliament), no. 4 (April 1976), p. 24.
16. *European Parliament Working Documents,* 222/76.
17. *Debates of the European Parliament* [*DEP*], no. 211 (January 1977) p. 188 and pp. 203—5.
18. *European Parliament Working Documents,* 513/76.
19. *European Parliament Working Documents,* 372/77: Report drawn up on behalf of the Political Affairs Committee on acts of terrorism in the Community: PE 50.974/fin.
20. *European Parliament Working Documents,* 327/77 rev and 328/77 rev respectively.
21. *European Parliament Working Documents,* 327/77 rev: PE 50.776, pp. 2—3.
22. *European Parliament Working Documents,* 328/77 rev: PE 50.777/rev, Clause 5, p. 2.
23. *Ibid.,* Clause 6.
24. *Ibid.,* Clause 8.
25. *Ibid.,* Clause 7.
26. *European Parliament Working Documents,* 372/77, p. 5.
27. *DEP,* no. 223 (15 November 1977) p. 67.
28. *Ibid.*
29. *Ibid.*
30. *Ibid.,* p. 68.
31. *Ibid.,* pp. 71—2.
32. *Ibid.,* p. 72.
33. *Ibid.,* p. 73. This was done with German war criminals after 1945.
34. *Ibid.,* p. 70.
35. *The Sittings* (November 1977), p. 9.
36. The United Kingdom introduced a levy on air transport estimated at £15 million per annum to finance better security at airports. See *DEP,* no. 223 (November 1978), p. 79.
37. *Ibid.* His party had introduced a bill in the Danish *Folketing* to this effect. Also see *ibid.,* p. 86.
38. *Ibid.,* p. 80.
39. *Ibid.*
40. *Ibid.,* p. 81.
41. *Ibid.,* p. 86.
42. *Ibid.,* p. 87.
43. *Ibid.,* p. 135.
44. *Ibid.* (March 1978), p. 23.
45. *European Parliament Working Documents* 50/78.
46. *The Sittings* no. 9 (November 1978).
47. See *DEP,* no. 229 (April 1978), p. 115. This was the second time that the European Council had mentioned a 'judicial area'.
48. *Ibid.,* p. 120.
49. *Ibid.,* p. 142—3.

50. *Ibid.,* p. 139.
51. *Ibid.,* pp. 149—52.
52. *Ibid.,* pp. 164—5.
53. *Ibid.* Also see, *The Sittings* (April 1978), p. 15.
54. For a summary of the European Parliament's tributes to Moro see: *The Sittings* (May 1978), p. 15.
55. *Ibid.,* p. 15 and p. 20.
56. *European Parliament Working Documents,* 284/78: Oral question 0-41/78: PE 54.137.
57. *The Sittings* (September 1978), p. 5.
58. Article 235 states 'Where action by the Community appears necessary to achieve, in the course of operation of the common market, one of the objectives of the Community, and where this Treaty has not provided for the necessary powers of action, the Council shall, by unanimous decision, on a proposal from the Commission and after the Assembly has been consulted, take the appropriate steps'.
59. Article 100 states 'The Council shall, by unanimous decision, on a proposal from the Commission, issue directives for the approximation of such provisions imposed by law, regulation and administrative action in Member States as directly affect the setting up or operation of the common market'.
60. Article 36 states 'The provisions of Articles 30 to 34 inclusive shall not preclude prohibitions or restrictions on imports, exports or goods in transit justified on the grounds of public morality; public policy ('ordre public'); public safety or security; the protection of health and life of humans, animals or plants; the protection of national treasures possessing artistic, historic or archaelogical value; or the protection of industrial and commercial property. Such prohibitions or restrictions shall not, however, amount to a means of arbitrary discrimination nor to a disguised restriction on trade between Member States'.
61. *Financial Times,* 11 October 1978.
62. *European Parliament Working Documents,* 663/78, PE 57.091/fin.
63. *Ibid.,* Annex.
64. *European Parliament Working Documents,* 513/76/corr. Also see, *Official Journal,* no. C30 (7 February 1977), p. 34.
65. *European Parliament Working Documents,* 372/77, and *Official Journal* no. C299 (12 December 1977), p. 24.
66. *European Parliament Working Documents,* 50/78, and *Official Journal* no. C108 (8 May 1978), p. 36.
67. *European Parliament Working Documents,* 663/78, *op. cit.,* para. z, p. 6.
68. *Ibid.,* para. 3.
69. *Ibid.,* para. 4.
70. *DEP,* no. 241, March 1979, p. 237.
71. *Ibid.,* p. 238.
72. *Ibid.,* p. 245.
73. See *EC Bulletin* (May 1979) points 2.2.64 and 2.2.65ff for details; and *EC Bulletin* (July—August 1979) points 2.2.51—55 and *EC Bulletin* (October 1979) points 1.3.1—1.3.5 on Lomé II signed on 31 October 1979.
74. See Klepsch Report, *EC Bulletin* (June 1978) point 2.3.17.
75. See *The Week,* 24—28 September 1979, p. 5.
76. *European Parliament Working Documents,* 1-288/79; Oral question 0-19/79, PE 59.182.
77. *DEP,* no. 245 (September 1979) pp. 170—1.

78. *Ibid.,* p. 172.
79. *Ibid.,* p. 182.
80. *Ibid.,* p. 172.
81. *Ibid.,* p. 182.
82. *Ibid.,* p. 173.
83. *Ibid.*
84. *Ibid.,* pp. 173—4.
85. *Ibid.,* p. 175.
86. *Ibid.,* pp. 176—7.
87. *Ibid.,* p. 179.
88. *Ibid.,* p. 180.
89. *Ibid.*
90. *Ibid.,* p. 181 and p. 184.
91. *Ibid.,* p. 182 and p. 185.
92. *Ibid.*
93. *EC Bulletin* (September 1979) point 2.3.15.
94. *European Parliament Working Documents,* 1-339/79/rev, PE 59.601/rev.
95. *DEP,* no. 245, *op. cit.,* p. 235.
96. *Ibid.,* p. 236.
97. *European Parliament Working Documents,* 1-370/79/rev, PE 59.624/rev.
98. *The Week,* 12—16 November 1979, p. 14. Also see the *Annual Report to Parliament on Political Cooperation* presented on 24 October 1979 by Mr O'Kennedy, chairman of the Conference of Foreign Ministers of the member states meeting in Political Cooperation, in *EC Bulletin* (October 1979) point 3.4.1., p. 137.
99. *European Parliament Working Documents,* 1-435/79.
100. *DEP,* no. 246 (October 1979), p. 325.
101. *Ibid.,* p. 327.
102. For details see Memorandum on the accession of the European Communities to the Convention for the Protection of Human Rights and Fundamental Freedoms (adopted by the Commission on 4 April 1979), *EC Bulletin* Supplement 2/79.

CHAPTER 8

Legal Responses to Terrorism: Towards European Cooperation?

David Freestone

Terrorism is not a legal term of art. It has been defined for national purposes,[1] and it is generally recognisable without difficulty, but for the lawyer — particularly the international lawyer — it presents a number of definitional problems.[2] These problems highlight the dependence of law upon the political order in which it operates, for successful definition must be based upon agreement as to the nature of the phenomenon to be described, and at an international level there is wide disagreement as to the circumstances in which it is legitimate to use violence for political ends.[3] Terrorist acts will generally be clear violations of national criminal laws, but the explicit political motives of the offender render them different in kind from other offences. This difference will plainly depend upon the observer's stance: the political motive may make the offence excusable, or it may make it appear more heinous than a comparable 'common' offence. This problem of stance — of, for example, effectively distinguishing between a terrorist and a freedom fighter — is the main obstacle to international attempts to take common action against terrorists. The purpose of this chapter is to outline the international legal framework within which states operate in their endeavours to control terrorism — or more precisely to apprehend terrorists — and to examine some of the more persistent difficulties that have faced Western European states, particularly when seeking international co-operation in the suppression of terrorism. It is not therefore the intention to compare in detail the various national counter-terrorist laws enacted by these states, although this would be a valuable task at a specialised level.

Nevertheless, at a legal level, the European states examined in this book do have a great deal in common. They have all chosen to join a common core of European regional institutions and to accept similar international constraints upon their legal systems. All are members of the Council of Europe.[4] All have accepted the standards of civil and political rights set out in the

European Convention on Human Rights,[5] which is intended to set out the basic civil and political rights that constitute the 'common heritage of political traditions, ideals, freedom and the rule of law'[6] of the member states of the Council of Europe. It specifically includes basic rights to personal freedom, fair trial, freedom of thought, expression and peaceful assembly, as well as certain rights to family life. All states have made the optional declarations under article 46 of the convention accepting the compulsory jurisdiction of the European Court of Human Rights (at Strasbourg) to decide 'all matters concerning the interpretation and application' of the convention.[7] All bar France have made similar declarations under article 25 accepting the right of an individual to invoke the machinery against them in the event of his being the victim of a breach of the rights protected by the convention.[8] The treaty regime thus established between states accepting both the compulsory jurisdiction of the court and the right of individual application represents an important step in the development of supranational (as opposed to international) mechanisms for the protection of human rights. When it was introduced, the right of individual application particularly represented a significant departure from traditional international litigation in which only states took part and in which the individual lacked the procedural capacity to bring claims, the enforcement of such rights as he had being dependent upon their espousal by an interested state.

In addition, all states are members of the EEC.[9] Apart from the obvious economic and political community of interest that membership of the EEC is intended to carry with it, there is a further legal bond in the common system of Community law that is binding upon member states. European Community law represents an even more radical departure from the tradition of international litigation referred to above. Under the terms of the treaties setting up the European Communities, individuals are given, in specified circumstances, the right to apply directly to the European Court of Justice in Luxembourg to complain of violations of Community law affecting them.[10] Community law also gives individuals specific rights that can be enforced by them in the courts of the member states and it obliges national courts to give precedence to those rights over conflicting rules of national law.[11] Significantly, the Luxembourg Court has suggested in a number of important judgments that the rights recognised by the European Convention form part of the common body of law upon which the more specific law of the EEC is based.[12] Thus, common membership of the two major European organisations — the Council of Europe and the EEC — carries with it common acceptance of an important body of civil and political rights.

Terrorism represents a significant threat to these shared liberal—democratic values. It has been argued that the very success of terrorism is itself 'a sort of back-handed compliment paid to the humanity and legalism of the bourgeois state' for 'it is not hard to imagine the reaction of an oriental despot or even a feudal ruler of medieval Europe to an attempt to change policy by the taking of hostages'.[13] Whatever the historical accuracy of this observation, it does bring into focus the considerable problems involved in maintaining common civil liberties while at the same time facing up to the threat to life and limb that terrorism represents. At best, the maintenance of all civil rights is a question of balancing the rights of one individual against the rights of another, or the interest of the state, which in a liberal democracy is taken to be the common interest. This balance is brought out in the text of the European Convention itself. Article 11 for example provides that 'Everyone has the right to freedom of peaceful assembly and to freedom of association with others . . .', but it subjects the exercise of this right to restrictions that are 'prescribed by law and are necessary in a democratic society in the interests of national security or public safety, for the prevention of disorder or crime, for the protection of health or morals or for the protection of the rights and freedoms of others.' Similar restrictions are also recognised in the exercise of other rights, such as 'freedom of thought, conscience and religion' (article 9) and 'freedom of expression', which includes 'freedom to hold opinions and to receive and impart information and ideas without interference by public authority and regardless of frontiers' (article 10).

Plainly the balancing of interests that these and other articles require is a difficult task, often involving explicit political factors that it has been argued should not be left to lawyers.[14] Nevertheless, given existing machinery, the interpretation of phrases such as 'necessary in a democratic society' and 'in the interests of national security' must of necessity involve a consideration of the atmosphere of the times. Here the *threat* of terrorism can have a particularly insidious effect if it shifts the centre of balance away from the rights of the individual and towards the interest of national security.

By way of extended example may be cited the legal responses to the troubles in Northern Ireland.[15] The problems faced there are unique and it would be wrong to compare the nature or the scale of terrorism there with any of the other states of Western Europe. Nevertheless, the emergency legislation enacted in response to the troubles in Northern Ireland by the Irish as well as the UK governments does demonstrate vividly the inroads that may be made into the civil rights protected by the European Convention at a time of terrorist-precipitated emergency, even by governments committed to the maintenance of liberal—democratic values. In fact, the nature of the emergency and the form the legislative response took led both the UK and the Irish governments at various times to derogate from their obligations under the European Convention.[16] This they were permitted to do 'in time of war or other public emergency threatening the life of the nation' provided the derogations did not exceed 'the extent strictly required by the exigencies of the situation' and were 'not inconsistent with [their] other obligations under international law' (article 15(1)).

The now substantial body of emergency legislation that has at various times been in force in Great Britain and Northern Ireland[17] (often with parallels in the Irish Republic[18]) has markedly shifted the balance of rights in favour of national security. Notably it has created entirely new offences like membership of a proscribed organisation,[19] collection of information likely to be helpful to terrorists,[20] and, in certain situations, mere failure to disclose information known or believed to be of assistance in the suppression of terrorism;[21] it has abolished jury trial for specified 'terrorist' offences;[22] and has given substantial powers to the executive, ranging from the right of the Secretary of State to proscribe 'any organisation that appears to him to be concerned in terrorism or in promoting or encouraging it' (a form of words that has been taken by the courts to effectively preclude review of his decisions),[23] to extended powers of entry and search, arrest and detention.[24] Such powers were described by one Secretary of State as 'Draconian' and one commentator has described the approach adopted by the UK government as a 'covert, non-justiciable military—security approach'.[25] These extensive executive powers have circumscribed the role the courts themselves can play in maintaining traditional common law values. In such an atmosphere, while commentators have commended the national judiciary for the standards of independence and impartiality they have maintained,[26] neither the United Kingdom nor the Irish courts, for perhaps understandable reasons, have been seen to spring to the defence of traditional civil liberties in their interpretation of widely drafted emergency legislation.[27]

In such a situation the European Convention does represent some form of stable yardstick against which to measure counter-terrorist measures. A number of actions have been started against the UK government using the machinery in Strasbourg, of which perhaps the most significant is the action by the Irish government itself.[28] This action led to the first ever inter-state case to reach the Strasbourg Court. The court found that the notorious 'five techniques' used at the Palace Barracks interrogation centre in Northern Ireland (i.e. wall standing, hooding, subjection to noise, deprivation of sleep, deprivation of food and drink) were in breach of article 3 of the European Convention in that they constituted 'inhuman and degrading treatment' (although not 'torture' as had been alleged by the Irish government and found by the European Commission in its initial inquiries).[29] The court also found that the nature of the situation in Northern Ireland did justify the derogation made by the UK government from articles 5 and 6 (relating to criminal process) and that 'extra-judicial deprivation of liberty' (internment) was not a measure disproportionate in the circumstances. Having made this finding, the Strasbourg Court did not see fit to use its powers to award any specific remedy (such as the award of compensation under article 50).

The significance of the case goes beyond the bounds of the judgment itself. The action took a long time to reach the court: the application was first made in 1971; judgment was given in 1978. Strong feelings were aroused in the United Kingdom by the decision of the Irish government to press the proceedings as far as the court, primarily because international litigation of this type puts considerable pressure on the defendant state, whose domestic laws and administrative procedures are held up for inspection against international standards. The effect of the protracted proceedings may be seen most clearly in the period prior to the 1978 judgment. In 1972 the UK government had of its own admission abandoned the 'five techniques', and although its policy of internment was to some extent vindicated in the court's judgment, that policy too had been abandoned in 1975, for reasons that, although not solely attributable to the Strasbourg proceedings, must plainly have taken them into account. In addition, it has been suggested that the Strasbourg proceedings may well have had a bearing upon the decision of the UK government to prosecute a number of soldiers and policemen against whom allegations of ill-treatment had been made, and to issue the security forces with new and detailed instructions on the treatment of persons under arrest and interrogation, emphasising particularly the prohibition on brutality and the risk of prosecution.[30]

The political implications of such inter-state proceedings are obviously considerable, hence their rarity. The fact that the Irish government was prepared to take up and pursue the action does reinforce what has been said about the unique character of the problems in Northern Ireland. Even so, the European Convention has broken new ground in its provisions allowing the right of individual application to the Commission of Human Rights and its potential should not be undervalued. There has been a general tendency throughout Western Europe to escalate penalties for 'terrorist' offences and to increase the powers the executive may hold in reserve for emergency situations. It is plainly important to make provision for effective counter-terrorist action, but in the heat of the moment the long-term effects of large-scale inroads into traditional civil rights may well be overlooked. Against this background the Strasbourg machinery provides an important and perhaps undervalued vehicle for the protection of these rights and, perhaps one might say tentatively in the light of *Ireland* v. *United Kingdom,* for the consideration of the proportionality of government action against a common European standard.

THE TRANSNATIONAL OR FUGITIVE TERRORIST

Domestic legislation is only one part of the role that law plays in the attempts of states to suppress terrorism. Terrorist activities do not always take place in the territory of the state against which the activity is directed, nor are terrorists always apprehended in the state where they have committed their offences. Effective anti-terrorist action therefore of necessity requires some degree of international cooperation, be it only the willingness of a state of refuge to extradite terrorist offenders to states that are willing and have the jurisdiction to try them. It should be noted that there is no general obligation imposed by international law upon such a state either to try or to extradite fugitive offenders within its borders. While a terrorist remains within the country of his crime that state will usually have the dominant, although not the exclusive, interest in bringing him to trial. In fact the right to exercise criminal jurisdiction over individuals within your territory is one of the cherished aspects of state sovereignty. Having said this however, in such a situation legal considerations may not be seen as the most pertinent. The territorial state may not wish to become involved in the trial or imprisonment of a terrorist for fear of reprisal or for political or even economic reasons. If, for example, the terrorist activities were directed at foreign nationals a state may wish to maintain a neutral stance. Such a stance might affect its willingness to prosecute the crimes in its own courts, although not necessarily its willingness to extradite the offender to another state with the jurisdiction to try them. Leaving aside for the present the issues involved in extradition proceedings, it may be useful at this point to examine the grounds under international law that may permit a state to claim jurisdiction to try criminal offences, bearing in mind the particular problems raised by the trial of terrorists.

The significance of jurisdiction in this respect is two-fold. From a national point of view a state's domestic courts will not have power to try offenders who are brought before them if, for example, the offences were committed in another country, unless national law specifically gives them that power. From an international point of view, extradition may be refused if the basis of jurisdiction over the offender on which the claim of the requesting state is founded is not recognised by the requested state. Whether such a request will in fact be refused is a matter for the domestic law of the requested state, but because states rest their claims to jurisdiction upon different principles it is obvious that anomalies are likely to arise. As will be indicated below, a state's approach to the issue of criminal jurisdiction is generally determined by its legal traditions. For this reason, if no other, states are unlikely to enact wholesale changes in their jurisdictional law. Clearly, a more flexible approach to jurisdictional claims might well close many of the more obvious loopholes through which it is possible for the terrorist as well as the common criminal to slip. The issues discussed below should, however, be kept in perspective. Criminal jurisdiction is unlikely by itself to solve any of the problems that result in terrorism, but it may have an important part to play in an overall strategy, particularly a strategy involving international cooperation. It also gives rise to particular problems of its own that in this context are worthy of examination.

Grounds for criminal jurisdiction

Primarily jurisdiction rests in the state where the offence was committed.[31] This is known as territorial jurisdiction, and territory for these purposes includes ships and aircraft registered in that state. For a number of reasons this is regarded as the most fundamental form of jurisdiction: it is drawn from a state's sovereign right to make and enforce laws governing its territory, but it also has obvious conveniences in that in most cases the offender will still be there, as will witnesses, etc.[32]

The second form of jurisdiction is based upon the nationality of the offender rather than the place where he/she commits his/her offence. This is known as personal jurisdiction. States with civil law systems (i.e. those loosely modelled on the French system) have commonly claimed such jurisdiction over their nationals, but it has not generally found favour with common law countries (i.e. those with legal systems based upon the English model, e.g. United States and the Commonwealth). Common law systems rest the majority of their jurisdictional claims upon territory, with the exception of a few offences like treason, murder and bigamy, for which they will claim extra-territorial jurisdiction over nationals. This division between the civil law and the common law countries can result in obvious anomalies. For example, civil law countries will claim jurisdiction over their nationals who commit offences in common law countries, but common law countries will not necessarily have the corresponding right to try their nationals who commit offences abroad. Should the common law state then refuse to extradite such an offender (e.g. because he/she *is* a national, or because his/her offence was political) then there will be a significant loophole in jurisdiction that may effectively prevent him/her from standing trial. Another anomaly of a rather different, albeit related, kind may arise between two common law states — for example, Ireland and United Kingdom. The Irish constitution forbids the extradition of political offenders, so that an individual who commits a political offence (which for these purposes means a 'terrorist' offence) in Northern Ireland and crosses the border into the Irish Republic cannot be extradited, nor under traditional common law theory can he/she be tried in the Irish Republic.

In 1975, in recognition of this particular anomaly, both the Irish and the UK governments introduced legislation expressly giving their courts extra-territorial jurisdiction to try such offenders for offences committed in the other section of Ireland and providing for cooperation in the provision of evidence, etc., for such trial.[33] In fact, these powers have only recently been used for the first time.[34] It is unlikely that this lack of use reflects the deterrent effect of such legislation. More likely explanations may be found in the technical difficulties in collecting evidence for extra-territorial prosecution, or in the fact that the number of such fugitives is somewhat smaller than the UK government suspects. This example does, however, put the issue of jurisdiction into perspective as it is only one aspect of an infinitely more complicated picture.

In addition to territorial and personal jurisdiction, jurisdiction is also claimed according to three other principles, all of which operate extra-territorially: the protective, the universal and the passive personality principles. Protective jurisdiction covers the right of states to try offences that threaten their security, institutions and national interests and that are committed *outside* their territory. A classic example of the use of the protective principle may be found in the French Penal Code prior to its amendment in 1975:

> Every foreigner who outside the territory of the Republic renders himself guilty, either as a perpetrator or as accomplice, of a felony or misdemeanour against the security of the State or the counterfeiting of the seal of the State or current national monies may be prosecuted and tried according to the provisions of French law if he is arrested in France or if the Government obtains his extradition.

It is, therefore, a form of extra-territorial jurisdiction, but it does not thereby give that state the right to enter the territory of another in order to seize an offender; it depends for its effectiveness upon the offender finding his way into the hands of the relevant authorities, either freely, by entering their territory, or by his formal surrender. Plainly, a state whose national interests have been affected is likely to press vigorously for his extradition from the state where the offence was committed, or from a third state.

The universal principle of jurisdiction allows states to try offences defined according to international rather than national law. Its origin lies in the universal right of states to try pirates apprehended on the high seas and hence outside any territorial jurisdiction. It has been extended to include jurisdiction over slave trading and in recent times has been claimed over war crimes,[35] genocide,[36] and even drug trafficking and apartheid.[37] Following the spate of aircraft hijacking that began in the 1960s,[38] it was suggested that hijacking could be regarded as a form of air-piracy and, therefore, could be prosecuted under international law on the basis of universal jurisdiction by any state, wheresoever or by whomsoever it was committed. This argument, for all its appeal to the anti-terrorist lobby, has not found general favour with states, although there has been some recognition of the advantages of such an argument in treaty law. Both the 1970 Hague Convention for the Suppression of Unlawful Seizure of Aircraft[39] and the 1971 Montreal Convention for the Suppression of Unlawful Acts against the Safety of Civil Aircraft[40] impose the obligation upon contracting states to adopt the necessary measures to assume jurisdiction over hijackers in such a wide variety of circumstances that the treaty regime has been described as establishing a 'quasi-universal jurisdiction over acts of aerial terrorism'.[41]

Both conventions recognise not only the territorial and nationality principles, but also the jurisdiction of the state where the hijacked plane first lands, of the state where the lessee of the aircraft has permanent residence or principal place of business, or, most significantly, of the state where the alleged offender happens to be.[42]

Under the passive personality principle, a state claims jurisdiction on the basis of the nationality of the *victim* of the offence. Because the application of this principle in practice will often overlap or conflict with other forms of jurisdiction, its exact status under international law is controversial. International law is drawn from two main sources: treaty and custom. In the absence of generally accepted treaty law regulating states' jurisdictional claims, such claims must be judged according to custom, by which is meant those practices of states that have been accepted either expressly or by implication as law. The passive personality principle, however, lies at the fringes of customary practice. It has found a degree of acceptance among civil law countries (e.g. article 4 of the German Penal Code[43]), but it has been consistently opposed by common law countries and by a number of important commentators.[44]

In 1927 its legality under international law was challenged by France in a case before the World Court — the *Lotus* case.[45] This arose from a collision between a French vessel of that name and a Turkish vessel, the Boz-Kourt. Turkish nationals were killed in the collision and article 6 of the Turkish Penal Code (which gave effect to the passive personality principle) was used to try the French officer of the watch when the SS Lotus arrived at Constantinople. France argued vigorously that international law did not permit national courts to claim such jurisdiction. In giving judgment however, the court did not reject the principle as illegal, but neither did it end the controversy, for it accepted Turkey's right to try the Frenchman on the alternative ground that the deaths took place aboard a Turkish ship and therefore on Turkish territory.

Since the *Lotus* case a number of international treaties have expressly prohibited the use of the passive personality principle — the most significant perhaps being the 1958 Geneva Convention on the Law of the Sea, which by article 11 prohibits its use in circumstances analogous to those of the *Lotus* case.[46] But these conventional rules are generally only binding upon contracting states. In the absence of a general rule of international law expressly prohibiting such a practice, it is difficult to argue that a state is acting illegally in exercising such jurisdiction. Recognising the difficulties, a commentator has recently suggested that although the passive personality principle may not be relied upon as the *sole* basis for jurisdiction over acts performed extra-territorially, it does provide a useful *additional* ground for jurisdiction. So that when linked, for example, with protective jurisdiction it may strengthen a state's claim to exercise extra-territorial jurisdiction in a number of useful situations, e.g. claiming the extradition of an offender in competition with another state.[47]

Significantly perhaps, it has been seen recently as an important weapon for states to have in their fight against international terrorism.[48] In 1972 it was specifically adopted for this purpose by Israel,[49] and in 1975, in one of the little ironies of history, by France.[50] After a terrorist attack on the French embassy in The Hague, an amendment was introduced to the provision of the French Penal Code quoted above, giving French courts the right to try foreigners who committed offences outside France against French diplomatic or consular agents or offices, if they were arrested in or extradited to France. The irony of this new law was pointed out by Deputy Jean Pierre Cot when the 1975 amendment was debated in the French Assembly. Cot took the opportunity of reminding Jean Foyer, Chairman of the Assembly Committee on Laws, which had supported the amendment, that France had opposed such jurisdiction in the famous *Lotus* case. In response, Foyer somewhat pragmatically reminded him that France had lost the case.[51]

Bringing the fugitive before the courts

So far, the discussion has concentrated upon the legal principles upon which a state may claim the right to try criminals. Of more practical significance perhaps is the question of how the fugitive offender is to be brought before those courts. In the absence of express consent, international law does not permit a state to exercise its criminal authority within the borders of another state and such consent is unlikely to be given.[52] Short, therefore, of illegal seizure or their voluntary surrender, the only way that such fugitives can be obtained is by their extradition or deportation, which is dependent upon the cooperation of foreign authorities. These two processes are by no means synonymous, for they are designed for different purposes: extradition is the formal surrender of a fugitive criminal to a requesting state; deportation is the summary expulsion of an alien.

Deportation
In Western Europe generally, extradition is a judicial procedure in which the various requirements of extradition law (which will be discussed below) have to be proved to the satisfaction of a court. Deportation, by contrast, is an executive act based upon a state's sovereign right to exclude or expel undesirable aliens. Such a right is not unfettered.[53] International law at the very least requires minimum standards of conduct in the handling of the deportation,[54] and treaty law has limited the right still further. Member states of the EEC, for example, have accepted definite limits upon their rights to deport nationals of other member states.[55] Nevertheless, deportation to a specified state in response to a prior request from that state is not contrary to international law. Should the deportee be a fugitive offender,

such action avoids all the technical difficulties of extradition (there is no need for treaty arrangements, no exclusion of political offenders) and is quicker and cheaper than extradition. Its advantages to the executive are obvious, but it should be stressed that in many of the states of Western Europe (including the United Kingdom) such a use of deportation is, if not actually unlawful, highly controversial.

To use deportation as a form of what has been called 'disguised extradition'[56] is a flagrant misuse of a civil administrative procedure; it avoids all the formalities, but also all the procedural safeguards of the Western European method of extradition. Such arguments against deportation do not, however, as one writer has commented, 'outweigh its convenience in practice'.[57] Even in the United Kingdom, where extradition is a judicial procedure, the courts have not in practice utilised their power to challenge such conduct by reviewing the grounds upon which a decision to deport is made,[58] or by imputing bad faith to a government decision to deport to a specified destination from where it is known that the deportee is a fugitive.[59]

A recent study has vividly demonstrated that deportation is an important method of bringing offenders to trial.[60] The study of 86 instances of efforts to apprehend international terrorists between 1 January 1960 and 30 June 1977 showed that 20 states requested the extradition of 87 persons from 21 states, but that only 6 requests were granted while 75 were denied (of whom more than half were subsequently prosecuted locally). In the same period, 145 people were deported by 28 states to 25 destinations. Disturbing as these figures may appear in the light of previous comments, it should be remembered that these figures are not restricted to Europe, that in some states extradition itself is an executive act and the distinction between the two procedures in practice is not as pronounced as it is in Western Europe, and that some of these deportations took place between states without extradition arrangements (e.g. Cuba/USA). They also demonstrate a surprising willingness by states to cooperate in the prosecution of terrorists, or at very least an unwillingness to harbour them, and must add considerable fuel to the argument that extradition procedures are in need of considerable simplification.

How then does extradition work, and what are the technical difficulties involved?

Extradition

Extradition,[61] or the formal surrender of fugitive offenders, has a history that can be traced back over 3000 years, but the modern practice of extradition between European states has its roots in treaties entered into in the eighteenth and nineteenth centuries.[62] In the seventeenth century, Hugo Grotius, who is often called somewhat loosely the 'father of international law', argued that the law of nations imposed a general obligation upon states either to surrender up or to try offenders within their borders — a principle known as *aut dedere aut judicare*.[63] However, by the nineteenth century, the establishment of the modern sovereign state had undermined much of the support for this proposition, as unfettered jurisdictional power became seen as an important facet of a state's sovereignty. In the absence of a general obligation under customary law, extradition came to depend upon a network of bilateral treaties entered into in a somewhat *ad hoc* fashion. Such general international law as there is on the matter must therefore be drawn empirically from the practice of states. By the mid-nineteenth century, in spite of this somewhat haphazard evolution, certain common principles had begun to emerge, based for a number of reasons upon the treaty-making practices of France.[64] As a result of this common model there is a surprising degree of consistency in the form and content of extradition treaties and national extradition statutes. That consistency, however, still bears some of the marks of its nineteenth-century origins and commentators are generally agreed that at a global level there is a pressing need for modernisation and harmonisation. An important start has been made in this process by the European Convention on Extradition,[65] but the fact that the United Kingdom is not a party highlights the fact that there are still differences in practice between civil law and common law countries, which although not insuperable are considerable obstacles to the sort of worldwide multilateral treaty that it has been argued is necessary for a complete rationalisation of international extradition. The system of extradition in the United Kingdom, for example, has recently been called a 'creaking steam engine affair'.[66] This judgement is based upon evidence that suggests that — transnational terrorism apart — extradition is not fulfilling its 'bread and butter' role of the recovery of 'common' criminals — be they train robbers, or persons accused of murder, theft or even exchange control frauds. For example, it has been reported that in 1978, of the 13 men whose extradition was requested by the British authorities, only 7 were returned. This low return was not regarded as exceptional; in fact it was said to have been a good year.[67] Small wonder then if the risk of extradition does not hold a great deal of fear for the terrorist, with or without powerful connections. In addition to procedural difficulties, the terrorist apprehended abroad may have further cards to play, in that political factors may influence the decision to extradite, even in those states where it is a judicial rather than a purely executive process.[68]

First, the majority of national systems permit the executive the final decision on whether an extradition is to go ahead. Even in those states where extradition is a judicial process, the practice is generally to permit the executive to overrule a positive decision to extradite (although not a negative decision). This power may well be exercised to protect the interests of the fugitive, but it can make the executive subject to political or terrorist pressure to veto extradition. Such pressure may even be evident in the judicial decision itself. The apparent impartiality of judicial proceedings may be a useful diplomatic device to shield a state that has refused extradition from the accusation of bad faith, but it would be naïve to suppose that the decision of a court on a matter of extradition is made in complete isolation from political factors. Such factors may be crucial. This is not necessarily to impugn the independence of the judiciary, but merely to acknowledge that judges, like any decision-makers, are subject to political pressures, whether explicit or implicit, whether as a result of their own political perspective or in recognition of the difficulties that may be faced by the executive if their decision is made in one particular way. Such factors may well have been dominant in the decision of the French court in 1977 to release Abu Daoud, a man alleged to have been an organiser of the massacre of Israeli athletes during the Munich Olympic Games in 1972.[69] The decision has been defended on certain narrow legal grounds, but it was certainly neither within the spirit of the extradition treaties with Germany and Israel (both of whom had requested Daoud's extradition) nor of the European Convention on the Suppression of Terrorism, which France had recently signed although not ratified. More significant perhaps was the current political atmosphere: France was courting the Arab countries; President Giscard d'Estaing was about to pay an official visit to Saudi Arabia to discuss oil supplies; a $150 million defence agreement was pending with Egypt; and the government was negotiating secretly through Libya for the release of the anthropologist, Madame Claustre, held by rebels in Chad.[70] Whatever interpretation one puts upon these facts, it is difficult to imagine that they did not influence in some way the controversial decision to release Daoud.

Second, one of the most enduring principles of extradition law has been the exemption of 'political offenders'. The definition of a 'political offender' has always been an issue of controversy, but terrorists for obvious reasons have been able to take advantage of this exception. Perhaps the most recent example at the time of writing was the decision in May 1979 of the US Federal Magistrate, Mr Frederick Woelflen, to refuse the extradition of the alleged IRA bomber Peter McMullen from California on exactly these grounds.[71] However, having acknowledged that the extradition of terrorists can be something of a special case, terrorists do provide the *causes célèbres* that give an immediacy to the need to overhaul extradition procedure generally and to find solutions to the more intractable problems.

What then does a state currently need to do in order to secure the extradition of a fugitive offender? Here again there is no one answer — it will depend upon the domestic laws of the requested state and the terms of any extradition treaty that may be in force between the two states. Subject, however, to these considerable caveats, it is possible to outline certain general principles underlying the extradition process, which should make the complexity of the task of general harmonisation apparent, and it will then be possible to consider the adaptions that have been made to existing procedures to facilitate the trial or extradition of terrorists.

Once a state has made a request for an offender, the extradition becomes a matter for the domestic law of the requested state. Here the first main divergencies in national laws can be seen. Common law systems are firmly based upon the requirement of treaty arrangements. The English Extradition Act 1870, for example, prevents extradition except in the presence of, and in accordance with the terms of, a treaty. In contrast, the French Extradition law of 1927[72] permits extradition in the absence of a treaty. Indeed, the 1927 act is only strictly necessary for situations where no treaty arrangements exist, as the French constitution gives properly ratified treaties the status of domestic law. It should be stressed, however, that extradition in the absence of a treaty is based upon international comity (goodwill) and is entirely discretionary. The French model is typical of most civil law systems, although the Netherlands will not extradite in the absence of a treaty[73] and Germany will only extradite on the basis of reciprocity (i.e. the willingness of the requesting state to extradite to Germany in the same circumstances).[74]

Closely linked to the national procedures for extradition is the problem of what constitutes an 'extraditable' offence. The English Extradition Act of 1870 requires that only persons charged with or convicted of offences specified in the treaty with the requesting state may be extradited. Other states adopt what is known as the eliminative method whereby all offences punishable by an agreed degree of severity (usually a minimum penalty) are extraditable.[75] Although this method (which is adopted by the European Convention on Extradition — article 2) is not free from difficulties, it is in some respects more convenient as it avoids the necessity of amending existing treaties when new crimes (e.g. hijacking) are created. It also avoids some of the technical difficulties that arise in relation to the next requirement — that of dual criminality. Dual criminality is the general requirement that the extraditable offence be a crime in both the requesting and requested states. Because the eliminative method does not rely, as the listing or enumerative method does, upon the naming of specific offences, it reduces the difficulties likely to arise from the different classification of offences in the two legal systems.[76] So, it does not matter what the offence for which extradition is requested is called, provided that in both states the behaviour it relates to is an offence that carries a sentence in excess of the agreed minimum. This in itself can cause difficulty where one state has penal policies out of line with other states or where the legal system does not always prescribe minimum or even maximum penalties, as is the case in Britain and many other common law countries. Harmonisation in this respect would involve very drastic changes indeed. By way of compromise, a commentator has suggested recently that a method of avoiding the difficulties of both the eliminative and the enumerative methods and at the same time maintaining the possible advantages that the dual criminality rule may have for the offender, would be to 'list the *non*-extraditable offences and to designate extraditable offences by type, category and dispositional method'.[77]

Once it has been established that the offence is extraditable, the next requirement leads naturally from that. This is the speciality principle: that the fugitive will not be tried for any offence other than the specific one for which extradition was granted (or an offence arising from the same facts) unless he/she is first given ample opportunity to leave the country again.[78] Were state practice to allow otherwise, the previous requirements would in many cases be somewhat pointless. Should a state try an offender in breach of the speciality principle then it has committed a clear violation of its obligations under international law, but the fact that such a violation has taken place is, it must be admitted, unlikely to assist the offender. He/she may or may not be able to plead the speciality principle as a defence under the national law of the state to which he/she has been extradited. Should he/she raise the question prior to extradition it will be unlikely that the extraditing state will presume bad faith in a foreign friendly state unless the offender is alleging in addition that the offence for which he/she will be tried on return will be a political offence rather than the offence of extradition. In such a case the request may be denied on the basis of the general exception of political offences rather than on the basis of the speciality principle.

However, before discussing the political offence exception in detail, there is one further exception to consider: the exception of nationals from the extradition process. It has been indicated that extradition has its roots in the nineteenth century, and the rationale for the exception of nationals has its roots in nineteenth-century national chauvinism. The wide variations in the standards of criminal justice of the nineteenth century are sparse justification for the continuation of this policy into the twentieth century, particularly between the countries of Western Europe.[79] The main proponents of this policy in recent times have been the civil law countries.[80] The common law countries have not as a general rule excluded their nationals from extradition, and it was Britain who pioneered the compromise position, whereby either party to an extradition treaty might 'in its absolute discretion refuse to surrender up its own subjects'. This compromise is the course adopted by the European Convention on Extradition (article 6), but a major study of extradition published in 1971 showed that such treaties are still very much in the minority.[81]

The exclusion of political offenders

The exclusion of political offenders from the process of extradition has probably been the single issue causing the greatest problems for states concerned to coordinate their activities for the suppression of terrorism. Ironically, the earliest forms of extradition treaty were specifically intended to secure the surrender of political rather than common criminals.[82] Political asylum is now one of the cherished values of Western liberalism, but the practice of excluding political offenders from extradition treaties can only be traced back to a Belgian treaty of 1833. Its widespread adoption is again attributable to the dominant influence of nineteenth-century French treaty-makers. In various forms it can now be found in the overwhelming majority of extradition treaties and national extradition laws. It is specifically included in the European Convention on Extradition, which gives states the option of refusing extradition for a 'political offence' or 'an offence connected with a political offence', or in circumstances where 'the requested state has substantial grounds for believing that a request for extradition for an ordinary criminal has been made for the purpose of prosecuting or punishing a person on account of his race, religion, nationality or political opinion, or that that person's position may be prejudiced for any of these reasons' (article 3).

Within these generally accepted guidelines, state practice differs and the problems of definition begin. The difficulties do not spring so much from the 'purely' political offences such as treason, sedition or espionage, which tend not to be included in extradition treaties anyway, but from what might be called the 'relative' political crimes, the common crimes committed for political reasons. It is in determining the circumstances in which exemption should be given to this latter group of offenders that the practice of national courts differs and a variety of factors may be taken into account, some subjective, some objective — even foreign policy considerations can be discerned. Some systems, such as France, Italy and Germany, give pride of place to the subjective motives of the offender. Others, such as the Netherlands, consider in addition the nature of the interests affected by the crime. The English courts also combine a consideration of the motives of the offender with what has in recent years become an increasingly restrictive notion of the circumstances in which a 'political offence' can be committed.

Judicial control of extradition started earlier in Britain than elsewhere, consequently the early interpretations of the relevant section (s.3) of the 1870 Extradition Act, which refers to 'an offence of a political character', played an important role in the general development of the concept. In *re Castioni*[83] in 1891, the fugitive, who had been a leader of an armed uprising in the Swiss canton of Ticino, had shot and killed a member of the canton council. The offence was held to be political as it was committed in the course of, and in furtherance of, a political disturbance. Three years later, in *re Meunier*,[84] the fugitive was an anarchist who had committed a number of bomb outrages in France, and a new element was introduced by the courts. 'In order to constitute an offence of a political character', said Mr Justice Cave in his judgment, 'there must be two or more parties in the state, each seeking to impose the government of their choice upon the other . . . if the offence is committed by one side or the other in pursuance of that object it is a political offence, otherwise not.'[85] An anarchist, therefore, as an 'enemy of all governments' did not meet these requirements and could be extradited.

This somewhat artificial but expedient definition reflected the nineteenth-century political scene. In the twentieth century, the English courts have explicitly stressed the need to respond to contemporary circumstances. In 1955, for example, at the height of the Cold War, Polish seamen who had mutinied and seized their ship in order to defect to the West were regarded as political offenders,[86] whereas in 1969, when Greece was still a member of the Council of Europe, such status was not granted to a fugitive opponent of the Greek military junta. He had been convicted in his absence of obtaining money by false pretences, but claimed that if extradited he would be further punished for his known political opposition to the military regime. The House of Lords held that such behaviour by the Greek government would be a clear 'breach of faith' and that an English court could not 'assume that any foreign government with which Her Majesty's Government has diplomatic relations may act in such a manner'.[87]

More recently, in *Cheng* v. *Governor of Pentonville Prison,*[88] the House of Lords referred specifically to the need to cooperate in the suppression of terrorism when it restricted the 'political defence' still further so that it could only be used by an offender whose only purpose was to 'change the government *in the state where [the offence] was committed*, or to induce it to change its policy, or to enable him to escape from the jurisdiction of a government of whose political policies the offender disapproved but despaired of altering'.[89] This requirement, that the offence must have been committed in the country whose policies the offender opposed, meant that Cheng, a member of a Formosan independence unit, who had tried to assassinate the son of Chiang Kai-Shek in New York, was extradited, even though as Lord Simon said in a strong dissenting speech it would not 'occur to anyone except a lawyer that the appellant's offence could possibly be described as other than of a political character'.[90] This flexible mix of objective and subjective criteria, of humanitarian as well as domestic and foreign policy considerations has, on the one hand, been the strength of the concept of asylum for political offenders but, on the other hand, it has also been the reason why the definition of a 'political offender' for international purposes has eluded treaty-makers.

TOWARDS EUROPEAN COOPERATION?

Having outlined some of the main difficulties that are likely to arise from the discrepancies between the jurisdictional and extradition practices of states, the main obstacles to effective action to tighten the net of criminal jurisdiction at a global level will be apparent. At a European level, however, the difficulties are not so pronounced. There still remain discrepancies between the practices and traditions of the civil law countries and the common law countries — particularly the United Kingdom. But there is a long tradition of cooperation in extradition matters that has to some extent been rationalised by the European Convention on Extradition, supported by the Convention on Mutual Assistance in Criminal Matters.[91] There is also a far greater degree of mutual trust and political consensus among the countries of Western Europe than is the case in much of the rest of the world. These factors must have played a significant role in the success with which the Council of Europe was able to sponsor a convention on the suppression of terrorism where other attempts have failed.

International attempts to deal with the problems of terrorism date back at least to the League of Nations, which in 1937 sponsored two conventions, one proscribing certain acts of violence, and the other setting up an international criminal court with jurisdiction over such crimes. Despite initial support, neither of these conventions ever came into effect.[92] The setting up of such a court would obviously pose major political as well as legal difficulties, but amongst international lawyers at least the project is not regarded as a dead issue.[93] Rather more successful have been the limited regimes established by the hijacking conventions. These are based upon a form of 'quasi-universal jurisdiction' discussed above (pp. 202-3), but again their complete success depends upon their enforcement by domestic courts and upon their ratification by those states that provide the traditional havens for hijackers. Attempts, as yet unsuccessful, have also been made to model a general anti-terrorist convention upon the approach adopted by these conventions.[94]

Against this background the European Convention on the Suppression of Terrorism[95] takes a conventional path, combining a number of traditional devices. It excludes certain (loosely speaking) 'terrorist' offences from the advantages of the political defence; it imposes strict obligations upon contracting states to extradite all fugitives who have committed such offences, or failing that, to submit them to the jurisdiction of their own courts; and it imposes a further obligation upon contracting states to extend their jurisdictional claims over criminal offenders in order to tighten the European jurisdictional net. What the convention does not do is attempt the difficult task of defining a terrorist offence. Article 1 provides that none of the listed offences (see pp. 170-1) shall, for the purposes of extradition, be regarded as a 'political offence or as an offence connected with a political offence or as an offence inspired by political motives'. In addition, the contracting states are given the option of also exempting from the political defence any other serious offence involving an act of violence against the life, physical integrity or liberty of a person, or any other serious offence against property that creates a collective danger for persons.[96] This legal fiction could well catch more in its grasp than those who would traditionally be called terrorists, for at most no serious act of violence may be regarded as a political offence. However, the traditional right of asylum is available in two forms.

First, under article 5 a state retains the right to refuse extradition for an offence included in articles 1 or 2 if it has 'substantial grounds for believing that the request for extradition . . . has been made for the purpose of prosecuting or punishing a person on account of his race, religion, nationality or political opinion, or that that person's position may be prejudiced for any of these reasons'. This is part of the formula adopted by the European Convention on Extradition and because it is directed at the circumstances of trial or punishment, rather than the motivation of the offender, it involves the rather delicate issue of having to impute bad faith into the motives of the requesting state.

Second, article 13 permits states to register a reservation that they retain the right to refuse a request for extradition on the basis that the offence is of a political character notwithstanding the fact that it is one of the offences listed in article 1. This, it has been claimed, effectively emasculates the convention by allowing contracting states to re-introduce the political defence by the back door. Although at first sight this does appear to be the case, there are a number of other provisions that should be taken into account. First, article 13 expressly obliges reserving states when deciding whether or not to classify a particular offence as 'political' to take into account any 'particularly serious aspects of the offence' including (a) that it created a collective danger to the life, physical integrity or liberty of persons; or (b) that it affected persons foreign to the motives behind it; or (c) that cruel or vicious means have been used in the commission of the offence. Second, any reservation made under article 13 is on the basis of reciprocity. This means that the effect of the reservation is to modify the treaty regime between the reserving state and other parties to the convention so that a reserving state cannot compel a state that has not made a reservation to extradite in circumstances where the reserving state itself would not be obliged to. Non-reserving states may well be prepared to ignore this provision but the reserving state does face the possibility of its own reservation being invoked against itself. Should that happen of course it would mean that the parties would be in the same position towards each other as they would have been without the treaty. The third point is particularly important. Where an offender is within the territory of a contracting state and that state receives a request for his extradition from another contracting state, if the requested state decides not to extradite (because e.g. it recognises the application of the political defence in article 5 or because there is a reservation in force under article 13) then it shall 'submit the case, *without exception whatsoever and without undue delay,* to its competent authorities for the purposes of prosecution'. The decision to prosecute shall then be taken in the same manner as it is with any serious national offence (article 7). This is a form of modified *aut dedere aut judicare* principle — in that the convention does not leave a free choice to the requested state, which is under an obligation to extradite or failing that to submit to prosecution. It is also important to note that article 6 imposes an additional obligation upon contracting states to amend as necessary their own national laws so as to be able to exercise jurisdiction over the fugitives that the convention obliges them to submit for prosecution.[97] Finally, the convention as a whole is subject to what is in effect a compulsory arbitration clause, which in the event of a dispute over the interpretation or application of the convention, and failing a friendly settlement, can be invoked by either party.[98]

All in all the convention does represent a wholesale condemnation of violent political acts, and having taken that position it cannot distinguish between the motives of the offenders. Nevertheless, in spite of the wide cast of articles 1 and 2, it cannot be said to undermine the concept of asylum — if this is understood to mean protection from political or other persecution. Even so, for those states that choose to reserve the power of granting the traditional defence to 'political offenders' (which it should be remembered has been a somewhat uneven form of protection) there is still a strict obligation to submit such offenders to prosecution, and a major terrorist trial may well be regarded as more politically embarrassing than the extradition of the offender.

Because of its somewhat uncompromising stance, the convention has aroused a considerable degree of controversy, and in spite of receiving the initial approval of seventeen of the member states of the Council of Europe, it has so far only been ratified by seven states: Austria, Cyprus, Denmark, Germany, Liechtenstein, Sweden and the United Kingdom.[99] Ultimately, the success of the convention is likely to depend upon the number of states that do ratify it and the success of the provisions obliging states to prosecute for offences committed outside their territory — the similar experiment in the Irish jurisdictions has not set an encouraging precedent. This issue is particularly important because of the number of states that have already indicated their reservations about the demise of the 'political offence'. Sweden and Denmark have already made a reservation under article 13, and France, Italy, Norway and Portugal made declarations in similar terms when initially signing the convention. Ireland has refused even to sign the convention on the basis that her constitution does not permit her to extradite political offenders. This argument is in fact based upon article 29 of the Irish constitution, which provides that 'Ireland accepts the generally accepted principles of international law as its rule of conduct in its relations with other states', and scholars have suggested that a rigid adherence to the practice of non-extradition of political offenders represents 'a narrow conception of the nature of international law and the process of its growth'.[100] In addition, the European Convention itself does of course provide expressly for reservations of this kind. At root the issue is plainly a political rather than a strictly legal one.[101]

CONCLUSIONS

The object of this chapter has been to outline the framework of international law within which the European Convention on the Suppression of Terrorism operates, and to point out the more obvious areas where political pressures may influence the form or operation of the law. From the discussion it should be clear that despite its grandiose name the European Convention has limited objectives. It aims simply to secure the extradition or trial of all persons convicted of, or charged with, offences of violence, loosely classified as 'terrorist' offences. It certainly does not seek to meet, nor to solve, any of the problems that give rise to terrorism. It should also be clear that the number of persons likely to be affected by the convention is not going to be large.[102] Nevertheless, the decision of the contracting states to abolish between themselves the availability of the 'political defence' does represent an important change in policy[103] and has provoked very different reactions. Spectators in the United States are reported to be viewing the progress of the convention with interest as a possible model for Atlantic, or even global, cooperation.[104] In France on the other hand, a group was formed calling itself 'France: Terre d'Asile' — dedicated to preventing ratification of the convention by France and to 'preserving the traditional and constitutionally acknowledged practice of political asylum'.[105] Critics of the convention see it as an international manifestation of the theory of the 'strong state' — that states hold in reserve strong and wide-ranging powers with which to suppress possible dissent.[106] Germany particularly, a state reported to have 'the most comprehensive system of police surveillance and anti-terrorist legislation in Western Europe',[107] is generally associated with this view, and along with the United Kingdom was one of the first to ratify the convention. In contrast, its promoters in the Council of Europe portray it as an instrument of peace enabling penal sanctions to be applied for serious criminal offences against the security of the state without affecting or sacrificing fundamental rights.[108]

In reality, neither view seems wholly justified. It is certainly true that the convention must be viewed in the legal and political context within which it is intended to operate. It is only open to signature by states that are members of the Council of Europe (article 11), all of whom are in fact parties to the European Convention on Human Rights (see pages 195-7), which it will be remembered protects the rights of fair trial. Even so it should be pointed out that there is a wide variety of national practice within the limits laid down by the Convention on Human Rights. Moreover, not all its parties accept the compulsory jurisdiction of the Strasbourg Court to pass judgment on their domestic legal systems, nor do they all accept the important right of the individual to invoke the machinery of the convention against them where necessary. *The Times* asked in 1978: 'Is it inconceivable that in spite of shared democratic values, a new tyranny may evolve where opposition

through scheduled offences is the only outlet for opposition?'[109] Such a
regime might well survive for some time within the Council of Europe
before being expelled or forced — as Greece was in December 1970 — to
leave in the face of expulsion. Having said that however, the important
territorial limitation in the convention itself, as opposed to national
implementing legislation (see e.g. the UK Suppression of Terrorism Act
1978, s.5 which gives the Secretary of State power to extend these provisions
to *all* extradition arrangements)[110] should not be underplayed. The
convention does *not* seek to abolish the 'political defence' in relation to non-
contracting states. Nor, should it be stressed, does it modify the procedures
by which national authorities (invariably the courts in Western Europe) will
consider requests (or requisitions) for extradition. Under English law for
example, a state requesting extradition must make out a *prima facie* case of
guilt against the alleged fugitive.[111] These provisions remain unchanged.

How far the right of asylum is affected remains arguable. The convention
abolishes the right to seek immunity from the operation of the criminal law
because the specified offence was politically motivated, but it does not
abolish the right to claim asylum where there is a risk of *persecution,* i.e.
where the prosecution itself is motivated by improper considerations.[112]
This change in policy may be seen as a statement of faith in the political and
legal systems of the contracting states. How far this faith is justified is not
within the scope of this discussion, but what is pertinent is how far the
operation of this limited right of protection from possible persecution is
itself adequately protected. It will be remembered that article 5 of the
convention, introduced apparently at the instigation of the UK government,
provides protection from extradition where there are substantial grounds
for believing that a requisition has been made 'for the purpose of prosecuting
or punishing a person on account of his race, religion, nationality or political
opinion, or that that person's position may be prejudiced for any of these
reasons'. It may be strongly argued that the very consensus of political
values that gives rise to the convention militates against the effective
operation of this clause. It has been suggested above that the imputation of
bad faith into the motives of a friendly state (i.e. a contracting state) is a
delicate political issue. Even national courts, protected by the doctrine of
judicial impartiality, have demonstrated considerable reluctance to make
such imputations and have accepted requisitions at their face value.[113] In
states where the executive retains the ultimate veto, government ministers,
at the forefront of political pressures, are likely to find the task of making an
objective assessment even more difficult. And of course the pressures are
exacerbated when the alleged offender is presented as a 'terrorist'.[114] Genuine
concern for the 'fair treatment' clause might have been more amply
demonstrated by a 'long stop' provision expressly enabling disputes,
particularly over article 5, to be submitted to the Strasbourg Court,
preferably by individual application.[115] It would be disingenuous to suggest

that the international judiciary is not itself subject to the sort of pressures discussed above, but they are at least at one stage removed from the inter-state political arena and by definition contain representatives of more than just the interested states.

Since the signing of the convention, the Ministers of Justice of the member states of the EEC have been meeting with a view to cooperation in 'fighting international terrorism', particularly in the light of proposals (apparently French) for the creation of a 'European judicial area'.[116] At the Dublin summit of November 1979 these ministers reached an 'arrangement' on international terrorism.[117] It is to be hoped, at a time when the European Commission is considering the accession of the EEC itself to the European Convention on Human Rights, that at the very least the basic 'fair treatment' safeguards discussed above will be incorporated into any long-term agreements or arrangements. European cooperation against terrorists is to be welcomed, but not at any price.

Notes and References

1. See e.g. Northern Ireland (Emergency Provisions) Act, 1978, c.5, s.31: ' "terrorism" means the use of violence for political ends, and includes any use of violence for the purpose of putting the public or any section of the public in fear.' The same 'definition' is used in the Prevention of Terrorism (Temporary Provisions) Acts, 1974, c.56, s.9(1) and 1976, c.8, s.14(1). Note the scope for judicial interpretation this 'definition' leaves.
2. See e.g. Terrorism and political crimes in international law. *Transactions of the American Society of International Law* (1973) pp. 87—111, particularly J. Dugard; Towards the definition of international terrorism. pp. 94—100.
3. See Ibrahim Abu-Lughad, Unconventional violence and international politics. *Ibid.,* pp. 100-11.
4. Statute of the Council of Europe *European Treaty Series [ETS]* no. 1 (with amendments).
5. *ETS* no. 5. The convention came into force on 3 September 1953. On 25 June 1979 all the member states of the Council of Europe were parties except Liechtenstein and Spain. Ratifications include: France (3 May 1974); FRG. (5 December 1952); Ireland (25 February 1953); Italy (26 October 1955); the Netherlands (31 August 1954); and the UK (8 March 1951).
6. *ETS* no. 5, the Preamble.
7. Ireland has made a declaration for an unlimited period from 25 February 1953. Declarations for limited, renewable periods include: France for 3 years from 3 May 1977; FRG. for 5 years from 1 June 1976; Italy for 3 years from 1 August 1978; the Netherlands for 5 years from 31 August 1974; the UK for 5 years from 14 January 1976.
8. Dates and periods as above (with the exception of France).
9. For a convenient collection of the principal treaties and other instruments

providing the legal basis of the EEC, and governing the accession of Denmark, Ireland and the UK see K. Simmonds (ed.), *European Community Treaties,* (London: Sweet and Maxwell, 3rd edn 1977).

10. See e.g. EEC Treaty, articles 173 and 175.
11. See G. Bebr, Directly applicable provisions of Community law: the development of a Community concept. *International and Comparative Law Quarterly, 19* (1970) p. 257. See the judgment of the European Court of Justice in case 26/62, *Van Gend en Loos* [1963] *European Court Reports* [*ECR*] 1 and, more recently, case 106/77, *Amministrazione delle Finanze dello Stato* v *Simmenthal S.p.A.* [1978] *ECR* 629. For the relevance of *Simmenthal* in e.g. UK law see D. Freestone, The supremacy of Community law in national courts. *Modern Law Review, 42* (1978) pp. 220—3.
12. Notably case 4/73, *Nold* [1974] *ECR* 491 and case 130/75, *Prais* v *E.C. Council* [1976] *ECR* 1586. Note also the proposal that the EEC itself become a party to the European Convention on Human Rights. See European Commission Memorandum, *EC Bulletin,* Supplement 2/79.
13. G. Hodgson, Terrorism. *Ditchley Journal* no. 1 (1979) pp. 35—44 at p. 36.
14. See e.g. from a UK point of view, P. Wallington and J. McBride, *Civil Liberties and a Bill of Rights* (London: Cobden Trust, 1970) p. 105.
15. For a detailed assessment of the part played by law in the emergency in Northern Ireland see K. Boyle, T. Hadden, P. Hillyard, *Law and State: The Case of Northern Ireland* (London: Martin Robertson, 1975).
16. For details of current and previous derogations by the UK government as a result of emergency legislation see Council of Europe, *Information Bulletin on Legal Activities* no. 4 (July 1979) p. 6. The Irish derogation was made after the passing of the 1976 Emergency Powers Act — see below note 27.
17. See Boyle *et al., op. cit.* The current legislation is the 1978 Northern Ireland (Emergency Provisions) Act [NI (EP) Act] c.5 and the 1976 Prevention of Terrorism (Temporary Provisions) Act [PT (TP) Act] c.8. For a consideration of the original PT (TP) Act 1974, see H. Street 'The Prevention of Terrorism (Temporary Provisions) Act 1974' [1975] *Criminal Law Review* pp. 192—9.
18. e.g. Offences Against the State Act, 1939 (as amended), the 1976 Emergency Powers Act and the Criminal Law Jurisdiction Act, 1976 (see below note 33). Note that the first case ever to reach the European Court of Human Rights concerned detention without trial under Irish emergency legislation, see *Lawless,* 3 *Yearbook of the European Commission on Human Rights* [*YBECHR*] (1960) p. 479.
19. NI (EP) Act, s.21; PT (TP) Act, s.1.
20. NI (EP) Act, s.22.
21. PT (TP) Act, s.11.
22. NI (EP) Act, ss. 6 and 7.
23. NI (EP) Act, s.21; PT (TP) Act, s.1; see also Street, *op. cit.,* p. 192. Cp. *McEldowney* v *Forde* [1969] 3 *Weekly Law Reports,* p. 179 and see Boyle, *et al., op. cit.,* pp. 14 ff.
24. NI (EP) Act, Part II, ss. 11—20; PT (TP) Act, s.12.
25. D. Lowry, Draconian powers: the new British approach to pre-trial detention of suspected terrorists. *Columbia Human Rights Law Review, 8/9* (1976—7) pp. 185—222 at p. 218.
26. Boyle, *et al., op. cit.,* pp. 12—13, 96—8, 131. But note their important criticisms of the operation of the criminal court system in emergency conditions (ch. 6).
27. E.g. *McEldowney* v *Forde, op. cit.,* and see Lowry, *op. cit.,* pp. 187—200.

Although for a number of 'tactical' victories in the UK courts see Boyle *et al.,* *op. cit.,* pp. 130ff. Given the different constitutional position of the Irish Supreme Court, note its 'balancing of interests' approach *in the matter of article 26 of the constitution and in the matter of the Emergency Powers Bill, 1976* [1977] *Irish Reports* [*I.R.*] 159 (a reference by the President for a ruling on the constitutionality of the Bill). See also D.M. Clarke 'Emergency legislation, fundamental rights and article 28.3.3. of the Irish constitution' *Irish Jurist, 12,* part 2, pp. 217−33.

28.   *Ireland* v *United Kingdom, European Court of Human Rights,* Series A, judgment of 18 January 1978. A second application by the Irish government concerning the 1972 Northern Ireland Act was abandoned when the UK undertook not to apply the act retrospectively. A number of individual applications have also been made, notably *Donelly and others* v *UK* 16 *YBECHR* (1973) p. 212. For a detailed consideration of the Northern Ireland cases, see Boyle *et al., op. cit.,* ch. 8, and H. Hannum and K. Boyle, Ireland in Strasbourg. *Irish Jurist, 7,* p. 329 and *11,* p. 243.

29.   19 *YBECHR* (1976), p. 512.

30.   Boyle *et al., op. cit.,* pp. 159−60. Although note the acquittal of Edward Brophy because a Belfast Crown Court could not be sure his 'confessions' had not been induced by 'torture and inhuman and degrading treatment'. *The Times,* 2 April 1980.

31.   On jurisdiction generally, see e.g. D.P. O'Connell, *International Law* (London: Stevens, 2nd edn, 1970) pp. 599ff. and M. Sørensen (ed.) *Manual of Public International Law* (London: Macmillan, 1968) ch. 6 (by M. Sahovic and W.W. Bishop). For an extremely detailed and up-to-date discussion, see D.R. Harris, *Cases and Materials on International Law* (London: Sweet and Maxwell, 2nd edn, 1979) ch. 6.

32.   See e.g. G. Williams, Venue and ambit of the criminal law. *Law Quarterly Review, 81* (1965) p. 276.

33.   Criminal Law Jurusdiction Act, 1976, No. 14 (Eire) and see the reference of the Bill to the Supreme Court by the President in [1977] *I.R.* 129. Criminal Law Jurisdiction Act, 1975, c. 59 (UK). This legislation was the result of an Anglo-Irish Commission that reported in May 1974 (Cmnd. 5627). See also A. McCall-Smith and P. Magee, The Anglo-Irish Law Enforcement Report in historical and political context. *Criminal Law Review* [1975] pp. 200−14.

34.   In 1979, a case was initiated in Dublin involving a shooting in Northern Ireland: *The Guardian,* 6 October 1979. This may well reflect the greater will to cooperate in the aftermath of the killings of Lord Mountbatten and the members of his fishing party and of the 18 British soldiers in August 1979.

35.   Claimed by the UN War Crimes Commission, 15 *War Crimes Reports* (1949) p. 26 and see Sørensen, *op. cit.,* pp. 365−8.

36.   Claimed by the Israeli court in *Attorney-General of Israel* v *Eichmann,* 36 *International Law Reports,* (1961) p. 5. But this claim does involve a controversial interpretation of the 1948 Genocide Convention (particularly article 6 − see para. 22 of judgment).

37.   Single Convention on Narcotic Drugs, 520 *United Nations Treaty Series* [*UNTS*] (1961) p. 204; Convention on the Suppression and Punishment of the Crime of Apartheid, 1973, article 1. For the text see 13 *International Legal Materials* [*ILM*] (1974) p. 50.

38.   For a compilation of all aircraft hijack incidents between 1 January 1960 and 31 July 1977 see A.E. Evans and J.F. Murphy, *Legal Aspects of International Terrorism* (Lexington, Mass.: Lexington Books, 1978) pp. 68−147. This work

also lists all national legislation relating to the control of hijacking and the states party to the aviation conventions relevant to hijacking.

39. For text see 10 *ILM* (1971) p. 133.

40. *Ibid.,* p. 1151.

41. C. Emmanuelli, Legal aspects of aerial terrorism: the piecemeal vs. the comprehensive approach. *Journal of International Law and Economics, 10* (1975) pp. 503—18 at p. 507.

42. Hague Convention, article 4; Montreal Convention, article 5. Note the similar approach adopted by the 1973 Convention on the Prevention and Punishment of Crimes against Internationally Protected Persons, including Diplomats, article 3: 13 *ILM* (1974) p. 42.

43. See also Mexican Penal Code, article 4 and the *Cutting* case, M.M. Whiteman, *Digest of International Law,* vol. 6 (Washington, DC: Government Printing Office, 1963—) pp. 104, 105.

44. E.g. Sørensen, *op. cit.,* pp. 368—72 and J.L. Brierly, *Law of Nations* (Oxford: Oxford University Press, 6th edn, ed. H. Waldock, 1963) pp. 299—304. But see *contra* O'Connell, *op. cit.,* pp. 828—9.

45. (France v Turkey) *Permanent Court of International Justice Reports,* Series A, no. 10 (1927).

46. 450 *UNTS,* p. 82.

47. M.C. Bassiouni, *International Extradition and World Public Order* (Leyden/ Dobbs Ferry: Sijthoff/Oceana, 1974) pp. 258—9.

48. See J.B. Gaynes, Bringing the terrorist to justice: a domestic law approach. *Cornell International Law Journal, 11* (1978) pp. 71—84 at p. 78. But see *contra* J.J. Paust, in Evans and Murphy, *op. cit.,* p. 395.

49. By an amendment to the Offences Committed Abroad Law, Law of 6th. Nisan, 5732 (21 March 1972). See Gaynes, *op. cit.*

50. Law of 11 July 1975, Law No. 75—624, Title III [1975] Journal Officiel [J.O.] 7220. See Gaynes, *op. cit.*

51. [1975] J.O. Débats Parlementaires, Assemblée Nationale 2763, cited Gaynes, *op. cit.*

52. See e.g. the consistent refusal of the Irish government to permit UK anti-terrorist activities in the Republic: *The Guardian,* 3 September 1979. Although note the recent concession in the wake of the Pope's visit to Ireland that British army helicopters be allowed to fly up to ten kilometres into Irish air-space: *The Guardian,* 6 October 1979.

53. It may well be subject to national rules. For UK practice see G.S. Goodwin-Gill, *International Law and the Movement of Persons between States* (Oxford: Oxford University Press, 1978) p. 269.

54. See generally, Goodwin-Gill, *op. cit.*

55. Free movement is one of the basic principles of the EEC. See EEC Treaty, Title III (articles 48—73) and note Council Directive 64/221. There is now a considerable case law upon the subject, see e.g. Goodwin-Gill, *op. cit.,* pp. 282—306.

56. See P. O'Higgins, 'Disguised extradition: the *Soblen* case. *Modern Law Review, 27* (1964) p. 521.

57. Alona E. Evans, 'The apprehension and prosecution of offenders: Some current problems', in Evans and Murphy, *op. cit.,* pp. 493—521, at p. 494.

58. See e.g. *R v Secretary of State, ex parte Hussain* [1978] 2 *All England Law Reports [All E.R.]* p. 424, and also *R v Secretary of State for the Home Department, ex parte Hosenball* [1977] 3 *All E.R.* p. 452.

59. See e.g. *R v Secretary of State for Home Affairs, ex parte Soblen* [1963] 1

Queen's Bench [*Q.B.*] p. 837. Note that Soblen had been convicted in the USA of an offence that was not extraditable from the UK. The plea of Crown privilege prevented him from access to government papers to prove bad faith.
60. Evans, *op. cit.,* pp. 494—5.
61. See generally Bassiouni, *op. cit.,* and I.A. Shearer, *Extradition in International Law* (Manchester: Manchester University Press, 1971). See also a brief survey by H. Schultz, 'The principles of the traditional law of extradition', in *Legal Aspects of Extradition among European States* (Strasbourg: Council of Europe, 1970) pp. 9—25.
62. Bassiouni, *op. cit.,* pp. 1—6; Shearer, *op. cit.,* pp. 5—19.
63. *De Jure Belli ac Pacis,* 1625, Book 2, c.21.
64. Shearer, *op. cit.,* pp. 16—19.
65. *ETS* no. 24. The convention came into force on 18 April 1960. On 25 June 1979 it had been ratified by 14 member states of the Council of Europe including FRG (2 October 1976); Ireland (2 May 1966); Italy (6 August 1963); the Netherlands (14 February 1969). France has signed but not ratified the convention; UK is not a signatory. Israel and Finland are also parties. See generally, *Legal Aspects of Extradition among European States, op. cit.*
66. *Observer,* 29 April 1979.
67. *Ibid.*
68. See e.g. Gaynes, *op. cit.,* p. 73.
69. For an excellent examination of the technicalities and the context of the case see T.E. Carbonneau, The provisional arrest and subsequent release of Abu Daoud by French authorities. *Virginia Journal of International Law, 17* (1977) pp. 495—513. See also Rapoport, Between minimum courage and maximum cowardice: A legal analysis of the release of Abu Daoud. *Brooklyn Journal of International Law, 3* (1977) p. 195.
70. Carbonneau, *op. cit.,* p. 501.
71. *The Guardian,* 14 May 1979.
72. Law of 10 March 1927. Shearer, *op. cit.,* pp. 27ff.
73. Article 4 of the constitution. Recently Pieter Menten was requested by Israel on the basis of common membership of the European Convention on Extradition. Extradition was refused because the constitution prevented extradition of nationals: Council of Europe, *Information Bulletin on Legal Activities,* no. 4.
74. Law of 23 December 1929, article 4(1); Shearer, *op. cit.,* p. 31.
75. E.g. see Bassiouni, *op. cit.,* pp. 314—21; Shearer, *op. cit.,* pp. 133—7.
76. Shearer, *op. cit.,* p. 135, found that after 1945, of the total of 50 extradition treaties registered with the UN, 33 adopted the eliminative method in preference to enumeration (cf. 80 out of 163 earlier treaties).
77. Bassiouni, *op. cit.,* p. 320.
78. See Shearer, *op. cit.,* pp. 146—9; Bassiouni, *op. cit.,* pp. 352—9.
79. For a discussion of the incidence and rationale of this policy see Shearer, *op. cit.,* pp. 94—131.
80. The laws of France, Germany and the Netherlands prevent the extradition of nationals; it is permitted by Italy if specifically provided for by treaty. See further Shearer, *op. cit.,* pp. 102—8.
81. Shearer, *op. cit.,* pp. 219—23.
82. For a detailed discussion of state practice in relation to political offenders see Shearer, *op. cit.,* pp. 166—93; Bassiouni, *op. cit.,* pp. 368—428.
83. [1891] 1 *Q.B.* p. 149.
84. [1894] 2 *Q.B.* p. 415.

222   *Legal Responses to Terrorism*

85.   *Ibid.*, p. 415.
86.   *R* v *Governor of Brixton Prison, ex parte Kolczynski* [1955] 1 *Q.B.* p. 540.
87.   *Government of Greece* v *Governor of Brixton Prison* [1971] *Appeal Cases* [*A.C.*] p. 250, *per* Lord Parker C.J. at p. 255.
88.   [1973] *A.C.* p. 931.
89.   *per* Lord Diplock at p. 945.
90.   at p. 951. It might be noted that prior to his arrival in London, Cheng had been extradited from Sweden — a country with allegedly a very liberal view of the political exception. See Bassiouni, *op. cit.,* p. 409.
91.   *ETS* no. 30. It came into force on 12 June 1962. On 25 June 1979 it had 14 parties including France, FRG, Italy and the Netherlands. It has not been signed by Ireland and France. Note also the Benelux Convention on Extradition and Judicial Assistance in Penal Matters, 1962 and the Nordic Treaty of 1962; see further Shearer, *op. cit.,* pp. 53—65.
92.   See M.O. Hudson (ed.), *International Legislation,* 9 vols (Washington, DC: Carnegie Endowment for International Peace, 1931—50) vol. 7, pp. 862, 865. For a brief review of attempts by the international community to control terrorism see R.A. Friedlander, Terrorism and international law: what is being done? *Rutgers Camden Law Journal, 8* (1977) pp. 383—92.
93.   See e.g. Evans and Murphy, *op. cit.,* 'General recommendations', p. 635.
94.   E.g. US Draft Convention for the Prevention and Punishment of Certain Acts of Terrorism, UN Doc. A/C.6/L.850 (25 September 1972), discussed in J. N. Moore, Towards legal restraints on international terrorism. In 'Terrorism and Political Crimes in International Law', *op. cit.,* pp. 88—94.
95.   *ETS* no. 90. It came into force on 4 August 1978. On 25 June 1979 it had been signed by all the member states of the Council of Europe except Ireland and Malta. The parties were (with dates of ratification): Austria (11 August 1977); Cyprus (26 February 1979); Denmark (27 June 1978); FRG (3 May 1978); Liechtenstein (13 June 1979); Sweden (15 September 1977) and UK (24 July 1978). For reservations see text below. For a discussion of the convention from a legal point of view see: Evans, *op. cit.,* pp. 497—9; J. Andrews, The European Convention on the Suppression of Terrorism. *European Law Review, 2* (1977) pp. 323—6; H. Golsong, E.C.S.T.: provocation or instrument of peace? *Forward in Europe,* no. 1 (1977) pp. 5—7.
96.   Both articles 1 and 2 include attempts to commit, participation as an accomplice in, and participation as an accomplice in attempts to commit, such offences.
97.   Article 6 is a complex provision. It does not appear to oblige all contracting states to subscribe to the same principles of criminal jurisdiction; it does however oblige them to ensure that they can try foreign nationals for the specified offences in all the circumstances in which they would have the right to try their own nationals — e.g. the UK enabling act, The Suppression of Terrorism Act, 1978, c. 26, s.4, extends territorial jurisdiction to the territories of the contracting states.
98.   Article 10. Note also that the convention provides for the widest measure of 'mutual assistance in criminal matters' relating to offences under articles 1 and 2 (article 8). This too is subject to the same political exclusion as extradition. Both Italy and Norway have declared their intention to reserve the right to refuse assistance in relation to what they regard as 'political offences'.
99.   See above note 96.
100. Evans, *op. cit.,* p. 499.

101. See notably the factors discussed by McCall-Smith and Magee, *op. cit.*, p. 200.
102. Even if Eire were to become a party, the Irish have always argued that the number of terrorists who use the Republic as a haven is far smaller than the British government claims.
103. For a fascinating discussion of the historical circumstances that fostered the growth of the defence in the UK see B. Porter, *The Refugee Question in Mid-Victorian Politics* (Cambridge: Cambridge University Press, 1979).
104. Evans, *op. cit.*, p. 498.
105. *The Times*, 7 February 1978.
106. E.g. G. Soulier, European integration and the suppression of terrorism. *Review of Contemporary Law*, no. 2 (1978) pp. 21—45.
107. *The Guardian*, 22 February 1980. See S. Cobler, *Law, Order and Politics in West Germany* (Harmondsworth: Penguin, 1978). See also D.N. Schiff, Astrid Proll's case. [1979] *Public Law* pp. 353—71 at p. 367.
108. Golsong, *op. cit.*, p. 5.
109. *Ibid.*
110. See *Hansard* House of Commons, vol. 948, col. 1575 and vol. 951, col. 524. Note how little *debate* this particular provision received.
111. See e.g. *Schtraks* v *Government of Israel* [1962] 3 *All E.R.* p. 529, 533. For the position in civil law states, see Shearer, *op. cit.*, pp. 157ff.
112. European Convention on the Suppression of Terrorism, article 5. Both these facets of the 'political defence' appear in s.3(1) of the UK Extradition Act, 1870. See further *Schtraks, op. cit.*, and *R* v *Governor of Winson Green Prison, ex parte Littlejohn* [1975] 3 *All E.R.* pp. 208, 209 (*per* Lord Widgery C.J.) (a case under the 1965, Republic of Ireland (Backing of Warrants) Act).
113. See e.g. *Government of Greece* v *Governor of Brixton Prison, op. cit.*, and *Atkinson* v *USA Government* [1969] 3 *All E.R.* p. 1317 where the fugitive alleged a breach of the speciality principle.
114. E.g. the suggestion of M. Simon (a judge of the Paris *Cour d'Appel*) and F.E. Dowrick, The effect of directives in France. *Law Quarterly Review, 95* (1979) pp. 376—85, at p. 384 that in the recent *Cohn-Bendit* case [1979] *Dalloz* 155, the *Conseil d'Etat* (the supreme administrative court in France) refused the proper effect of an EEC directive in France because 'sharing the Government's pre-occupation with the suppression of terrorist activities' it may have wished to maintain complete discretionary powers regarding deportation, even of Community nationals. And as a general example see *Hansard* for the debates of the Suppression of Terrorism Act (note 110 above).
115. The European Convention on Human Rights protects fair trial by articles 5 and 6, while article 14 guarantees that the rights of the convention shall be exercised without any form of discrimination (including political).
116. *EC Bulletin* Supplement 1/79, 'European union — annual reports for 1978', p. 14.
117. For text see HMSO, Cmnd. 7823. The agreement (which comes into force after it has been ratified by all the EEC Member States) extends and modifies the regime of the European Convention on the Suppression of Terrorism in its application between EEC member states. It does this in two ways. First, EEC member states accept that in extradition proceedings between two member states the European Convention will apply in full (i.e. without reservation) *even if* one or both of the states are not party to it, or if one or both have made the 'political defence' reservation permitted by article 13 (see above p. 213). Second, the agreement seeks to restrict still further the effect between EEC member states of such reservations. Hence, where member states party to the

European Convention have made 'article 13' reservations, those reservations will not apply in extradition proceedings between EEC member states unless a further declaration to that effect is made under article 3 of the agreement (addressed to the Department of Foreign Affairs of Ireland, with whom instruments of ratification etc. must be deposited). Also under article 3 those member states that are not party to the European Convention because they have not signed it (e.g. Ireland), or have signed it but not yet ratified it, are required to indicate by declaration if they wish to retain the 'political defence' in extradition proceedings between EEC member states. So far Italy, France and Denmark have made declarations under article 3.

CHAPTER 9

Concluding Remarks

Juliet Lodge

Individual states in the EEC have taken a number of measures designed to counteract terrorism. These have usually involved improving air- and seaport security procedures, improving intelligence services, screening processes using computer technology, police cooperation, and the exchange of information and cooperation at an international level. In addition, punitive measures regarding search and arrest procedures have been tightened and strengthened. A range of different tactics has been employed by authorities facing terrorist action. These have included the use of specially trained anti-terrorist commando-type forces, psychological techniques based on exhausting terrorists' resilience, reserves and resources, a mixture of weak and strongarm techniques to secure the release of any hostages, and the adoption of strategies committed either to securing the release of hostages after a period of negotiation with terrorists or to resisting terrorist demands at all costs. More recently, in Ireland, media coverage of terrorist attacks has been restricted to the post-crisis period when hostages have been safely recovered.

In all instances, the authorities have been faced with the need to demonstrate their credibility in combating terrorism without either resorting to the wholesale introduction of repressive measures intolerable and alien to liberal—democratic values, or acquiescing to public pressure for tough reprisals including the reintroduction, in some cases, of the death penalty.[1] Governments may not always have been as vigilant as they might have been to ensure that those responsible for apprehending and interrogating terrorist suspects (many of whom have subsequently gone free, or been set free by their colleagues in further terrorist attacks, even when judged to have, or having admitted to having, committed certain terrorist offences) respect their human rights. If procedures concerned with the apprehension and questioning of terrorist suspects are seen to be inhumanely or unjustly administered, not only may terrorists make capital out of this via the media, but the credibility of those enforcing those procedures and their accountability to a government committed to upholding the liberal—

225

democratic state may be queried. Aware of this, there is among the EEC states widespread acceptance of the need to ensure that the authorities do not add fire to terrorist rhetoric and allegations of a given state's 'repressiveness' whose overthrow by violent means is justified.

As the Italian and West German case studies revealed, care has to be taken to ensure that any latent authoritarian potential is not mobilised in response to pressure to combat terrorism lest liberal—democratic values are, thereby, severely threatened and undermined. Indeed, the West German experience especially indicates how, when tighter anti-terrorist measures are contemplated by the government, aspersion may be cast on the mere articulation of dissent even via the accepted and normal parliamentary and political channels.

There is, moreover, broad though not unanimous agreement that terrorism constitutes a criminal offence, that its use is an illegitimate means of advancing political goals, and that except in certain cases (involving, *inter alia,* the quest for political asylum) non-prosecution of the offence should not (though, of course, it might, and has been) be vindicated on the grounds of it being politically rather than criminally motivated. In this respect, most Community member governments refute terrorist suggestions that if terrorists act within a political tradition based upon resisting oppression, legitimacy accrues to their 'movement' and their terrorist actions, which they portray as the pursuit of honourable and legitimate goals beneficial to the 'masses' in a society subject to 'state violence'.[2] This can be explained by the fact that terrorists neither use nor respect accepted channels of communication with the authorities; that they are often scornful of liberal—democratic norms and infringe them with impunity; and that they contest the legitimacy of the state's authorities. Furthermore, apart from directly attacking the state or targets deemed to represent or embody the state (including 'innocent' airline passengers, for example, if the terrorists perceive them as 'representatives' of a given state or target), terrorists frequently engage in activities that not only contravene accepted codes of civil behaviour regarding the expression of discontent or dissent, but include the commission of acts, such as bank robberies or kidnappings, for financial gain that are recognisable as criminal offences. The French have relied heavily on criminal law to control terrorism. While it is possible, as the Italian case study argued, to separate terrorism *per se* from terrorist acts having political intent, all the case studies that have been presented here are concerned with political terrorism. As the authorities' responses in each case study reveal, the ostensible 'political' character of the terrorist act is not universally regarded as a mitigating circumstance. Instead, terrorism is seen as a criminal and illegal but politically inspired activity. This, in turn, has influenced governments' reaction to terrorism.

For the most part, governments have been preoccupied with discerning and developing anti-terrorist measures rather than with engaging in the kind of scrutiny of the causes of terrorism (assuming that these can be isolated reliably in the West European advanced technological societies) advocated by some members of the European Parliament.[3] This preoccupation derives from their perception of their primary duty and immediate concern being the need to protect their societies and innocent people from terrorism. It obviously also owes something to time and financial constraints, a government's priorities and the fact that the majority of the population accepts the government's authority as legitimate and repudiates terrorist claims to the contrary. Moreover, liberal democrats are not much impressed by analyses of society's ills and the government's alleged repressiveness and violence being dressed up in terrorist rhetoric either genuinely inspired by or masquerading as Marxist in origin. This is not to suggest that such analyses may not isolate problems in society. Rather it is to argue that, as recent history has shown, liberal—democratic governments, and often the public, in the EEC have not found them convincing. It would be useful to consider briefly the limits of Community cooperation and further areas for consideration regarding the fight against terrorism.

Apart from endeavouring to extract agreements on extradition and the denial of landing rights to terrorists from developing countries associated with the EEC, there are a number of areas that Community members could explore with a view to intensifying their cooperation. The establishment of a European judicial area would certainly assist in the development of a Community-wide penal system. At a minimum, it might prompt thorough investigation of the feasibility and desirability of establishing such a system and of harmonising prosecution procedures regarding terrorist suspects, permissible delays between the apprehension and prosecution of suspects, and sentences imposed upon those judged guilty of terrorist offences.[4] While local authorities obviously require a good deal of discretion in coping with terrorist incidents, and while the need for speedy political decisions demands that the ultimate authority for dealing with the situations as they arise remains in the hands of the respective heads of government or state and any crisis and cabinet teams convened to assist them, some uniformity might prove useful.

However, uniformity or harmonisation for their own sake will not necessarily prove major deterrents to the commission of terrorist offences in EEC member states. But the authorities might be able to deal more effectively with terrorists, in terms of ensuring their prompt prosecution, if the member governments agreed to minimise delays and to lend each other such moral and logistic support as necessary. This need not entail disregard for civil and human liberties if they adhered, as MEPs have suggested, to a common EEC citizens' bill of rights. Yet, it would undoubtedly prove very difficult to draft a bill acceptable to all EEC member states and incorporating the safeguards enshrined in some of their constitutions. Similarly, the establishment of some common system of penalties for certain terrorist acts might be deemed logical, desirable and warranted, so implying above all that terrorism is perceived as a criminal offence. The problem lies in the fact that none of these areas can be isolated completely from broader aspects of national domestic criminal law. If EEC law is to take precedence over national law, and if new laws impinge either upon aspects of law not covered already by EEC regulations or upon matters where ambiguity arises, then notwithstanding any intention to secure the speedy prosecution of terrorist suspects the process may be held up by the need to refer ambiguous issues for interpretation to the Court of Justice, which would result in lengthy delays even if the Court were to give priority to such issues. Moreover, skilful lawyers might be able to manipulate any ambiguities to good effect in decelerating a terrorist suspect's trial.

Another area of terrorist activity that, on the surface, might appear amenable to uniform treatment concerns matters like policies towards the taking of hostages, kidnapping and the payment of ransoms. Some EEC member states have suffered a greater incidence of certain of these crimes than others and attitudes towards dealing with them vary. If it were deemed desirable to harmonise legislation on these matters, then common rules governing the authorities' response to any such crimes would have to be implemented. Yet, this could lead to potentially counterproductive rigidity regarding the authorities' response to terrorist demands. For example, militating against a ruling that the payment of ransoms is illegal would be not only the need to preserve the greatest degree of flexibility on the part of local authorities confronted with such a ransom demand (whether levelled directly at them or at a citizen or organisation in their country) but also the competing need to try and ensure that any hostages should not be harmed.[5] Furthermore, decisions to refuse to bargain, to bring in anti-terrorist commando squads or to adopt a 'wait-and-see' tactic may be appropriate for one but not another situation. In no event can a peaceful outcome be guaranteed. Nor can terrorist responses be accurately predicted for each situation — advance planning, simulation and scrutiny of possible terrorist actions and responses, and government or authorities' tactics notwithstanding.[6] Harmonisation would very probably prove both unobtainable and unacceptable.

Any measures to be invoked by counter-terrorist task forces across the EEC might also be unacceptable. Not only does a Community-wide task force not exist, but there is no ultimate source of supranational authority in the EEC to which it could be held accountable. While it is easy to suggest that its source of authority should be EEC Ministers of the Interior and/or Justice and/or heads of government or state or their deputies, in times of crisis, when flexible and speedy responses may prove critical, the time required to contact and call together even a tele-conference of the relevant ministers and officials, coupled with the time needed to prepare briefs for them, and any EEC Commissioner(s) or member(s) of the Court of Justice invited to participate in any team would militate against effective and speedy decision-making. This, in turn, might mean that the task force could not become operational fast enough to apprehend suspects. This highlights the obvious unsuitability of existing Community decision-making processes for dealing with matters for which the EEC was not designed. It also shows that perhaps the most fruitful way of proceeding in these areas is by means of comparable bilateral accords and understandings between the member governments, their police and security forces. Not least among the problems in this area is the need to maintain the functional division between the security service activities of the security and counter-terrorist services themselves, and the police forces at both the national and transnational levels. However, the mechanisms for bilateral and multilateral cooperation between anti-terrorist and police forces already exist, and mutual assistance has been rendered when appropriate.

Another area open to intergovernmental agreement rather than EEC regulation might be that regarding the suppression of media coverage of terrorist acts pending either the release of hostages (by either the kidnappers or special commando forces), payment of ransoms or acquiescence of either party to the other's demands. It has often been argued that terrorists rely on the media to transmit their demands, to draw public attention to their activities, to instil fear in a section of the public, organisations or authorities, or to incite the latter to pressurise the respective target authorities to concede terrorist demands.[7] So it might seem logical to advocate curbs on media coverage of terrorism until after the event;[8] this would have to extend to all member states given that television and radio transmitters can pick up programmes from neighbouring states. The problems here lie not simply with the fact that terrorist organisations having international links might be able to circumvent such restrictions by securing coverage via other national networks or via any transmitters they set up or take over themselves. Rather, each of the member states has different rules regarding the surveillance of the media and freedom of the press. Even if it were possible to get the media's compliance with restraints on coverage during terrorist sieges, any mandatory application of this across the EEC could prove counter-productive. Instead, it would probably be better for the media to exercise self-restraint when called upon to do so, for there may well be instances when the government or local authorities might find media coverage essential to their purposes, as well as a means of communication with the public and terrorists.[9] This suggests, again, that any measures must be sufficiently flexible to allow local authorities room for manoeuvre and the ability to adapt to changing circumstances. Moreover, as the Italian case study demonstrated, from the terrorists' point of view publicity may not always be useful except as an intermediary objective to the attainment of their goals. Nevertheless, in the past, terrorists have often demanded the transmission of their statements on national broadcasting networks in order to secure mass awareness both of their demands and of their 'leaders' or 'heroes'.

In conclusion, it can be seen that within the EEC's confines there has been emphasis on combating terrorism by establishing the principles of it as a criminal offence whose perpetrators should be prosecuted (or extradited for that purpose). Even so, it has not been easy to persuade all member governments of the merit of such an approach. Not until November 1979 was there governmental acceptance of such principles, and the process for securing parliamentary ratification of a formal agreement to this effect has still to be completed.

Notes and References

1. C. Dobson and R. Payne, *The Weapons of Terror: International Terrorism at Work* (London: Macmillan, 1979), p. 150.
2. These notions are well known and well documented in many of the texts cited in the select bibliography to chapter 1.
3. See C. Fletcher-Cooke, *Terrorism and the European Community* (London: European Conservative Group, 1979), p. 23.
4. For discussion of similar issues in a US context, see J.B. Wolf, Controlling political terrorism in a free society. *Orbis, 19* (1975—76) pp. 1289—308.
5. See E.F. Mickolus, Negotiating for hostages: a policy dilemma. *Orbis, 19* (1975—76) pp. 1309—25.
6. *Ibid.,* pp. 1314—24.
7. See, for example, W. Laqueur, *Terrorism* (London: Weidenfeld and Nicolson, 1977), p. 109.
8. See C.C. O'Brien's speech in the Seanad as Minister for Posts and Telegraphs introducing the Broadcasting Authority (Amendment) Bill, 27 March 1975, in his *Herod: Reflections on Political Violence* (London: Hutchinson, 1978), pp. 110—27.
9. This is examined, along with other counter-terrorist measures, in Dobson and Payne, *op. cit.,* pp. 130—50.

Select Bibliographies

Chapter 1:

Alexander, Y. *Terrorism: National, Regional and Global Perspectives.* New York: Praeger, 1976.

Arendt, H. *On Violence.* London: Allen Lane, The Penguin Press, 1970.

Arendt, H. *On Resolution.* London: Faber, 1963.

Arey, J.A. *The Sky Pirates.* New York: Scribners, 1972.

Becker, J. *Hitler's Children.* London: Michael Joseph, 1977.

Bowyer Bell, J. *The Secret Army: The IRA 1916—1970.* Cambridge, Mass.: MIT Press, 1974.

Bowyer Bell, J. *On Revolt: Strategies of National Liberation.* Cambridge, Mass.: Harvard University Press, 1976.

Bowyer Bell, J. *Transnational Terror.* Stanford, Calif.: AEI—Hoover Institute, 1978.

Burton, A.M. *Urban Terrorism.* London: Macmillan, 1975.

Carlton, D. and Schaerf, C. (eds) *International Terrorism and World Security.* London: Croom Helm, 1975.

Clutterbuck, R. *Living with Terrorism.* London: Faber and Faber, 1975.

Clutterbuck, R. *Terrorism ohne Chance.* Stuttgart: Seewald Verlag, 1979.

Clyde, P. *An Anatomy of Skyjacking.* London: Abelard Schuman, 1973.

Coogan, T.P. *The IRA.* New York: Praeger, 1970.

Crozier, B. *Ulster: Politics and Terrorism.* London: Institute for the Study of Conflict, 1973.

Dobson, C. *Black September.* London: Hale, 1975.

Dobson, C. and Payne, R. *The Carlos Complex.* London: Hodder and Stoughton, 1977.

Dobson, C. and Payne, R. *The Weapons of Terror: International Terrorism at Work.* London: Macmillan, 1979.

Edler Baumann, C. *The Diplomatic Kidnappings: A Revolutionary Tactic of Urban Terrorism.* The Hague: Nijhoff, 1973.

Eckstein, H. *The Evaluation of Political Performance: Problems and Dimensions.* Beverly Hills and London: Sage, 1971.

Funke, M. (ed.) *Terrorismus.* Düsseldorf: Athenäum Verlag, 1977.

Gaucher, R. *The Terrorists: From Tsarist Russia to the OAS.* London: Secker and Warburg, 1968.

Gurr, T. *Why Men Rebel.* Princeton, NJ: Princeton University, 1970.

Gurr, T. and McClelland, M. *Political Performance: A Twelve Nation Study.* Beverly Hills and London: Sage, 1971.

Havens, M. *et al. The Politics of Assassination.* Englewood Cliffs, NJ: Prentice Hall, 1970.

Hyams, E. *Terrorists and Terrorism.* London: Dent, 1975.

Jenkins, B. *International Terrorism: A New Mode of Conflict.* Los Angeles: Crescent, 1975.

Jenkins, B. and Johnson, J. *International Terrorism: A Chronology 1968—1974.* New York: Rand Corporation, 1975.

Laqueur, W. *Guerilla: A Historical and Critical Study.* London: Weidenfeld and Nicolson, 1977.

Laqueur, W. *Terrorism.* London: Weidenfeld and Nicolson, 1977.

Lineberry, W.P. (ed.) *The Struggle Against Terrorism.* New York: Wilson, 1977.

MacFarlane, L.J. *Violence and the State.* London: Nelson, 1974.

Nardin, T. *Violence and the State: A Critique of Empirical Political Theory.* Beverly Hills and London: Sage, 1971.

O'Brien, C.C. *Herod: Reflections on Political Violence.* London: Hutchinson, 1978.

Parry, A. *Terrorism: From Robespierre to Arafat.* New York: Vanguard, 1976.

Rapoport, D.C. *Assassination and Terrorism.* Toronto: Canadian Broadcasting Corporation, 1971.

Rose, R. *Governing without Consensus: An Irish Perspective.* London: Faber and Faber, 1971.

Scorer, C. *The Prevention of Terrorism Acts 1974 and 1976.* London: NCCL, 1976.

Servier, J. *Le Terrorisme.* Paris: Presses Universitaires de France, 1979.

Walter, E.V. *Terror and Resistance: A Study of Political Violence.* London: Oxford University Press, 1969.

Wilkinson, P. *Political Terrorism.* London: Macmillan, 1974.

Wilkinson, P. *Terrorism and the Liberal State.* London: Macmillan, 1977.

Chapter 2:

Aus Politik und Zeitgeschichte, articles on Germañ terrorism in issues of 27 March 1976, 19 June 1976, 15 October 1977, 20 May 1978 and 24 June 1978.

Becker, J. *Hitler's Children: the story of the Baader—Meinhof gang.* London: Granada, 1978.

Federal Ministry of the Interior, Bonn, annual reports on *Verfassungsschutz.*

Funke, M. (ed.) *Terrorismus: Untersuchungen zur Strategie und Struktur revolutionärer Gewaltpolitik.* Bonn: Schriftenreihe der Bundeszentrale für politische Bildung, no. 123, 1977.

Funke, M. (ed.) *Extremismus im demokratischen Rechtsstaat.* Düsseldorf: Droste Verlag, 1978.

Geissler, H. (ed.) *Der Weg in die Gewalt: geistige und gesellschaftliche Ursachen des Terrorismus und seine Folgen.* Munich: Günter Olzog Verlag, 1978.

Paczensky, S. von (ed.) *Frauen und Terror: Versuche, die Beteiligung von Frauen an Gewalttaten zu erklären.* Reinbek bei Hamburg: Rowohlt, 1978.

Shell, K. 'Extraparliamentary Opposition in Postwar Germany'. *Comparative Politics, 2* (July 1970).

Vinke, H. and Witt, G. (eds) *Die Anti-Terror-Debatten im Parlament: Protokolle, 1974—1978.* Reinbek bei Hamburg: Rowohlt, 1978.

Chapter 3:

Acquaviva, S.S. *Guerriglia e guerra rivoluzionaria in Italia.* Milan: Rizzoli editore, 1979.

Bocca, G. *Il terrorismo italiano.* Milan: Rizzoli editore, 1979.

Bologna, S. *La tribu delle talpe.* Milan: Feltrinelli, 1978.

Bonanate, L. Dimensioni del terrorismo politico. *Comunità,* no. 177, 1977.

Brigate Rosse, Risoluzione della Direzione Strategica, febbraio 1978. *CONTROinformazione* no. 11—12 (July 1978) pp. 76—95.

Flamigni, S. *et al.* (eds) *Sicurezza democratica e lotta alla criminalita, Atti del Convegno organizzato dal Centro studi per la riforma dello Stato 25—26 febbraio 1975.* Rome: Editori Riuniti, 1975.

Hutchinson, M.C. The concept of revolutionary terrorism. *Journal of Conflict Resolution, 16,* no. 3, (September 1972) pp. 383—97.

Negri, A. *Il dominio e il sabotaggio.* Milan: Feltrinelli, 1978.

Sciascia, L. *L'Affaire Moro.* Palermo: Sellerio editore, 1978.

Silj, A. *'Mai piu senza fucile!' alle origini dei NAP e delle BR.* Florence: Vallecchi editore, 1979.

Tessandori, V. *BR, Imputazione: banda armata.* Milan: Aldo Garzanti Editore, 1977.

Chapter 4:

The secondary literature on terrorism in France is almost non-existent, and there is no general work surveying the field. Of French newspapers, *Le Monde* provides the most complete factual coverage, but has a deliberate policy of underplaying the more sensational aspects of terrorist incidents. The right-wing press, especially *L'Aurore* and *France-Soir,* employs the notion of terrorism more widely.

A philosophical consideration of the traditional interrelationship of 'terror' and French political history can be found in L. Dispot, *La machine à terreur.*

Paris: Bernard Grasset, 1978.

Peripheral references to terrorism occur in the report of the Peyrefitte Commission, *Réponses à la violence,* 2 vols. Paris: Presses-Pocket, 1977.

The legal context is surveyed in 'L'Europe de la répression, ou l'insécurité d'état', *Actes,* special edition, supplement to no. 17 (Spring 1978).

Certain philosophical, literary and artistic aspects of terrorism are dealt with in 'Territoires de la terreur', *Silex* no. 10 (Autumn 1978).

R. Gaucher, *Les terroristes, de la Russie tsariste à l'OAS.* Paris: Albin Michel, 1965, is also available in English, *The Terrorists: From Tsarist Russia to the OAS.* London: Secker and Warburg, 1968.

On the *Cagoule* and the OAS, see J.-R. Tournoux, *L'Histoire secrète.* Paris: Plon, 1962; on the *barbouzes,* see P. Chairoff, *Dossier B . . . comme barbouzes.* Paris: Alain Moreau, 1975.

The distinction between the use of criminal law and special legislation for terrorists is considered in V.V. Stanciu, Terrorisme et crime politique. *Revue politique et parlementaire, 74,* no. 832 (May 1972) pp. 28−37.

But most useful of all is the series of short articles in the monthly journal of political documentation published by the League of the Rights of Man, Le Terrorisme. *Après-demain* no. 211 (February 1979).

Chapter 5:
No important work on South Moluccan terrorism in the Netherlands exists in English. Amongst the literature dealing with the South Moluccans are:
Bagley, C. *The Dutch Plural Society; a Comparative Study in Race Relations.* London: Oxford University Press, 1973.
Department of Information Service of the Republic of the South Moluccas, Confrontation with a quarter of a century of discrimination of the South Moluccan right of self-determination. Eindhoven, 1975.
Wittermans, T. and Gist, N.P., The Ambonese nationalist movement in the Netherlands: a study in status deprivation. *Social Forces, 40* (1962) pp. 309−70.

The literature in Dutch on South Moluccans and terrorism is extensive and can be grouped under three headings:
(1) *Governmental documents, including:*
Ambonezen in Nederland. Report of the Verwey-Jonker committee, The Hague: Staatsuitgeverij, 1959.
Gebeurtenissen rond de treinkaping te Beilen en de overval op het Indonesisch consulaat-generaal te Amsterdam. *Handelingen 1975−1976,* 13756, no. 1−4.

De Gijzelingen in Bovensmilde en Vries. *Handelingen 1977—1978,* 14610, no. 1—2.

De problematiek van de Molukse minderheïd in Nederland. *Handelingen 1977—1978,* 14915, no. 1—2.

Handelingen 1977—1978, 14968.

(2) *Material produced by the South Moluccans, of which the most important works are:*

Nota van de Badan Persatuan. The Hague: Badan Persatuan, 1978.

Zuidmolukse tegennota betreffende de RMS problematiek. Republik Maluku Selatan, 1978.

Maluku Selatan; Zuid Molukken; een vergeten bevrijdingsstrijd. The Hague: De Populier, 1977.

(3) *Academic literature, including:*

Amersfoort, J.M.M. van, *De sociale positie van de Molukkers in Nederland.* The Hague: Staatsuitgeverij, 1971.

Amersfoort, J.M.M. van, *Immigratie en minderheidsvorming; een analyse van de Nederlandse situatie 1945—1973.* Alphen a/d Rijn: Samsom, 1974.

Chachet, A. De Molukse Minderheid in Nederland. *Sociale Wetenschappen, 20* (1977) pp. 124—37.

Ellemers, J.E. Minderheden en beleid in Nederland: Molukkers en enkele andere categorieën allochtonen in vergelijkend perspectief. *Transaktie, 7,* no. 1 (1978) pp. 20—40.

Mariën, M.H. Actuele Beschouwingen, Het Zuidmolukse radicalisme in Nederland; nationalistische of emancipatiebeweging? *Sociologische Gids 18* no. 1 (1971) pp. 62—76.

Persijn, J. Uit de schaduw van het verleden, legende en realiteit in het Molukse vraagstuk. *Internationale Spectatar 30* (1976) pp. 103—10.

Veenman, J. and Jansen, L.G. Molukkers in Nederland: beleid en onderzoek. *Mens en Maatschappij,* no. 2 (1978) pp. 217—29.

Chapter 6:

Bowyer Bell, J. *The Secret Army.* Cambridge, Mass.: MIT Press, 1970.

Bowyer Bell, J. *A Time of Terror.* New York: Basic Books, 1978.

Boyle, K. *et al. Law and State: The Case Of Northern Ireland.* London: Martin Robertson, 1975.

Burton, F. *The Politics Of Legitimacy.* London: Routledge and Kegan Paul, 1978.

Evelegh, R. *Peacekeeping in a Democratic Society.* London: Hurst, 1978.

O'Brien, C.C. *States Of Ireland.* London: Panther, 1974.

Wilkinson, P. *Political Terrorism.* London: Macmillan, 1974.

Wilkinson, P. *Terrorism and the Liberal State.* London: Macmillan, 1977.

Chapter 8:

On terrorism:
Bassiouni, M.C. (ed.) *International Terrorism and Political Crimes.* Springfield, Ill.: C.C. Thomas, 1975.
Evans, Alona E. and Murphy, John F. (eds) *Legal Aspects of International Terrorism.* Lexington, Mass.: Lexington Books, 1978.

On the European Convention on Human Rights:
Beddard, R. *Human Rights and Europe.* London: Sweet and Maxwell, 1973.
Fawcett, J.E.S. *The Application of the European Convention.* Oxford: Oxford University Press, 1969.
Jacobs, F.G. *The European Convention on Human Rights.* Oxford: Oxford University Press, 1975.
Robertson, A.H. *Human Rights in Europe,* 2nd edition. Manchester: Manchester University Press, 1977.

On international Law:
Greig, D.W. *International Law,* 2nd edition. London: Butterworths, 1976.
Harris, D.R. *Cases and Materials on International Law,* 2nd edition. London: Sweet and Maxwell, 1979.
O'Connell, D.P. *International Law,* 2 vols, 2nd edition. London: Stevens, 1970.
Sørensen, M. (ed.) *Manual of Public International Law.* London: Macmillan, 1968.

On extradition:
Bassiouni, M.C. *International Extradition and World Public Order.* Leydon/ Dobbs Ferry: Sijthoff/Oceana, 1974.
Shearer, I.A. *Extradition in International Law.* Manchester: Manchester University Press, 1971.

Index

237